Bruce Springsteen
and Philosophy

Popular Culture and Philosophy®
Series Editor: George A. Reisch

Popular Culture and Philosophy®

Bruce Springsteen and Philosophy

Darkness on the Edge of Truth

Edited by

RANDALL E. AUXIER

and

DOUG ANDERSON

OPEN COURT
Chicago and La Salle, Illinois

Volume 32 in the series, Popular Culture and Philosophy®, edited by George A. Reisch

To order books from Open Court, call 1-800-815-2280, or visit our website at www.opencourtbooks.com.

Open Court Publishing Company is a division of Carus Publishing Company.

Printed and bound in the United States of America.

Library of Congress Cataloging-in-Publication Data

Bruce Springsteen and philosophy: darkness on the edge of truth / edited by Randall E. Auxier and Doug Anderson.
     p. cm. — (Popular culture and philosophy ; vol. 32)
    Summary: "Essays examine philosophical aspects of rock musician Bruce Springsteen's music, lyrics, and legacy"—Provided by publisher.
    Includes bibliographical references and index.
    ISBN-13: 978-0-8126-9647-9 (trade paper : alk. paper)
    1. Springsteen, Bruce—Criticism and interpretation. 2. Rock music—United States—History and criticism. 3. Music and philosophy. I. Auxier, Randall E., 1961- II. Anderson, Douglas R.
ML420.S77B78 2008
782.42166092—dc22

                                          2008004034

To all the folks in all our
garage bands over the years

Contents

V *Greetings from . . .*   279

"I Got this Guitar and I *Learned* How to Make It Talk"

RANDALL E. AUXIER AND DOUG ANDERSON

Hardly anyone, no matter how well trained in philosophical dialectic, could argue with Bruce Springsteen's claim in this lyric from "Thunder Road." His guitar talks indeed. But what does it say? Let's begin with something Bruce once said with his voice and see whether we can learn to understand the language of the guitar. When Bob Dylan was inducted into the Rock 'n' Roll Hall of Fame, on January 20th, 1988, Bruce Springsteen was called on to speak at the ceremony. On that occasion he said:

> When I was a kid, Bob's voice somehow thrilled me and scared me, it made me feel kind of irresponsibly innocent . . . Dylan was a revolutionary. Bob freed the mind the way Elvis freed the body. He showed us that just because the music was innately physical did not mean that it was anti-intellectual."[1]

This is a highly suggestive thought, and quite complex. Bruce Springsteen is wicked smart. And he packs a lot into a few words, which is, after all, the songwriter's craft— to suggest in three verses and a chorus as much as a novel says. Here, the first sentence depicts Bruce's *embodied* response to a sound— thrilled and scared. And then the jarring juxtaposition of this response to a surprising generalized feeling that results: irresponsible innocence. Being thrilled and scared at the same time is powerful—and we all know what this is like; it's like making

---

[1] Quoted in the entry "Bob Dylan," in Gary Graff, ed., *The Ties that Bind: Bruce Springsteen A to E to Z* (Detroit: Visible Ink Press, 2005), 117.

love for the first time. And that is also how we might understand "irresponsible innocence," which is a phrase that fairly captures much of Springsteen's own early music.

But quickly Bruce moves on. "Elvis freed the body." And that is certainly true, even if it might be more precise to say that Elvis communicated a sense of jubilant embodiment to white urban and suburban youth that already existed in African American culture. But to "free" the body, one needs to assume that it was somehow imprisoned or trapped, or stuck. White America through the 1950s still lived zombie-like under the lingering and deadening influences of Calvinism, Victorianism, and later fundamentalism: no music, no dance, no touch, no kiss, no sex. Everyone feared her own scarlet letter, a world of form without substance. Were we Americans all stiff in 1954? It's good to remember that the bodies of Americans had been sacrificed in great numbers less than a decade before, and that the hoped-for *freedom* for which we sacrificed a million sons and daughters of our own (and still more of the enemy's sons and daughters), was plunged into immediate danger by the Cold War, a war that was not yet over when Springsteen spoke these words. The past was awash in blood, and the future was a black hole. The bodies of our children were trained to "duck and cover" in the event of a nuclear attack. When one tries to imagine the bodily prison that Elvis sprung us from, it is tempting to imagine children cowering beneath their school desks, hoping they get a chance to grow up, and that there will still be a world in which to do so. Yes, Elvis—innocently—freed their bodies from that. Bruce is right.

But in light of this, Bruce offered an analogy—Dylan had done for the mind what Elvis did for the body. The mind, also, was apparently imprisoned, or stuck, or trapped. How can we understand *that?* Again, the American mind was locked into the historical disjunctions of a rigid world: religious or not, patriotic or not, white or not, communist or not. No ambiguities. When Dylan sang "Mr. Tambourine Man" for a "topical" song workshop at Newport, and when he sang "Maggie's Farm" electrified, he brought ambiguity with him. He unsettled the disjunctive traditionalists—folk music or not. He was the master of ambiguity; he set minds on fire. In the 1950s we could ask, were our minds beneath our school desks too? Were we unable to think? In a sense, perhaps so, but that is too simple. A complex psychology results from such universal fear, but are we under our desks because we are afraid, or are we afraid because we are under our desks? What happens to the mind that puts it under a desk to begin with, and then what happens to a mind that has to deal with the guilt and fear of having ducked and covered? If *you* knew then what you know now, is it just possible that you would refuse to go under your desk when the teacher said it was time for a drill? Clearly the nation was ripe for a revolution of the mind.

Bruce is saying, it seems, that Dylan was *building* on what Elvis had done—not that the body and mind are two different things, but rather that music remained "innately physical," and that where our bodies went, our minds would surely follow. In short, you are not under your desk because you are afraid, you are afraid because your body is under a desk. Just crawl out from under it, stand up straight, and see how that changes your thinking. Dylan was not attempting to *deny* the physicality of musical experience and substitute for it some sort of mental revolution; he was, according to Springsteen, attempting to show that existing in and as a body does *not* mean deadening your mind, or sinking into hedonism.

The gain of embodied freedom is *not* the loss of intellectual development—and if the mind is to be free, such a revolution grows out of a freed body. And Dylan showed us that this could be done. Bruce is right again. We cannot be too far from talking guitars when we realize that intellectual understanding can be built from embodied experience. A guitar is, after all, a few of planks of wood with some silvered steel stretched over them. That is a body, but under the right circumstances, it lives and talks. We are not so different from it. Flesh stretched over bones, talking.

But the revolution was not finished. There is more to a human being than just body and mind, and the liberation of those only makes us more acutely aware of what remains caged beneath the desk. And it's here that Springsteen took the lead and *learned* to make the guitar talk. In addition to bodies and minds, human beings have hearts and souls. Free bodies and minds yearn for still freer hearts and souls. We might fairly understand Springsteen's early songs as "heartwork," and beginning with *Nebraska* in 1982, he began his "soulwork." We do not think Elvis or Dylan did *this* work, and it might even be accurate to observe that they foundered as they approached the task. They might have known it needed doing, but it wasn't their gift.

Springsteen learned about the body from Elvis, among others, and about the mind from Dylan, among others. He learned from Elvis that it was alright to have fun, that living *as* a body is not a curse. He learned how to play all night, and that it ain't no crime being glad you're alive. And from Dylan he learned that he didn't have to deny his mind—that ideas concretized in words and images are the very embodiment of power. To build on and incorporate the Free World of body and mind required great learning. But Bruce soon discovered that the heart and the soul are more deeply imprisoned—harder to find and harder to free.

So Springsteen asked questions of the heart—is love wild, is it real? And the more questions he asked, the more he saw that everywhere our hearts were simply broken. He brought us to close quarters with our own fragility. And there was no escape route, not Route 9, not the Jersey Turnpike, not Highway 26, even if the State Trooper lets you pass. Why? Even love grows old, and we can't escape from who and what we are. Like Janey, we lose heart and we want to give up, no matter how much we are told not to. We can't love our country, we can't love ourselves, and we can't love each other, since all have disappointed us too many times. And if this human heart disease is chronic and incurable, what hope can there be for the soul?

As Springsteen matured, he came up against questions no sage or seer can answer, and he put his questions and the *non-*answers straight into his songs. Madame Marie had disappeared, and even she wasn't always right. So the body grows old, and the mind dulls, and neither of them has the power to unbreak our hearts or cheer our souls. We are inconsolable. The best we can do? There is, Bruce thinks, a spiritual hope for the soul, in hard work and basic decency, and for the heart there is the blessing of family and the old fashioned art of conversation. But there is no *freedom* for either. The world does not have room for it. The revolution fails, but not for lack of a leader. The leader is just a man with a talking guitar—a guitar that talks *with* and not *at* its audience. It is saying "don't lose heart, because it'll take your God-filled soul and leave you with devils in your mind and dust where your body used to be." That is good advice.

When Bruce plays, we all know that the guitar language comes to more than smart music emitted from a vintage Fender plank. We know this because our hearts leap and our souls touch. We are thrilled and scared, and it is like making love. And we feel, for a time, irresponsibly innocent. If that doesn't heal your broken heart, at least it makes you glad to have one. And if your soul is not lifted to heaven, at least it is filled with music. And that's revolution enough. We hope you enjoy these chapters as much as we enjoyed writing them for you.

I

*Born to Run
the USA*

1
Prophets and Profits: Poets, Preachers, and Pragmatists

RANDALL E. AUXIER

> Perhaps this is the issue that frightens the prophets. A people
> may be dying without being aware of it; a people may be able
> to survive, yet refuse to make use of their ability.
>
> —ABRAHAM JOSHUA HESCHEL, *The Prophets*

I have always thought there was something beyond the usual
going on in Bruce Springsteen's music, and I was reaching for a
word to describe it. Clearly he is a poet, but the forms and subject matter point to something beyond poetry. Clearly
Springsteen is not a philosopher; he does not fill his free time
studying Aristotle and formulating clear ideas about knowledge,
being, and the good life. Yet, here is someone who can ask
"what if the things you do to survive kills the things you love?"—
someone who observes that the power of fear can "take your
God-filled soul" and "leave you with devils and dust." I was
tempted by the word "prophet" to describe him, and I was not
the first. Is there something prophetic about Springsteen's
approach to music? What is a prophet anyway?

The question led me to the philosopher who has spoken
more about prophecy in recent years than any other. It seems
that each generation gets one such philosopher, and not much
more than one. In the present it is Cornel West, philosopher, ora-
tor, public intellectual, lay preacher, and Hollywood film actor—
West had a small role as "Councillor West" in all three *Matrix*
movies. West loves music—George Clinton, John Coltrane, Miles
Davis, and yes, Bruce Springsteen, whom he has called a

prophet. As philosophers go, West is much quicker to credit the crucial role played by popular music in culture than almost any philosopher in Western history. So here's someone who speaks reverently of popular music and culture, and spends the rest of his time talking about prophecy and hope. It is logical to consult West on what has been bugging me about Springsteen.

Taking a look at what West says about prophets, prophetic thinking, prophetic action, I began to think that this was indeed the right word for describing a voice like Springsteen's—and I want to make it clear that Springsteen is not the only figure who bugs me in this regard. Paul Simon, for example, seems to be cut from similar cloth. But there are precious few who really occupy this company. West says that four things go into prophetic thinking. Let's look at them.

Four Chords and a Cloud of Dust

The first element is "discernment," by which West means that a prophetic figure has a "nuanced historical sense," remaining "attuned [yes, *attuned*] to the ambiguous legacies and hybrid cultures in history." And so attuned, the prophet is able to "keep track at any social moment of who is bearing most of the social cost." This really is one of Springsteen's strong suits. From "The Ghost of Tom Joad," to "Born in the USA," to "My Hometown," to "Devils and Dust," Springsteen is engaged in a continuous act of prophetic discernment and tracking who is carrying the social cost. He never backs down, and he is never wrong.

The second element for West is what he calls "human connection," by which he means placing great emphasis upon empathy, where empathy is understood as "the capacity to get in contact with the anxieties and frustrations of others."[1] This also seems apt in considering Springsteen. He writes in the first person, boldly, constantly, and describes conditions and burdens that simply never were his own—a homeless worker, an ex-con trying to go straight, a Reno hooker, a gay man dying of AIDS. I very much doubt that Bruce ever camped by the railroad tracks with "no home, no job, no peace, no rest," but I certainly

---

[1] Cornel West, *Beyond Eurocentrism and Multiculturalism, Volume 1: Prophetic Thought in Postmodern Times* (Monroe: Common Courage Press, 1993), p. 5.

feel that he knows what it is like, and I don't doubt him when he says "wherever somebody's struggling to be free, look in their eyes Mom, and you'll see me." On the other hand, I have never endured such a situation either. Yet, those who have been through the ordeals he describes are the very bedrock of Springsteen's public. He sees and feels their lives, and gives it back to them not only as art, but as truth. This is the power of empathy, and the result of the effort is human connection, "never losing the humanity of others," as West puts it.

The third element in West's scheme is what he calls "tracking hypocrisy," but doing so in a "self-critical" rather than "self-righteous mode." West continues that the prophet accents "boldly and defiantly the gap between principles and practice, between promise and performance, between rhetoric and reality." Of many choices, I think of Springsteen's new song "Your Own Worst Enemy," which says "the times, they got too clear, so you removed all the mirrors." Assuming the moral high ground so as to call out the hypocrisy of others is a slippery business. It invites people to take pot-shots at the messenger. Springsteen has always shielded himself by trying to remain down to earth, unpretentious, humble, grateful to his audience, and prepared to admit his own faults. As West says, we have to recognize that "we are often complicit with the very thing we are criticizing" (p. 6). The constancy of Bruce's effort at humility over four decades has given him unusual moral authority in the eyes of the public. Where Paul Simon often gave in to cynicism, Bruce just keeps coming back and speaking truth to power, and one of those truths could be summarized as saying to such people the moral equivalent of "you power brokers and pundits think that ordinary people don't see you for what you are, but they do."

For West, the final element in someone prophetic is hope. West says that "to talk about human hope is to engage in an audacious attempt to galvanize and energize, to inspire and invigorate world weary people." Sounds like a fair description of a Springsteen concert. The seats fill with people whose jobs "leave them uninspired," and Bruce and seven of his dearest friends take them into the living room on E Street and talk about a train that carries saints, sinners, losers, winners, whores, gamblers, lost souls, souls departed, kings and fools, and on *that* train "faith will be rewarded . . . hear the steel wheels singing, bells of freedom ringin'." I can't think of a modern troubadour who can show us so much despair and human misery without taking away our hope, our shot at freeing ourselves.

Rising and Falling

Springsteen, quite possibly more than any other figure in the English-speaking world, embodies all four of the elements West combines to make a prophet. And there is so much more. This is not a songwriter who offers a few prophetic moments, it comes album after album, concert after concert, a drumbeat of prophecy as steady as Max Weinberg's right foot. In his latest release, Bruce tells us of the future:

> Now there's a fire down below
> But it's comin' up here
> So leave everything you know . . .
> There's bodies hanging in the trees
> This is what will be, this is what will be.

I'm not sure what the prediction is, but it isn't good news. And as I consider the lyrics of "The Rising," I find the label "prophet" tempting indeed:

> Wearing the cross of my calling . . .
> Spirits above and behind me
> Faces gone, black eyes burning bright
> May their precious blood forever bind me
> Lord as I stand before your fiery light.

This is a New York City fireman bravely facing his end and dreaming of the resurrection. Who but a prophet dares to discern the historic moment of 9/11, to write the words in first person of one who perishes, who audaciously finds hope in the blackness, and tells us of a rising? I am sorely tempted, but somehow I just know something is missing here. This is powerful stuff, the best we have, but it is not quite prophecy.

Pragmatists, Poets, and Preachers

Sometimes philosophers have silly arguments, sometimes they don't. One argument they've been having for about twenty years (you decide if it's silly) is the future and direction and meaning of the philosophical school called "pragmatism." I would tell you what pragmatism is, if I could, but it turns out that *this* is what people are arguing about. It's somewhat easier to say what pragmatism *was*, but all participants in the argument seem to agree that it doesn't ultimately matter, since none of them is willing to be bound by some strictly historical sense of the term.

There are lots of people arguing over the term and its meaning, but the three main choices seem to be Richard Rorty, Cornel West, and Hilary Putnam. They all agree that pragmatism is supposed to be practical in some way, but beyond that, they don't have so much in common.

Rorty is currently at a disadvantage in the debate because he recently died. And since he didn't believe in God, we can assume that if he was correct, he is out of the debate; and if he was wrong, he is out of the debate for a different reason. But he has many supporters who, we may assume, are not exactly praying for him, but they still read his books and speak his lingo. Rorty, calling himself a pragmatist, spent nearly thirty years trying to convince everyone that philosophy was not much use, and that the real hope for democratic civilization lay with the work of *poets*. Poets create words and whole vocabularies; they sort of go fishing for the future and bring back a stringer of fresh marks and noises, the fish of the future, providing the rest of us with linguistic sustenance. Because so much depends on language (*everything* does, according to Rorty), a great deal of weight is given to those who *make* the words (or find them, or reel them in, or whatever it is they do). Today's poetic metaphors become tomorrow's literal truths and common sense, Rorty says. Let's call this "poetic pragmatism."

If poetic pragmatism is like fishing for the future, the ocean that such poets set out upon is one of possibilities for living, for thinking, for being. And if the poet is the one who braves this sea and brings back a hold of fishy words, those words are cleaned, cooked and consumed first by the masses (from the semi-literate dockworker to the college graduate, who is also sometimes semi-literate). The political leaders eventually digest the innards, and the philosophers then sit around discussing the discarded bones. At least, that is Rorty's story, as abridged.

On the other hand, Cornel West says that pragmatism should be *prophetic*. By this he means that not just poets, but philosophers (and others) should speak to the masses, make their own contributions to the market-place of words, use philosophy to change and improve society. Such philosophers sort of preach their moral message and pitch their preaching to the sonic tastes of the masses, especially those members of society whose voices are not heard by the powerful. In a sense, the "prophetic" part of West's pragmatism has to do with one special aspect of prophecy: the tradition of excoriating those who ignore and mistreat the needy from motives of greed and self-satisfied power. The prophetic pragmatist goes fishing with the poet, reels in a few of his own, and shares the responsibility for cleaning and cooking them, making the powerful digest the guts, and then discussing the bones with the philosophers, but not too much of the last. All this activity keeps a body busy. As I said, West calls this "prophetic pragmatism," but I will call it "preachy pragmatism," for reasons that will be clear shortly.

Then there's Hilary Putnam. He is a nice man. He doesn't think philosophers should wax poetic or sermonic. He thinks philosophers contribute "reasonableness" to any discussion of human problems, unpretentiously, humbly, but assertively. His philosophers can ride on the fishing boat, even cast a line in the water, but in the end, he is saying "don't underestimate the need for a well-ordered and productive discussion of the bones." This is why he will not win the debate. He might even be right, but it doesn't matter because this is not going to capture anyone's imagination, except bone collectors', no matter how well he makes the case. We can call his kind of approach "sober pragmatism," but the consumers of philosophy usually want a little wine with their meal. In the public mind, the contest is between poets and preachers. Teetotalers need to find themselves a good meeting with the friends of Bill W.

A Pop Quiz

The debate over pragmatism has been raging for a quarter of a century. West is ahead, as measured by books sold, movies and CDs made and consumed. Rorty has a strong enclave in the academies. Putnam has a good AA meeting going for people who are trying to shed their addiction to analytic philosophy, one day at a time. But all pragmatists insist on something practical, and that a philosophy has to pass the test of "experience."

I want to run such a test. The true poets of the present culture are not those who publish highbrow verse and teach in English departments; they are the songwriters. And among these, any number might be identified as poets of the type Rorty praises—the creators of vocabularies that inspire the mass imagination, and whose lyrics suggest possibilities for living. But in order to test Rorty's vision against West's we need someone who is also at least arguably prophetic—takes up the cause of the dispossessed, the outcast; someone who speaks truth to power, identifies the sins of greed and the consequences. In short, we need a poet who has found a way to preach, and has achieved the ear of the public.

This requirement narrows the choices. In fact, beyond Bob Dylan and Bruce Springsteen, I can't think of anyone at all in the present. Dylan has preachy songs, but there is no consistency of worldview or message. Where Dylan created a persona, Springsteen revealed himself as a person—or at least, that's how it feels. To his public, Springsteen *is* what he seems to be, in the sense that he never attempted to shroud his origins or his perspective in a myth. Springsteen is the better test case. (Some people will mention Steve Earle in this company. I actually agree that he might be an even better test case, but he simply does not command the public's attention in the same ways or at the same level.)

But here we encounter a serious problem. Rorty knew almost nothing about poetry, apart from what he happened to like. West knows a bit more about prophecy, but his perspective on it neither is nor claims to be deeply informed. For him, the idea of prophecy derives from contemporary sources—Reinhold Niebuhr's call for a prophetic Christianity in the 1930s, Martin Luther King's oratory and leadership in the Civil Rights movement, various Christian Marxist voices. It would be handy to know something a little more thorough about both prophecy and poetry—where they come from and how they have been inherited in the Western world.

Prophets Proper

I needed someone who could tell me more about prophets. Enter Abraham Joshua Heschel (1907–1972). Heschel probably knew more about the prophets than any person in the twentieth century. But among the many things he said and wrote, he took some trouble to distinguish poets from prophets. The confusion of poet and prophet goes as far back as human history, partly because both are clearly moved by a spirit of some kind, be it a Muse or a divinity; partly because prophets do not hesitate to write in verse, and both bring words to the masses; and partly because prophets and poets often share such a broad range of social and religious concerns. We've seen above how a voice like Springsteen's addresses this shared territory, and in much the way West requires. Heschel calls this "the profound kinship of prophetic and poetic imagination."[2]

The confusion of poet and prophet is understandable. As Heschel reminds us, Ezekiel complained that he was to the people "like one who sings love songs with a beautiful voice and plays well on an instrument, for they hear what [I say], but they will not do it" (*The Prophets*, p. 387; *Ezekiel* 33:32). No one feels obliged to do what Springsteen tells them to do, no matter how well he sings it or plays the guitar. At least in this respect, he isn't different from Ezekiel. Furthermore, Heschel, in what may be the most notorious and controversial part of his account, compares the "call" or "appointment" of the prophet to an act of seduction of the prophet by God (pp. 113–15). Most people don't think of God as a seducer, or worse, a rapist, as Heschel contends. The relationship of the poet to the Muse is often described as the seduction of the poet by the Muse, but not as rape.

But according to Heschel, there are some deep and crucial differences between poets and prophets, and we should not underestimate their importance. First, what the poet calls "inspiration," the prophet calls "revelation." While the poet is grateful for the words, the prophet often receives them with dread. And the poet doesn't know what power inspires the words, but the prophet knows exactly Whose message he is to bring. And while the poet wants the job, the prophet doesn't. There's no profit in being a prophet. The image of rape, used in *Jeremiah* 20:7, indicates, according to Heschel, the "sense of being ravished or carried away by violence, of yielding to over-powering

---

[2] Abraham Joshua Heschel, *The Prophets* (New York: Harper and Row, 1962), p. 268.

force against one's will. The prophet feels both the attraction and coercion of God, the appeal and the pressure, the charm and the stress" (p. 114).

Fishing with Bruce and Jonah

I mentioned the fishing trip. This is a good place to take an imaginary one. Many of you will recall the story of Jonah, but you may be fuzzy on the details. God shows up and tells Jonah to drop everything and go to Nineveh and "cry out against it, for their wickedness has come up against me" (*Jonah* 1:2). Let me translate. God shows up in Asbury Park and tells Bruce to go to New York City and stand on a street corner and cry out against its wickedness. What is the response? Jonah heads for Tarshish. Let me translate. Bruce heads for Nebraska.

You know what happens next. Bruce catches a flight for Omaha and God starts doing a Buddy Holly re-run with the weather, and Bruce confesses to the passengers and crew that *he's* the problem. So they hand him a parachute and push him out over Lake Erie. Miraculously, Bruce is caught in the net of the last solvent fishing boat in the upper Midwest, spends three days in the hold with the rest of the fish, does some serious praying and repenting, and gets spat out in Buffalo. Seeing the error of his ways, he hitches a ride to Manhattan, stands on the corner of Broadway and 42nd Street, and explains in tones an octave too high that if the people of Sin City don't repent in forty days, God is going to make New York look like, well, like it did on September 11th, 2001. But, in this case, the good people of New York *believe* Bruce, repent in sackcloth and ashes, and God relents. No September 11th. Yet, Bruce is not happy about this. He feels like a fool and goes off to F. Scott Fitzgerald's fabled Ash Heap and pouts (until God tells him not to be such a pansy).

This is all pretty hard to picture; a fable. But the key feature of it is the call, the appointment—the seduction *and* coercion. Prophets resist their calling because it isn't good news. It means a life of ridicule and rejection, a life on the profitless margin of acceptability. And this is true *even if* the people actually repent—which they usually don't. As Heschel puts it, "the mission [the prophet] performs is distasteful to him and repugnant to others; no reward is promised him and no reward could tem-

per its bitterness" (p. 18). The prophet is afforded no life of his
own, no leisure to follow a dream, and no escape from a town
that rips the bones from his back. The prophet knows exactly
Who has put him where he is, and it isn't a welcome Muse. For
the same reason, poets don't usually profess to grasp the full
meaning of their own words, but according to Heschel,
prophets definitely do (p. 388).

"Honey, Let's Invite the Prophet to Dinner"

When people think of prophets in the abstract, or from the
pages of books, they often seem to think it would be nice to
have such people around these days, what with all the greed
and wickedness and idolatry abounding. Upon serious consideration, the truth is otherwise. It is hard to have a dinner party
with a prophet, you don't want one in your neighborhood—and
especially not in your church or synagogue or mosque. They
may wear animal skins, marry prostitutes, and name their children things like "Not-pitied" and "Not-my-people" (*The
Prophets*, pp. 52–53; *Hosea* 1:6-9). Springsteen named his kids
Evan, Jessica, and Sam. If you're thinking you'd like to have the
Springsteen family over for dinner, it is because Bruce *isn't* a
prophet.

Prophets have what we would call, in today's favored psy-
chobabble, "boundary issues." No matter what you've done, it
isn't good enough, and prophets don't hesitate to inform you of
it. As Heschel points out, prophets exaggerate our sins and
aren't known for being especially realistic about things (p. 14).
You think you've done okay in this life? Bruce might agree, but
Hosea and Amos and Jeremiah aren't impressed, with you *or*
Bruce. The boundary issue is clearest when it comes to matters
of religion—what Rorty calls the great "conversation stopper."
Now poets may speak of religion, indeed, they often do, and so
much poetry draws upon religious imagery and religious sensi-
bilities that it is not easy to imagine poetry without them. But
even John Milton and William Blake stop short of prefacing their
poetry with the phrase "Thus says the Lord . . ." (p. 389). You
want to talk about a conversation stopper. What would even
Cornel West do with a prophetic pragmatist who begins his
speech with "Thus says the Lord"—especially when the rest of
the message is likely to be very, very bad news?

Give Me the Bad News First

We looked at Springsteen's response to 9/11 in *The Rising*. It admittedly seems like something a prophet might or would say. But something's missing. Let us drop back to the issue of Viet Nam for a moment before we examine the more recent wound to the American psyche.

Heschel points out that "a tribal god was petitioned to slay the tribe's enemies because he was conceived as the god of that tribe and not the god of the enemies. When the Roman armies were defeated in battle, the people, indignant, did not hesitate to wreck the images of the gods" (p. 12). We have never, in the USA, hesitated to petition our God to help us defeat our enemies, even when we fought *one another*. But in Viet Nam, we lost the war. Why did no one blame God for failing us? Why would we not wreck the sanctuaries of church and synagogue and mosque to show our displeasure with a God who had not brought us victory? Most of us (not I, not Bruce, but *most* of us) were certainly convinced that the enemy was godless, that our struggle was divinely sanctioned, and that our victory would be a victory for truth, justice, and freedom. But perhaps we, and Springsteen, know that the relevant God is *not* a tribal god, and does not condone violence—Martin Luther King and Abraham Joshua Heschel, had certainly made the point.

But there's more. As Heschel says:

> The prophets of Israel proclaim that the enemy may be God's instrument in history. The God of Israel calls the archenemy of his people "Assyria, the rod of My anger" (*Isaiah* 10:5) . . . "Nebuchadnezzar, the king of Babylon, My servant" whom I will bring 'against this land and its inhabitants' (*Jeremiah* 25:9; 27:6; 43:10). Instead of cursing the enemy, the prophets condemn their own nation. (*The Prophets*, p. 12)

I can recall many people, including Springsteen and King condemning the US government for the foolish adventure in violence that was Viet Nam, but I cannot recall them or anyone else saying Viet Nam was the rod of God's anger, or Ho Chi Minh was God's servant, giving the United States *exactly* what it had earned by acting as though the commandments of its God were mere suggestions. I can easily, in my own prophetic mode, believe that the US deserved exactly what it got, but our recent behavior in Iraq suggests that we haven't yet learned our lessons about greed, empire, violence, lies, and the misuse of God for the debased ends of idolaters who pretend to sanctity.

But here's a question worth considering. What would happen to Springsteen if he were to have written a song depicting the 9/11 hijackers as instruments of *our own* God sent to take down our towers of Babel and our monuments to greed, and depicting Osama bin Laden as the servant of *our own* God, giving us exactly what we had earned, in our greed and faithlessness? Yet, Isaiah and Jeremiah were saying something comparable to this in their time. And when you think about it, Springsteen would have had a stronger case, since Bin Laden, unlike the kings of Assyria, professes to worship *the same God* we claim as ours. And indeed, the worse news is that, between the two of them, Bin Laden's language is closer to the language of the prophets than Springsteen's. I can hardly imagine a less comfortable observation, but I think it is wise to be chastened by it, and to use the words "prophet" and "prophetic" with greater care than we typically do. I will point out that Bin Laden cannot be a prophet either, for the prophet comes from within the people, and is never *himself* the instrument of violence. But if Springsteen were to say the very things Bin Laden says, that would be pretty close to the language of prophecy as employed by Amos, Hosea, Jeremiah, and Isaiah.

And the Good News Second

But here's a more comforting thought. "The Rising" is not prophecy, but it *is* lamentation. The greatest lamentations in Western history were written by a prophet, Jeremiah. This is a more productive point of overlap, a place where the poet and the prophet may console one another, for the prophet does not *want* his warnings to be fulfilled any more than the poet or the philosopher wants it. I wonder if Springsteen might be willing to sing:

> How lonely sits the city
> That was once full of people!
> How like a widow she has become,
> She that was great among nations . . .
> She took no thought of her future;

Her downfall was appalling,
With none to comfort her.
"Oh Lord, look at my affliction,
For the enemy has triumphed!"
(*Lamentations* 1:1, 1:9)

But there are no prophets now who, like Jeremiah, have seen
the warnings fulfilled. The United States stands, at least for the
present. There are only poets and pragmatists and politicians
and people with feelings of foreboding. And even if a prophet
should appear, God forbid, we should remember that sometimes God withholds the Mighty Hand of Justice. I do not think
the United States *deserves* a better end than did Israel and Judah,
and I do not think our current president is morally better than
Ahab. But Ahab and the children of Israel *tolerated* Elijah. The
current administration wouldn't even tolerate Ambassador
Joseph Wilson, and he wasn't exactly saying the terrorists were
God's servants, or calling the President a faithless and adulter-
ous idolater. The United States has indeed earned a worse punishment than Israel and Judah, war by war, torture by torture,
conquest by conquest. Ill-gotten gain abounds, but God is, as
Heschel put it, anthropopathic—God has human-like feelings,
and the prophets tell us what they are. God, if there is one,
surely understands our weakness, and why, against the advice
of conscience and our betters, we have insisted upon a King and
an empire. Heschel and Cornel West and Bruce Springsteen
have done all they can do to enlighten us. Now it's up to the
rest of us. The question is open, and God's furious judgment,
while it has been well-earned, is not yet pronounced. Surely a
prophet will appear to warn us before that happens, and looking around, I see none.

2

Who's the Boss?
Springsteen on the
Alienation and Salvation
of Work and Labor

STEVEN MICHELS

Few artists have earned as much of a reputation for championing the working class as Bruce Springsteen. His songs are replete with references to thankless jobs and grudging bosses that just plain screw up an otherwise decent life. But where among the philosophers of labor should we place him?

Perhaps the most prominent voice on the subject belongs to Karl Marx (1818–1883). The great error (and evil) of capitalism, he teaches, lies with the separation or "alienation" of the individual from the product of his labor, which is co-opted by the bourgeoisie, as the owners of the factories and equipment necessary for capitalist production. In plain language, that means you don't own what you work to produce. This "contradiction" will be the undoing of the great capitalist machine and the cause of a socialist revolution, Marx says. Those unable to see this ("scientific") truth in history have been brainwashed or deluded by the powers-that-be—suffering from "false consciousness," in the Marxian vernacular—which is why workers need to be led away from their doldrums by the more enlightened and revolutionary members of the elite. (Marx has himself and his friends in mind.)

On the other end of the spectrum, we find Professor Max Weber (1864–1920), author of countless works, including *The Protestant Ethic and the Spirit of Capitalism*, his most well-known text. Echoing the focus on the individual and labor in the classical liberalism of John Locke (1632-1704) and Adam Smith (1723-1790), Weber believed that capitalism prospered in certain countries of the West due to their Protestant heritage. Protestants view work as something to be embraced, he argued, as an activity consistent with their religious and public identities, which helped those societies develop economically.

Also relevant is the writing of Hannah Arendt (1906–1975), the last of our German philosophers, and what she says about the distinction among labor, work, and action in her book *The Human Condition*. "Labor" is repetitive and continuous, she writes; it satisfies our most basic physiological needs, but it's essentially the stuff of slaves. "Work," by contrast, is a more permanent act of creation that shapes the material world. Both labor and work fall within what she calls "the private realm." But the final realm, action, is public; this is the realm of freedom. It is in this sphere that people fulfill their purpose as citizens.

So where does Springsteen fit in? Is he sympathetic to Marx's historical materialism? Does he agree with Weber's account of the possibility of salvation through manual labor? Or is his account more nuanced, as we find in Arendt? This chapter examines Springsteen's lyrics to determine his position on these issues, with particular emphasis on *The Ghost of Tom Joad*, which takes work and labor as its theme. Let's survey the way that work and labor are depicted in each phase of Springsteen's career so that we can form an overall sense of his view, and we'll save our conclusions for the end.

Now My Boss Don't Dig Me 'cause He Put Me on the Night Shift

The scant attention to work and labor in Springsteen's early recordings is surprising, given the reputation he has earned as an advocate for the working class. On his first album, *Greetings from Asbury Park, NJ*, the only song where work is mentioned is "Mary Queen of Arkansas." The lyrics are vague but clearly political. The occupations Springsteen lists only serve to elaborate on the elitism of Mary. The suitor-narrator of the song is worthy of Mary's attention because of or despite how he spends his day. But loneliness is hardly alienation, and as we'll see later in "Wild Billy's Circus Story," even a bad day at the circus is better than a good day at the factory.

Also noteworthy on this first album is "It's Hard to Be a Saint in the City," if only for the fact that it does not include work or

unemployment as part of the moral challenges Springsteen identifies. "It's so hard to be a saint when you're just a boy out on
the street," he sings. If Springsteen were truly sympathetic to
Marx's critique of capitalism, we would expect to see poverty
and exploitation as reasons behind the ethics of the street. In *The
Communist Manifesto* and elsewhere, we should recall, Marx
alleges that capitalism reduces even the family to an economic
relationship. They stay together because they have to divide their
labor between earning wages and caring for children.

We do find that view in one of Springsteen's strongest statements on work and labor, the piano-driven balled "Factory,"
from his fourth album, *Darkness on the Edge of Town*. It's sung
from the perspective of a son about his "daddy." The harsh realities of an industry are summed up in the second verse: "Factory
takes his hearing / factory gives him life." Work provides for the
family, but not without consequence. The final stanza is the
most shocking, however, for "someone's gonna get hurt
tonight." Springsteen suggests that "the working life" exacts a
toll not only on those who are paid for sacrificing their bodies,
but on spouses and children, too. No names are given here;
Springsteen does to his characters what the factory does to its
workers: he takes their identity. Springsteen packs an incredible
amount of realism into a song that clocks in at 2:19.

Springsteen's view of human nature comes to the fore in *The
River*'s "Hungry Heart." It begins with one of the more dramatic
lines in all of rock 'n' roll: "Got a wife and kids in Baltimore,
Jack / I went out for a ride, and I never went back." But the
remainder of the verse—"Like a river that don't know where it's
flowing / I took a wrong turn, and I just kept going"—suggests
Springsteen might be pointing out a certain degree of irrational-
ity. (Can a river really not know where it's going?) The things
his characters do sometimes don't make sense, but he allows his
listeners to pass judgment or feel empathy. It's remarkable that
so many can relate so closely to characters who cry out for judgment or emotional distance. Nevertheless, in this song and others Springsteen has tapped into a common if not universal
emotion: restlessness and longing—for its own sake.
(*"Everybody's* got a hungry heart.")

Springsteen penned the song at the request of Joey Ramone.
(It was Jon Landau who convinced Springsteen to record it for
himself.) It's interesting to ponder how Springsteen's writing

might differ when he is not limited by his own style or voice.
(It's also impossible to hear the song without thinking how the
Ramones would have done it differently.) In any event, this
commentary on human nature is essential to understanding his
more specific thoughts on economics and labor.

Springsteen revisited the theme of working-class escapism on
"Born to Run." Alienation has never had a more perfect anthem.
At the same time, it's frank, tender, and moving. Plus, it just
rocks. It builds on the theme of "Hungry Heart," but this time the
main character is not alone; he does not wish for isolation. His
image of a better place includes his fellow tramp, "Wendy." (On
the album itself, the song is followed by "She's the One.") Also
noteworthy is that Springsteen does not detail exactly the *where*
to which they are running. It doesn't seem to matter. Many have
criticized Marx for not spelling out more explicitly his vision of
communist society; the same could be said for Springsteen here,
since all he promises Wendy is a walk in the sun.

The final release in this stage of Springsteen's career is the
stark yet impressive *Nebraska*, an album he recorded at his
home on a four-track machine. The third song, "Mansion on the
Hill," depicts a big house "on the edge of town" that overlooks
a factory. Unlike the town it sits above, everyone there is happy
and content. It is not clear what is most offensive about the
mansion and its inhabitants—the fact that it's distant, elevated,
or just big? Is it that its inhabitants are happy? It could also be
the rare (or even impossible) combination that is so deserving
of our contempt.

Nebraska's "Highway Patrolman" is an example where work
is contrasted with the law, a theme Springsteen uses quite often
and with maximum effect. This song is unique, however, in that
Springsteen sings from the perspective of authority. Joe Roberts,
a policeman, is conflicted between his duty to uphold the law
and the loyalty he feels toward Franky, his troubled brother. The
early refrain "Man turns his back on his family / Well, he just
ain't no good," which had once applied to Franky's treatment of
his family, now becomes the rationale for Joe's decision to let
his brother escape. It is a moral repeated from the other perspective in "The Line." This song (from *The Ghost of Tom Joad*)
depicts an immigration officer, Carl, who loses his job after he
falls in love with an immigrant and unwittingly helps her brother
smuggle drugs across the border.

Nebraska's "Open All Night" is most typical of Springsteen's treatment of work. The main character is someone who drives for a living. For some reason, he has run afoul of his boss, so he's stuck driving though the night. He can't wait till the dawn so he can visit Wanda, whom he met at Bob's Big Boy Fried Chicken on Route 60. He is not oppressed and the work is not terrible, but he'd rather be with his girl. Until that time, his only solace is the radio. Springsteen uses the same plot, imagery, and even some of the lyrics in *Tracks'* "Living on the Edge of the World." In the first phase of his career, it seems that Springsteen's view of work is that it's an ambiguous but tolerable part of life—it gets in the way, it's often drudgery, but it's no cause for revolution.

I Bought a Bourgeois House in the Hollywood Hills

"Born in the U.S.A." made Springsteen a huge star, even if it meant his politics were sometimes confused or obscured. Springsteen's message is biting—but hardly radical. The guy in the song just can't get a job. It's tragic insofar as he put his life on the line in Vietnam.

Springsteen makes the same point in "Out of Work." The song begins with the main character at the unemployment agency. It's bad enough that it eats at a man's pride, but it also interferes with his love life, when the father of his girlfriend asks him what he does for a living. Also telling is the third and final verse, which is an appeal to the president—not for a check, but for a job. The president appears rather sympathetically as someone trying to help the less fortunate, but maybe he needs a driver. Perhaps the greatest irony is that "Out of Work" itself never found employment: it was never released.

Aside from the title track, *U.S.A.* also contains the upbeat "Working on the Highway," which in many respects, tells of the worst job possible. As part of a road crew, there is little that you can call your own. You are out in the open, exposed to the elements, and on display for all to see. The product of your labor is used by tramps, gypsies, criminals, and star-crossed lovers. The best you can do is wave as they use your finely paved roads to get to where they need to go. It would be a tragic song, were it not saved by its tempo and its sense of humor and irony. Our hero falls in love with an under-aged girl he meets at the union hall, whom he promptly takes on a little road trip across state lines. He is hunted down by the girl's brothers, who come with the authorities, and he is arrested and sentenced to prison for kidnapping. The song comes full circle as he returns to the highway to work as part of a prison gang. Marx would not be surprised to know that time spent in prison so closely resembles freedom, but Weber might have some explaining to do. Is this the reward for a Protestant work ethic? But then again, Springsteen isn't a Protestant (perhaps the girl was . . .).

In those rare instances where Springsteen writes from the perspective of the upper class, it is often to reveal dissatisfaction. *Tunnel of Love*'s "Ain't Got You" heralds love as the most important thing. Fame and fortune have left him unsatisfied. The anti-materialist message is reaffirmed on "When You're Alone," where he sings, "When you're alone, you ain't nothing but alone."

The superficiality of material success comes to the fore again in *Human Touch*'s "57 Channels (And Nothin' On)." In this song, the main character, John, pays cash for a huge house and settles in with his wife for a life of comfortable amusement and elitist socializing only to find it wanting—so much so that his wife leaves him. The only thing left to do is an Elvis impersonation—that is, shoot the TV. The last lines of the song show John defending himself against a charge of disturbing the peace by blaming the lack of quality programming on television. (He wouldn't be convicted by a jury of *anyone's* peers.)

Springsteen released *Lucky Town* and *Human Touch* on the same day in March 1992. Together, they produced six singles. *Lucky Town*'s "Better Days" too has a strong materialist message. It begins on a somber note—"Well, my soul checked out missing as I sat listening / To the hours and minutes tickin' away"— but it is a more serious and hopeful reflection on life and happiness. The impatience and despondency of the first verse are eventually replaced by assuredness and a renewed sense of purpose by the song's end.

The title track from that album returns to the idea that things might be better elsewhere. This time around, the place has a name. (If you can't make it in Lucky Town, you can't make it anywhere.) Also noteworthy is that the main character is "going down" there just to catch a break; he wasn't simply "born to run." He begins from a more mature perspective, so the song concludes with a more mature lesson than we find in Springsteen's earlier work: "When it comes to luck, you make your own / Tonight I got dirt on my hands, but I'm building me a new home."

Despite his place in the history of rock 'n' roll and his ability to craft the perfect song song, Springsteen has never had a number-one single. ("Dancing in the Dark" came the closest, when it hit #2.) His luck was not about to change, but he kept on working.

I Would Not Do Heaven's Work Well

Springsteen has put places in the titles of his albums (Asbury Park, Nebraska, U.S.A) but *The Ghost of Tom Joad* is the only one for which he thought it proper to put a character in the title. It might not be Springsteen's most personal album—that designation probably applies to *Tunnel of Love*—but it is his most *personalized*.

Joad is an interesting selection, given that he is a character borrowed from someone else (John Steinbeck's *The Grapes of Wrath*) and he appears in spirit form. What is more, *Ghost* comes with a reading list and homework. Listed in the liner notes are a pair of book and news items Springsteen took as inspiration. It is interesting that Springsteen also lists John Ford's 1940 film adaption of Steinbeck's novel in the liner notes to *Joad*, rather than the novel itself.

The first three songs are reflections on work and the law. The title track opens with a man on the run who is visited by Joad. That Joad comes as a ghost suggests there is no rest for the working class weary, even in death. The most moving part of the song is its final verse, where Springsteen uses Joad's parting words to his mother as he heads off in search of understanding—and to evade the law.

In "Straight Time" the main character—his uncle calls him "Charlie"—is reflecting on the drudgery of work and his family life since he was released from prison: "Got a cold mind to go tripping 'cross that thin line / I'm sick of doing straight time." By the end of the song, Charlie finds his release by committing an unnamed criminal act. He is not fearful of being caught because, as he says of prison, "You get used to anything / Sooner or later it just becomes your life."

"Highway 25" completes the trilogy by echoing the storyline of "Working on the Highway." In both instances, the song begins with a man at work. The main character is a shoe salesman, who meets a woman and heads off with her to Mexico. We're not told why they run, but they are able to avoid the law—since they happened to rob a bank along the way. Throughout the song, Springsteen suggests that the woman tapped in to some dormant emotion in the man. He too must have a hungry heart.

In many ways, "Youngstown" is a standalone song in that it is a transition from the introductory material on work and the law to a sequence on immigration and the American dream. The song is a rare instance in which Springsteen refers to the distant past: he mentions 1803 as a significant point in the town's founding and development. But Springsteen is no historian. Typically, things are meaningful only insofar as they affect the present. Here, he describes a town, a people, and a family inextricably tied to the past. The song is sung from the perspective of a man so distraught that he wishes eternal damnation on himself: "When I die I don't want no part of heaven / I would not do heaven's work well / I pray the devil comes and takes me / To stand in the fiery furnaces of hell." It is a remarkable commentary on the despair of the working class and one of the most moving images in the whole Springsteen catalogue.

"Sinaloa Cowboys" begins a sequence of six interrelated songs, which Springsteen often played in order during his solo acoustic tour in support of the album. The song depicts brothers Miguel and Louis immigrating from Mexico to California. The pair soon tires of life in the fields, when they have an opportunity to make methamphetamine. The song ends with Miguel kissing the body of his dead brother, after an explosion in a lab. The most telling part of the story is the warning they received from their father before leaving home: "For everything the north gives it exacts a price in return." In the end, however, it wasn't competitive spirit of "the north" that cost Louis his life; it was his own senselessness and greed that put him and his brother at odds with the law and in harm's way.

The sequence ends with the stirring "Across the Border," a song about someone preparing to immigrate to the United

States—a theme Springsteen revisits on *Devils and Dust*'s "Metamoras Banks." They are not "born to run"; they are running from "pain and sadness," and they are driven by the same ambition that brought them from their homes. Springsteen also spends more energy detailing what that life will be like in this song than he has elsewhere. The American dream is alive and well, we must conclude, despite Springsteen's earlier reflections on it. Were it not, these would be pathetic characters, and Springsteen is not that cruel.

"Galveston Bay" parallels "Youngstown," in that it frames the immigration sequence, but also because it serves as a commentary on the social and economic life of a particular locale. Whereas "Youngstown" ends with no hope for escape (not even in the afterlife), "Galveston Bay" illustrates (in an almost Weberian sense) how devotion to one's trade can redirect racism and violence to more productive pursuits.

The album ends with the brief and purposefully trite "My Best Was Never Good Enough." The lyrics, which also could have been written by Forrest Gump, are a compilation of seemingly random clichés that are in stark contrast to the gravity of the rest of the album. In this sense, Springsteen's album on work closes with him at play. It is a curious choice for his last words on such a serious theme. In it, Springsteen questions whether he is worthy of devotion. It's just as much about love and acceptance as it is about work and labor. The song would be sad were he not reassured by the object of his disaffection. That the song feels thrown together, however, suggests that the problem is more with not trying than with trying and failing. His "best" is really nothing of the sort; rather, he is rendered immobile by his lack of confidence and fear of rejection. The problem with work in this song is with the self-inflicted dejection or isolation that comes with a sense of inadequacy.

Joad was the first post-*Born in the U.S.A* studio album by Springsteen to sell less than a million copies. In the United States, it sold only 500,000 units, dwarfed by the fifteen million he sold of *U.S.A*. Columbia Records was probably none too pleased, but artistically it reveals a songwriter-novelist at his peak. Marx might approve of the message, but even he might have been bothered by the drop in sales.

I Keep My Heart in My Work,
but Trouble's in My Head

Springsteen never again devoted a collection of songs to work. It's not surprising that the releases immediately following *Joad* are almost completely devoid of references to that theme. This is particularly striking in the case of *The Rising*, Springsteen's reflections on a post-9/11 America. There's also a chance that he's learned a lesson from *Born in U.S.A.* about having his message misconstrued by his political rivals.

Springsteen released *Tracks*, a four-CD set of unreleased material, in 1998. Apart from "Living on the Edge of the World," it also contains "Car Wash," a rare instance where Springsteen sings from a woman's perspective. She is devoted to her kids, hates her boss, and has dreams of being a singer. Perhaps the most telling line of the song is what she says of the cars she cleans: "From Mercedes to VWs / I do 'em all, and I don't favor none." It is a highly egalitarian sentiment, and Weber would approve. She takes pride in her work and does not single out the wealthy, even if they don't show her the same respect.

There are two other songs of note from this period. "The Fever" and "The Promise" close out (the edited) *18 Tracks*. They are the final two songs on the album, but interestingly, neither song is on *Tracks*, the full box set. The first song is one of infatuation, but Springsteen places the possible romance within the context of work and economic troubles. The main character cannot enjoy the typical after-work amusements because of his obsession with "this girl." Nor are his economic difficulties a source of trouble. ("Nothing that a po' boy can do" when he's got "the fever.") He doesn't see his job as a way to distract himself from the thoughts of this woman. And after they finally get together, his focus is on her, not on his job. It is his life with her that animates him and gives him purpose.

This sense of hope is completely abandoned in "The Promise." Springsteen sings as a man shut out of the "American dream." The main character laments how closely he has been following the path to success he's seen in the movies—in this case, represented by how skillfully he builds his car, only to have to sell it later. The Land of Opportunity has failed him so completely that he struggles with the notion that it's even possible. In the final verse, he makes reference to a time when "won big once"—only to realize the hollowness of the success you feel when others are left behind. The promise of America is not simply the chance to make something of yourself; it's bigger than that. "When the promise is broken you go on living / But it steals something from down in your soul."

Devils and Dust's "Maria's Bed" again contrasts work with love. This later commentary, however, is more positive, in terms of how work is presented. The main character, like so many others, works on the highway, but comes as close to Weber's work ethic as any character in Springsteen's songs. "I ain't complainin' / it's my job and it suits me right," he sings. However much he identifies with his labor, he still finds a greater purpose with his woman: "I keep my heart in my work but trouble's in my head / And I keep my soul in Maria's bed."

The most significant of Springsteen's post-*Joad* commentaries on the working class appears on *We Shall Overcome*, his collection of Pete Seeger covers. Springsteen does a version of Seeger's "Jesse James," which turns the outlaw into Robin Hood: "Jesse James was a lad that killed many a man / He robbed the Danville train / He stole from the rich and he gave to the poor / He'd a hand and a heart and a brain." In addition to idolizing James, the song refers to Robert Ford as a "dirty little coward," for betraying James and shooting him in the back of the head. The notion that James was anything other than a thief has been thoroughly discredited. Of course, the fact that Springsteen recorded and released the song is not necessarily an endorsement of that view, and it's hard to take it too seriously since it appears alongside "Froggie Went A-Courtin'."

Springsteen's most recent statement on the working class is *Magic*'s "Gypsy Biker"—a story of a soldier lost in the Iraq war. It recounts the devastation of a family and friends who lose a loved one. While overtly political, the song contains a few references to economics and the condition of the working class. The first line in particular—"The speculators made their money on the blood you shed"—takes seriously the economic consequences (and motives) of those in power. It's an alternate version of the storyline from "Born in the U.S.A.," in which the soldier doesn't come back alive. Evidently, there are fates worse than coming home from a war unemployed.

Quittin' Time

A life-long Democrat, Springsteen has stumped for Democratic candidates and, in a recent *Rolling Stone* interview, he mentioned Howard Zinn's *A People's History of the United States* among the books that have inspired him. He's clearly a man of the left, but he is no Marxist. And we can't forget that "The Boss" has never had a job other than playing and recording music.

Perhaps if Springsteen had spent any time on the clock, he would have been more appreciative of Marx's class analysis. Springsteen is highly attentive to the travails of the working class, but it is not necessarily with other classes that they struggle. Much of the time, it is with each other, and sometimes it's with themselves. Springsteen sees human nature as far too restless—as we've seen in "Born to Run," "Hungry Heart," and "57 Channels." The wealthy are not oppressors; they too can suffer their own bourgeois malaise. What is more, a class *perspective* is hardly to be equated with recognition of class *conflict.* In "Born in the U.S.A." and "Out of Work," work is sometimes most problematic when you can't get it.

As far as Weber goes, the most we can say is that Springsteen's characters see their work as necessary to, though not the essence of, their well being and happiness. Even if you take pride in your work, it's not what makes you who you are. What is more, songs like "The Factory" reveal something brutal about the condition of the working class, which is treated with more sympathy by Marx and Arendt. There are also instances where the fact of work leads to a life of crime. And you can just as easily identify with things that are unhealthy, including life in prison, as we learn in "Straight Time."

Finally, Springsteen doesn't seem to share the distinction between the slavish nature of work and the more purposeful labor that Arendt describes. The real problem with most work— *Born to Run*'s "Night" makes this point explicitly—is that it takes time away from doing other stuff. In sum, Springsteen does not share Arendt's vision of the good life. For her, the realm of action is public and virtuous, but for Springsteen it's unapologetically middle class: cruising around in a cool car, hanging out with your best friends, or getting with your favorite girl. And whatever the particulars, the human condition is insufferable without a radio.

3

They Play Guitars All Night and All Day: On the Ethics of Encores

STEVEN GIMBEL

You feel the sweat under your shirt. It's been an amazing show. The dark of the stage brings out the lighters, the silence is giving way to the building rhythmic applause. Deep voiced calls of "Bruuuuuuce" randomly dot the audience like flash bulbs at a press conference. Then the lights come back up and, bam, a fifteen minute rendition of "Rosalita," that by itself is worth the price of admission. Any other show and you'd be on your way to the parking lot glowing. But you've got another thirty or forty minutes ahead. A "Badlands" or "Jungleland" you didn't think you were going to get. ZZ Top, Mitch Ryder, and Credence Clearwater Revival covers that have the hell rocked out of them. Bruce goofing and telling stories between or in the middle of songs, they won't be leaving for good until every last ounce of energy, every drop of sweat is left out there on the stage. While other groups may play encores, the E Street Band plays **ENCORES**.

Most bands hold back one of their songs that received the most radio play in order to re-emerge and put a solid, pre-calculated exclamation point at the end of their show. Seasoned Springsteen fans, on the other hand, have come to expect something different; multiple encores, each one its own little set. But what does it mean? What significance should we attach to encores? Is an encore just an expected little treat that is part of the structure of a contemporary rock show like the fortune cookie after dinner at a Chinese restaurant? Is it an authentic expression of gratitude from the band, like a tip left for a hard-working waitress on a busy night? Is it part of the unspoken contract between artist and audience or is it something the audience has to earn? The difference in the approach to encores that we see between most bands and Bruce Springsteen allows us to ask questions about the nature and obligations of an artist for his audience and of the audience for the artist.

The Hunters and the Hunted: The State of Nature and the Social Contract

One approach to ethics is based on the notion of a "social contract." This has been a very popular theory since the seventeenth century in the Western world, and some people think it's robust enough to provide a basis for human social life.

The argument against the King of England in the U.S. Declaration of Independence follows the social contract theory, for example. According to contract theorists such as John Locke (1632–1704), human life can be conceived of as beginning without society, without culture. We were just like every other animal out there just trying to survive, just doing whatever we had to do make it through another day. When things are tough, you have to be, too.

Of course, trying to survive in this "state of nature" may mean having to take something helpful from someone else who is also trying to survive. Anything that would be useful to *you* would also be useful to the next guy, and he's eying it all the time, looking for the chance to snatch it. And if he can't snatch it while you are around, he'll do whatever he has to in order to make sure you are not around. The all-out scramble for the things you need to survive turns everyone against everyone else in a state of war, each individual against all others. Life in this state means "no home, no job, no peace, no rest," in Bruce's words, or, as Thomas Hobbes (1588–1679) put it, a life that is "solitary, poor, nasty, brutish, and short." Hobbes had a darker version of the state of nature than the other contract theorists, but a devilishly clever argument.

As reflective beings, though, humans come to see the irony of the situation. When all claim the right to take anything that would help them survive, including taking the lives of competitors, it doesn't actually help us survive; on the contrary, it actually makes it more likely we'll die sooner. The state of war that we enter into in order to grab what we need to live makes it more likely that we won't live long or well.

So what we need to do, according to the social contract theorists, is figure out how to come together to organize ourselves in a way that really would be advantageous for all of us, a way to make sure that we leave our corners, throw away our switchblade knives, and kiss each other good-bye. We need to reach an agreement by which we determine what *I* have that *you* can't touch and what *you* have that *I* can't touch, and who can do what to make sure that if you *do* touch what is mine, you sure as heck won't do it again. This is called the social contract and by willingly being a member of a society, you agree to play by its rules for the good of yourself and everyone else. At least, this is what social contract theorists claim. The structure of the society requires that everyone accepts certain ground rules and by agreeing to follow these rules, you get the rights that come with community membership.

One of the keys to this contract is that it allows individuals within the society to interact in mutually beneficial ways. We can make deals in which I'll do something to help you if you do something to help me. My worry, of course, is that once I do my part for you first, you're not really going to follow through and do your part for me. The social contract guarantees that you *will* by creating obligations (and in some cases, enforcement mechanisms to ensure that you do what you are obliged to do).

The clearest sort of social interaction of this sort is economic. If you give a store the proper amount of money, you've fulfilled your part of the bargain. The people who run the store then have to give you the merchandise as advertised. If they don't give you anything, if they try to pull a bait and switch and give you the wrong thing, or if the purchased item doesn't do what they said it would do, they've violated the contract you entered into with them and they need to give you your money back or replace the lemon with a working version.

Okay, so let's put the social contract theory to the test. You've been out in the ticket line for hours. You got there absurdly early and there were already people waiting, some in sleeping bags. Finally, the line starts moving and after paying a ridiculously excessive service fee, you have your tickets in hand, good seats, too. You're stoked.

Now, what did you just buy? You just entered into a contract by putting down your hard earned cash, but for what? The ticket is a promissory note, a rock 'n' roll IOU. What do you have a right to expect in return? When you cash in your "good for one rock show experience" coupon, what needs to be done by those on the other side of the transaction?

On the ticket, it gives a date, a seat number, and a band name. It doesn't say a thing about how long they'll play, whether they'll come back out for an encore, even whether or not they'll be any good. It is not unheard of in the history of rock music for the performer to come out drunk or stoned and perform a very short show. Jimi Hendrix did it in 1970 at Madison Square Gardens with Band of Gypsies and Steven Tyler of Aerosmith did it in 1982, to give just a couple of examples. You may have gotten a lousy show, a short show, less of a show than you hoped for, but you got the show you bought a ticket for.

Trying to Learn How to Walk Like Heroes: The Basis for Moral Obligations

So maybe you don't have a right under the *financial* arrangement to an encore, much less three, but still you have reason to be pissed if the band doesn't come out. You feel betrayed, not just cheated. The snub is personal. It just wasn't right. Let's follow the social contract theory a bit further to see if it is any help.

The social contract not only sits beneath financial obligations, but moral ones as well, according to these theorists. By entering into the social contract, something you do by being a member of the society, you also come to acquire certain ethical obligations. Different sorts of interpersonal relationships come with different sorts of responsibilities. Think about the narrator in "Hungry Heart." The man's got a wife and kids in Baltimore, Jack, he deserves to be strongly condemned for going out for a ride and never coming back. When you get married, when you have a child, you enter into relationships that bring with them contractual moral duties, one of which is not to find yourself back in that bar in Kingstown again. Could it be that the performers who don't come back out for an encore are violating their ethical responsibility in an analogous way?

This question immediately gives rise to two others. The first is "what are the moral responsibilities of an artist who has agreed to perform for a ticket buying audience?" If the expectation of an encore is not based on the financial arrangement of buying a ticket, maybe there's a contractual *moral* basis for it.

But there's another question here. If the contract is not purely about the ticket anymore, do we have a responsibility beyond buying the ticket? The narrator in "Hungry Heart" acquired his spousal duties by saying "I do." But that relationship is symmetric. There was a moral agreement, a covenant between him and his wife and they both came to have duties to each other. So the second question is "As an audience member, what is your responsibility to the performer at the show?"

The artist's obligation seems to involve playing music at a professional level. Technically, by paying for your ticket, the contractual obligation may have been filled by a single short set, but clearly when you went to see Jimi Hendrix, you didn't sign up to go and look at Jimi Hendrix as if you were seeing the giraffe at the zoo; you were going to see Jimi Hendrix *be* Jimi Hendrix. When Bob Dylan pulled out an electric guitar at the Newport Folk Festival in 1965 and was roundly booed for it, it was because there had been an agreement between Dylan and the audience about what they were coming to see. The sense of betrayal was felt because while he played and "sang" Bob Dylan songs, he did it in a way that was not being "Bob Dylan, the folkie" which is what the implicit arrangement was reasonably thought to be by those who purchased tickets.

So an artist has a responsibility to play a show respectful of the expectations of the audience, but what is the audience's responsibility? Musicians don't perform sequestered off in a bubble (with the possible exception of *Spinal Tap*'s bass player Derek Smalls). The relationship between the performer and the audience is a real one. If the audience is not into what is being played, it will affect the show. A dead crowd will kill a concert. A hostile crowd can do even worse. Joni Mitchell's encore-less performances often result from what she perceives as rudeness by those in the seats. Miles Davis was famous for turning his back on or insulting audiences he thought were insufficiently serious, respectful, or enthusiastic. On the other hand, when the energy is there, when everyone is going nuts, bands feed off of it. The performer doesn't just play *to* the audience, but *with* the audience. What sort of "contract" is this?

So, if the audience members play a role in the *success* of a show, don't they then also have an obligation to do their best to do what they can to make everything go off well? And if you hold up your end of the bargain, or indeed go above and beyond the call of duty, don't you deserve a little extra treat? Should we, therefore think of encores as something extra, an additional little free show being offered up as a thank you by the band for being a helpful audience? On this view, the performer has satisfied his or her moral obligations to the audience by playing an acceptably professional show: end of the show, end of the obligation. Anything more is purely out of gratitude, out of the goodness of the performer's heart—not only a thank you note, but several thank you choruses.

The problem here, on this "moral" version of the contract theory, is that the encore isn't something "extra." When a band comes out and plays an encore, no one thinks, "Hey, what's this? I thought they were gone. How cool, more music." The point of a gift is that it is not something expected. If it truly is something the artist does out of gratitude and not obligation, there would be no lighters, no expectation there, no anger and disappointment, should it not come to be. The "gift" does seem moral in some way, but not quite contractual in the sort of frame in which we've been casting it.

You May Wonder How Come I Love You: Care and Ethics

Maybe the reason we're not quite getting to the heart of the matter here is that the contractual approach we're using *lacks* heart. It's all so calculated with contract theories. Maybe there's another way of looking at the relationship between performer and audience that better captures its nature and better accounts for the obligations on all sides.

Some contemporary philosophers, like Sarah Ruddick and Nel Noddings, have argued exactly that. While it may be true that *some* of our ethical obligations arise from the sort of contractual picture of human relationships, there are other kinds of relationships that give us obligations but don't fit into that mold. If we move out of the marketplace and around the kitchen table, the nature of the relationship is quite different, and the nature of the obligation that comes from it as well.

In a contractual relationship, as we ordinarily understand it, the terms and obligations are clearly set out and once you have satisfied your end of the bargain, you are freed from the relationship. You walk into the music store and put down your money on the counter, you get to walk out with the CD. Then, it's done. The relationship is over. You may choose to buy more music from them, you may not. They may decide to close up shop or switch to classical only, they may not. In a purely contractual relationship, there are no expectations beyond the immediate transaction required by the contract you have both agreed to be part of. Once you've discharged your end of the bargain, you are freed from the obligation and the relationship. It strains the idea of the "contract" to think of all moral obligations in those terms.

There are some relationships that are based on care instead of contracts and care-based relationships play by completely different rules. When you enter into a contractual relationship, you do your best to negotiate a fair or advantageous contract, that is, one whose terms get you what you want or need at the lowest price, in terms of money or obligations. Your thoughts, in this case, are about your own well-being and what you need to do for someone else to have those needs or wants satisfied.

But when you're in a care-based relationship, your consideration is not just about you, but about what you can do to further the other person's well-being. To care about someone is to take that person's needs and happiness and attach them to your own, or indeed to put them before your own. You act in a way that you think will be advantageous to the other person, not because you will ultimately get something out of it, but because he or she will. Parents or lovers act in the interests of the children or the beloved because they are genuinely concerned about making their lives better, even if it means some sacrifice on their own part.

It's precisely the "human touch" that Bruce sings of when he says:

> Oh girl that feeling of safety you prize
> Well it comes at a hard hard price
> You can't shut off the risk and the pain
> Without losin' the love that remains
> We're all riders on this train.

The risk that you are willing to take, the way you allow yourself to be vulnerable in order to give to another—this is what is meant by "care."

It's what makes the song "Pink Cadillac" so funny in its absurdity. Despite the fact that the narrator finds his lover annoying, she gets on his nerves, but yet he says, "I love you for your pink Cadillac." Perhaps he loves her Cadillac, that would make sense enough; but if he loves *her*, it would be an internal sense in which he considers her happiness important, something he clearly doesn't. It's *his* happiness, "cruisin' down the street, waving to girls, feelin' out of sight" that is operative here. You can love someone, you can love her Cadillac, but you can't love her *for* her Cadillac. Love, as far as it entails care, is just the wrong word for it.

Care, then, can be the basis for moral responsibility in certain sorts of relationships. Of course, not every relationship you have is care-based. You couldn't care about everyone (unless, perhaps, you are Bono) and there are clearly cases in which the relationship between people is correctly described as being merely contractual. But when the relationship is the kind that involves deep personal interaction, now you are in the realm of care.

The question for us, then, is whether the relationship between performers and audiences is that sort of relationship or is it the more arm's length contractual sort? Like so much else in philosophy, the answer is "it depends." When you hear a tune you like on the radio by a band you'd never heard of, you might check out their CD and then decide to go see them live. By doing this, there's not necessarily much there other than, "I paid my money, play some good music." If they're good and their music touches something inside, if it really speaks to you, you might get more heavily into them. Or you might not. If not, hey, you gave it a shot, thanks for coming.

But this is very different from the relationship we have with our favorite bands, especially if there is one in particular that you are really into. There is a level of appreciation, a degree of dedication, where your favorite band becomes part of your identity, part of who you are. Your life would not be the same if the music weren't there. When you have all the albums, some t-shirts, if you've ever framed a photo or hung a poster somewhere, checked on blogs or chat-groups dedicated to discussions about them (or read a copy of *Your Favorite Band and Philosophy* . . .), there is more there than just a casual acquaintance.

This is why it comes off as personal when you go to see a show and there's no encore. Many of the people in the seats did more than buy a ticket. Their investment is more than just the price of admission. As a loyal fan, one who stayed with the band through great and mediocre albums, who patiently waited for guitar players to come out of rehab, who stayed when yet another lead singer was introduced into the line up . . . and then, after all of that, they don't have the decency to really lay it all out there?

The nature of Bruce Springsteen's music makes that bond between artist and audience even stronger. In a rock 'n' roll world where the is so much posing and image making, Springsteen has made a career writing songs that reflect the joys, fears, passions, failings, triumphs, and hopes of so many working people. His fans see themselves and people they know in his lyrics. There is a depth and an intimacy there that is so deeply personal because it is so dead on target. The relationship seems more personal because it seems like he is singing *to* you *about* you.

And it goes in the other direction as well. Springsteen is not only aware, but thoughtful about the life he has been privileged to live and his ability to share his dream. The man loves his work and but for those devoted fans, he'd be another guy working a straight job like so many in his songs. It is common during the course of a show (especially if you catch one in the New York-Philadelphia area) for Bruce to joke about what he would be doing if he hadn't taken up annoying his family by playing his guitar. There is not only an awareness of the role his fans have played in giving him the life he has, but an authentic gratitude. When Bruce steps on stage, he not just playing his music, he's giving it back to the people who allow him to keep making music.

From both sides, there is a sense of care. There is a legitimate sense of concern and a special relationship. Crowds at Springsteen shows are wound up like nowhere else. The energy in the room is amazing. And from the stage, Bruce is goofing like he's with his best friends in someone's living room, albeit a very, very large living room. He's going to keep going and going because those aren't just people who deserve their money's worth, they are his people and he's going to give to them regardless of what they paid, but especially when he knows they paid a lot.

When he agreed to play a series of anti-nuclear benefit concerts in the early 1980s, the band worked up a ninety-minute set that blew the roof off of Madison Square Garden. They completely stole the show. It went over so well that the band thought a precedent had been set.

"After those shows went over so great, I just figured that that's what we'd be doing on this tour," remembers E Street guitarist Steve Van Zandt. "Just ninety minutes, a couple of ballads, and make people as crazy as you can, like the old days. We can do that. But not Bruce. What we ended up doing was just adding that ninety minutes to the show we always did" (Interview with Dave Marsh, *Musician*, February 1981).

The idea of paring back his show, of giving less to the fans he cares so much about because they've cared so much for him was not even a question.

There's a relationship between bands and their most dedicated fans that is more than the contractual relationship between strangers conducting business. The fans allow the band members to live a life pursuing their music, and if commercially successful, to live a life of fame and luxury. In the other direction, the music and the image then contribute to the lives of the fans, bringing them joy and community, shaping their identity. This sort of relationship is deeply personal, even if those involved have never actually met each other. This sort of connection requires care and this means concern for the desires of the other party and for the artists that concern is manifested in the performances they give to those fans. The relationship they have fostered means they have to care and that means they have to give back.

Are encores required? In a sense. Are they gifts? In a sense. Should you expect multiple encores the next time you go see Springsteen? Do you expect presents under the tree when you wake up Christmas morning? When you buy those tickets, man, you already know Santa Claus is comin' to town.

4

Where Were You Born, Bruce Springsteen, and What Does It Matter?

JOHN SHOOK

Your origin in space and time makes all the difference to what you are, and what you can become. Great poets and songwriters have long built their bright visions of what is, and what can be, upon the cold facts of location and context. Where were you born?

We know that Bruce Springsteen was born in the U.S.A. More precisely, in Long Branch, New Jersey, on September 23rd, 1949. The Boss traveled a long way from that place. Let us be transported into the past so we can see where he arrived: still in the U.S.A., achieving amazing fame in his home country. His song "Born in the U.S.A." was born on June 4th, 1984 when the album of the same name was released. Springsteen's evocative lyrics launched him into new territory—where was he headed?

Things really started moving fast. The tour buses were waiting. Three weeks later, on June 25th, Patti Scialfa was hired as a backup singer and joined the tour just in time for its opening date at the St. Paul Civic Center in Minnesota on June 29th. The album reached Number One on the Billboard chart on July 7th, a day when the tour was traveling through Ohio for a concert at Richfield Coliseum in Cleveland. Before arriving in East Rutherford, New Jersey, for a home stand of ten shows in early August, the tour had played in Chicago and Detroit, where the blue-collar message resonated with fans old and new.

Word was getting out that this tour was something different. Springsteen and the band didn't need to be told. They could see which song whipped up the audience into the greatest frenzy. The anthem song was obvious, so "Born In The U.S.A." moved up the set list, dramatically starting each New Jersey concert during mid-August. An immense American flag. The pounding drum kicks in the beat. Bruce Springsteen in leather and jeans, bandanna around his neck, a black headband holding back his hair, his fist hammering the sky. Over the crashing of the music, what could be heard? Something about middle-American troubles and muddled Vietnam regrets. No vagueness about the refrain, though, when Springsteen explains where he was born with manly patriotic pride. The crowd, chanting along with gusto, always seemed to sympathize and understand where this tough-looking singer was coming from.

A real American phenomenon was evident during that summer of 1984. When Springsteen hit the nation's capital on August 25th, playing at the Capital Centre near Washington, D.C., the mainstream media really began to pay attention. Morning news shows and radio talk shows scrambled for something to say. This was Ronald Reagan's morning in America, and the Republican Reagan was running for re-election against Democrat Walter Mondale. Media pundit George Will, a voice of conservatism and informal advisor to Reagan, went to a concert and came away impressed. The tour had moved on to Philadelphia by September 13th, when Will's column in the *Washington Post* proclaimed his witness to "A Yankee Doodle Springsteen." Here were traditional American values cheerfully proclaimed, Will explained, even if he couldn't pin down Springsteen's politics.

Tipped off, Reagan politicos asked if the song could be used for the campaign, but Springsteen refused. Reagan's speechwriters were undeterred. While the tour was headed to Pittsburgh, Reagan's stump speech in Hammonton, New Jersey, on September 19th, included new words: "America's future rests in a thousand dreams inside your hearts; it rests in the message of hope in songs so many young Americans admire: New Jersey's own Bruce Springsteen. And helping you make those dreams come true is what this job of mine is all about."

A week later, as the Born in the U.S.A. tour finished up its eastern leg in Buffalo and headed to the west coast, Mondale said that *his* campaign had Springsteen's endorsement. Springsteen had to deny that, as well—he wasn't ready to be used as a political tool. But what was Springsteen trying to say about America, and who was taking his carefully composed lyrics seriously? Where could Springsteen be located on the cultural landscape?

By mid-December, the single had reached its peak of Number 9 on the Billboard Hot 100 chart, and the tour went south for shows in Alabama, Tennessee, Kentucky, and Georgia. The hastily assembled video was put on the air for the MTV generation, who saw concert footage of Springsteen and the E Street Band interlaced with working class scenes of celebration and disappointment, of unkempt Vietnam vets and neat cemeteries. And that huge flag at the video's start and finish. The video's scenes accurately imitated the images conjured up by the song's lyrics. Yet this video, like the staccato chorus of "Born in the U.S.A.," may have simplified the poet's message too much. It was too easy for the media and the pundits to categorize Springsteen now. Forget that dark and complicated album *Nebraska*. Such a huge flag! The huge crowds, now waving their own flags. The masses couldn't be smart enough to penetrate into the lyrics, so why should the media bother?

The storyline seemed obvious: Springsteen has decided to go to any extreme as the popular poet-demagogue, speaking up for the dumb and down-and-out. Plenty of other musicians, from rock and pop stars to country and western crooners, had their own laments for the suffering working class. But none of them draped and clothed their visual image with the American flag like the Boss. This was new—and not to be seen again until more tough-looking white men, sporting cowboy hats this time, crooning glorifications of an Iraq war almost twenty years later. But the motif is the same: what better to put the fight back into a bruised and dazed citizen than prideful patriotism? The war eagle and the flag is flying, so chin up! Just the mid-1980s way of warming up the lower and middle classes during the frosts of a prolonged Cold War and an endless wage freeze. Crystal clarity in a song: working class values is American. Pride in testosterone strength is where the U.S.A. is at. If you were born in the U.S.A., like the Boss, you knew your identity. At least that's what many people thought was going on with this song. But could Springsteen really be pinned down so easily?

Identity Politics

Suffering can help to create identity, just as much as place of birth. The white working class, swept up into the conservative revolt of the Reagan revolution, was certainly suffering. Union jobs were disappearing faster than the industrial factories, while stagflation stole away real earning power. But the white working class was hardly the first segment of America to suffer. African Americans knew all about suffering, as did other ethnic groups. And women too, also recently integrated into the man's world. The list could go on and on.

The many social movements of the 1950s and 1960s treated the suffering of disenfranchised and neglected subgroups with the medicine of pride in one's identity. This was not identity as an individual, not old-fashioned rugged American individualism. In the post-war turbulence of big corporate America, no one could stand alone anymore. The type of identity offered by that era's social consciousness was the identity of the group, the salving balm of sameness. Unions understand the power of identity. So do church denominations, and civil rights leaders. So do politicians.

Too many politicians achieve power by dividing the country. If a politician can forge a unity for a sub-group, and convince that sub-group to make him their champion in a fight against other sub-groups, clinging to office election after election is much easier. To many cynical or lazy eyes, Springsteen appeared to be speaking for the white working class. Many politicians thought they had found an ally. But no one who carefully listened to this musician's albums should have reached that conclusion. Springsteen, drawing on his vast appreciation for rock 'n' roll's roots in the traditions of blues and country, located himself midstream, trying to articulate the shared experiences of the entire Vietnam generation. Allusions and echoes of great artistic predecessors, black and white, permeate "Born in the U.S.A." The song's video is faithful to that integration effort, showing men and women of multiple races sharing a common fate. Whatever your ethnic or gender origin, your birth in the U.S.A. at a certain time and place throws you onto the nation's stage for a performance together with the rest of your cohort. Whatever your specific role in that drama, you are all transformed by your common experience. Is your generation going to experience triumph, like the "Greatest Generation," Tom Brokaw's moniker for the group who fought World War Two, and thereafter feel a solidarity of confidence? Is your generation going to experience defeat, like the people represented in Springsteen's "Born in the U.S.A" narrative? Suffering can forge a identity no less powerful than triumph.

The politics of suffering can arouse vast energies and organize mass movements. If democracy does anything well, it opens the opportunity for transforming suffering into hope and then possibly into action. But the suffering must be identified as a common factor. People have to look past differences to see the shared suffering. Poets can direct people where to look, by supplying the images for the head and heart to focus on. Poetic songwriters, forced to compress their verse into four and a half minutes, snap together intense and unforgettable images.

Is "Born in the U.S.A" trying to help forge an identity of suffering? The song's narrative captures plenty of suffering, as recounted by a man who was born with nothing and has been kicked around from the very start. No surprise that he gets into a little hometown trouble. Crime is always to be found in a dead end town. Judges often offered military service instead of jail, so off to Vietnam he goes, to kill the hated "yellow man." His only luck is that he gets to come home, but what does he come home to? His hometown is even more dead to him. The refinery won't explain why he can't be hired. His Veterans Administration bureaucrat doesn't want to have to explain why either. Plenty of Americans apparently have enough hate left over from Vietnam to spend on him now too. The only love in the song is the love between his unlucky dead brother and a Saigon woman, and he can see that love in his treasured picture of them. He can't see any future for them, and he can't see any future for himself. No one will talk to him now. Trapped between the cold penitentiary and the burning refinery, he knows that he has nowhere to go. His origin entirely decides his true identity, and then it seals his fate.

Unlike many other Springsteen songs, pregnant with hope and the possibility of redemption, "Born in the U.S.A." ends with hopelessness. This song's America has been delivered to a tragic dead end. No escape down a highway to some better place—this man is born to an early grave. He may have thought he was born to run, but now he's reached the end of the road, right where he started. This song's dramatic images are about more than suffering. This song is about a kind of living death. That's what it is like for this man to be born in the U.S.A. And that is what the song's video ultimately fails to convey. Who'd want to identify with the hopelessly living dead? Possibly the bleakest and most despairing tune to climb the heights of the hits charts in modern American music, "Born in the U.S.A." is not just another protest song. It arrives too late to be a protest song about the Vietnam War, and too late to be a protest song about the demise of the blue collar union job. The working class doesn't matter anymore, but no one wants to talk about it. It's just too late to be born in the U.S.A.

Few people grasped the full extent of the irony. Sure, it was silly for Reagan to try to attach himself to the weight of the working class blues, since his fast-rising conservative movement sought the demise of unions and deep cuts to social programs that kept the heads of the poor just above turbulent waters. And it was just as silly for liberals to make the opposite mistake of supposing that Springsteen's song held out hope for progressivism either. "Born in the U.S.A" is about the common suffering of the Vietnam generation, yanked from the ranks of the working class, caught in a terrible crossfire of two wars, home and abroad. The jungle war and the class war get jumbled together in the song's images. There are no answers as to why the ultimately misguided and profitless foreign war could be relevant to the interests of the working class in America. The humiliating defeat across the Pacific Ocean, as overloaded helicopters flew away from Vietnam cities, was followed by the humiliating defeat across America's blue collar towns, as factory jobs fled out the country. And there are no answers either for why the working class must bear the brunt of capitalism's unsteady globalization. How ironic that a song about defeat and depression generated such optimism and pride in so many fans.

In "Born in the U.S.A" there just isn't any hope for an America that has already pretty much gone and died. If there is an America that this song celebrates, it is located only in the past. Maybe you can sympathize and identify with the Americans located in that singular cultural place. What sort of mood does this song put you in?

Patriotic Nationalism

Most people bellowing out the refrain of "Born in the U.S.A." at the Boss's rock concerts aren't feeling defeat, humiliation, or despair. Their chant feels cathartic, releasing the built-up energy created by the tension between the militaristic music and the sad narrative, just as Springsteen intended. What is not clear is whether Springsteen intended for the audience's reaction to be mostly celebratory. His fans needed to direct their erupting energies towards something, anything—and there was that huge flag. Very convenient. More than a few skeptical observers concluded that all that passionate patriotism must be just heated emotion without any real substance. An empty patriotism, having no real answers about what actually makes America great or what could be done to make it better, seems just cheap and easy.

The entire irony of this song's refrain is only revealed upon realizing that passionate nationalism is nothing to be proud of. What does it matter now that you were born in the U.S.A.? According to the song's lyrics, you're just going to die like the man trapped in the song. If you are seeking an identity here, you will only find a hopeless identity, the identity of all those marching together in lock-step towards an early grave. Not much in the song's deflating words to construct a positive identity or to energize a real movement of concrete political activism. But the concert and video images are another story, inflating idealized visions of national unity. The flag flying high represents the national life, still vibrant with pride. If you only focus on the proud refrain, and ignore the shameful reality down on the ground, "Born in the U.S.A." will serve as a new national anthem. Yet we must ask, is this airy and empty pride, attached to no reality but just a symbol, really good for anything? What does it really matter?

National pride can matter. It can matter greatly. Patriotism is usually viewed as the "quick and dirty" means of uniting people, according to twentieth-century liberalism. Liberal theory, in the United States and in England, has been powerfully shaped by Europe's convulsions through two horrible world wars. Passionate nationalism was precisely the method of Germany's leaders for energizing and controlling its population. Strikingly similar to past centuries of bloodshed powered by religious and ethnic strife, twentieth-century hatreds were born in the pride of identity, national identity this time. Is patriotic nationalism good for any country? That depends on the kind of country one wants to have. Germany became obsessed with its perceived weakness, in the face of threatening neighbors. The devastating defeat of World War One, and the resulting economic collapse, delivered a severe blow to German self-esteem and drove the German people towards a collective paranoia. Adolf Hitler's stunning rise to power through democratic elections cannot be fully explained without accounting for this fertile soil which eagerly received his patriotic rhetoric about the destiny of the "Aryan race." Hitler's dictatorship used every quick and dirty means of capitalizing on the poverty and demoralization of the German people. What really is the German nation? It must simply be the German people, the *Volk*, united by blood and suffering and destiny. Origin matters, especially if it becomes an obsession.

One of the most strident and forceful intellectuals who diagnosed national pride as the carrier of hatred was Carl Schmitt (1888–1985). During the 1920s, this German professor of law and politics drew attention for his claim that real democracy was not constitutional democracy. Constitutions distribute political power too thinly among citizens; constitutions create a forum for too much parliamentary debate that goes nowhere; constitutions place too much restraint on the sovereign's power for doing the country's necessary business. Genuine democracy happens for Schmitt when there is an identity of rulers and ruled, as *The Crisis of Parliamentary Democracy* (1923) claims. What is that identity like? No representative deliberative body should get between the sovereign executive power and the good of the people: Germany needs a popular dictator. Throughout the 1930s, Schmitt applauded Hitler's rise to power through elections that gave the Nazi party its life, Hitler's ensuing dominance over Germany's Reichstag legislature, and his subsequent suspension of the constitution. Schmitt especially appreciated how Germany's new dictator justified his suspension of the constitution by declaring a state of national emergency that only the executive office could deal with. In Schmitt's political theory, the modern nation-state survives only by constantly living in the state of emergency, in a state of war. A war needs an enemy—an internal enemy or a foreign enemy. Where do you find an enemy?

Well, finding the enemy is the dictator's problem. Arousing enough hatred for the enemy, so that the dictator's war and state of emergency gains mass approval, is also the dictator's problem. National pride is an obvious solution. Suffering peoples, despairing peoples, can be fertile soils for the seeds of anger, hatred, and violence. Schmitt was convinced that he had discerned the emotional fuel for national pride. Now you have all the ingredients for totalitarian fascism: supreme power for a beloved dictator who promises to lead the fight against the nation's common enemy. To achieve national unity, Schmitt demands not just national identity, but its logical extreme, national uniformity. In his books Schmitt keeps talking about democracy, but only in his perverse sense. *The Crisis of Parliamentary Democracy* anticipates the German fever of ethnic cleansing and genocide when he says, "Democracy requires, therefore, first homogeneity and second—if the occasion arises—elimination or eradication of heterogeneity." How could Schmitt really be talking about democracy? Fear of the heterogeneous—the xenophobic fear of anything different—is no longer democracy.

During the 1930s, Schmitt gave up all pretext of describing how democracy should work, defining politics and government in terms very far from democracy's original meaning. Just as the Nazi party was really gaining momentum, Schmitt's *The Concept of the Political* (second edition, 1932) announced that "the political" boils down to "the distinction between *friend* and *enemy*." Your friends are all of your fellow citizens who are just like you, while the enemy is anyone else whose differences threaten your inclusive group. The point of politics, for Schmitt, is not to prevent war, but to deal with it practically, since it is inevitable. There is nothing in Schmitt's political theory designed to reduce or prevent hatred and war. Government can only manage it, for the good of the country, which means that the sovereign power must correctly identify the enemy and strenuously lead the war effort. Since countries only hold together as unified political states during times of war, politics is about nothing but constant war. If an internal civil war successfully exterminates the enemy within, then an external war must be fought as well, so the government is always in power and the country stays united. But how could this be the fate of democracy? Friends of democracy around the world watched with horror as the meaning of democracy was so brazenly perverted beyond all recognition.

Classical liberalism since the mid-1700s has always meant unity from diversity, not unity from eliminating diversity. America's Founding Fathers envisioned a democracy proud to welcome all immigrants who wanted to join the American journey. Since this country's origins, conservatives and liberals may have disagreed over how much assimilation and conformity should be expected of immigrants, but they all pretty much agreed that once immigrants are in the U.S. legally, the Constitution protects their rights and liberties. Modern liberal theory embraces both the conservative and liberal, because this foundational political theory is about protecting the individual's rights and freedoms from other citizens and from the government, something that liberals and conservatives alike agree about. Not everyone has wanted to be liberal in this broad sense, of course. Indeed America has seen its share of fringe fanatics of hate calling for deportation or genocide for people who don't look like them, or talk like them, or dress like them, or pray like them. There was plenty of that sort of politics of hatred throughout the nineteenth century. But early twentieth-century liberals (again, encompassing both "Republican" and "Democrat" thinkers) supposed that no modern state would ever again be tempted to wield national pride and national unity as a lethal weapon. Those liberals thought wrong. Schmitt and other Nazi cheerleaders signaled the green light for the paranoid hatred of Hitler's politics of national pride. Hitler told the German people exactly why they should be proud to be Germans, who was to blame for their suffering, who they were supposed to hate, and the people listened and saluted back with adoration. The dark angry side of passionate nationalism cast a long shadow across Europe, and then lit the fires of genocide and war.

Ever since World War Two, liberals have shuddered with worry: does democracy, no matter how favorable its origins, always end up getting trapped down this dead-end of tragedy? What can prevent that sort of fate? Some political thinkers didn't see the big problem. Didn't America successfully fight those wars without resorting to angry patriotism? Well, there was a tremendous amount of patriotism, and plenty of wartime propaganda shaping and directing that patriotism. German Americans were the special target of much of the hatred that such patriotism spawned. There is nothing special about being an American that makes a person immune to the perverse power of patriotism's ability to arouse hate for an enemy. Are Americans, simply because they are born in the U.S.A., really any different from the Germans? Could Schmitt's tactics of political warfare apply universally, for all peoples and countries?

Does It Still Matter Where You Were Born?

People who reflected on the aftermath of two World Wars wondered if the German experience was a special strange case, or instead revealed something about universal human nature. It was hard not to notice that many dozens of countries throughout the twentieth century experienced the rise of dictators following a similar recipe for mixing together nationalistic patriotism, xenophobic hatred, and endless war. Accordingly, much of twentieth-century liberal theory veered away from patriotism and nationalism. Attempting to stay true to the ideals of democracy, and its protection of individuals despite their differences, liberals decided that where you are born should not matter very much. Do your rights really depend on the fact that you happened to have been born in a particular country? Do only Americans have rights that deserve respect and protection? If rights are universal, and if you deserve to have them protected regardless of where you were born, then politics is ultimately not about nations or nationalism.

Democracy cannot be about pride in one's own country, then, either—if you admire democracy, if you want democracy to spread around the world, then nationalistic patriotism is a poor vehicle to transport this kind of politics. Ultimately, the proliferation of proud nations, facing off against each other in a global game of competition and survival, is antithetical to democracy and must surrender to democracy. What democracy needs instead of divisive patriotism is a unifying cosmopolitanism: a world in which people think of themselves first and foremost as citizens of the world, and not merely citizens of some particular country. In cosmopolitan liberal theory, people may vote locally, but they should think globally. It really shouldn't matter to people that they were born in the U.S.A., or anywhere else. If people were more concerned about what is good for people globally, instead of simply what is best for one's own country, then countries would stop trying to dominate and control each other. Dictators would no longer be able to arouse passionate hatreds in the masses, and could no longer justify their extraordinary powers for fighting needless wars. Some liberal

cosmopolitans imagine a future world where countries surren-
dered their authority to a global government designed to protect
global rights. Other liberal cosmopolitans are satisfied with
visions of international federations of democracies which merge
their powers into an overwhelming force for peace and justice.
There is even a version of this liberal cosmopolitanism which
casts America as the lone superpower shouldering the entire
burden of promoting democracy around the world.

No matter which version of cosmopolitanism one may sub-
scribe to, it only works if the problem of diversity, pluralism,
and multiculturalism is finally resolved. Obviously, cosmopolitanism would not solve this problem by promoting assimilation
and homogeneity, like Schmitt. Citizens should be respected for
their differences, not for how well they conform to some identity. Should cosmopolitanism therefore celebrate the uniqueness
of each individual, the individual who is, after all, the bearer of
rights? Traditional liberal theory took that individualistic
approach, arguing that the government must only seek to protect individual rights and must be blind to pluralism—all of the
ethnic, religious, gender, and other differences that make us
individuals. Individual rights must be the same for everyone. But
doesn't this approach sound like a confusing paradox? After all,
the primary reason why people have been so worried about
their *rights* is because they have been treated as *wrongs*: their
ethnic or religious or gender identities have been disrespected
by their fellow citizens and by their country. Liberalism started
out as a dignified philosophical argument for individual rights,
but has evolved as a continual series of ugly street fights for
group dignity and group civil rights. If modern liberal theory
was supposed to evolve into cosmopolitanism, to avoid the
democratic trap of prideful patriotism, it instead got derailed
into the divisive politics of pluralism.

Take, for example, the emergence of multiculturalism in the
1980s. Multiculturalism in theory relies on traditional liberalism's
respect for individuals as individuals, but multiculturalism in
practice depends on novel group identities forged in a common
struggle for group rights. What makes people so energized with
anger that they are willing to take to the streets in protest? Not
their identity as mere individuals—it is instead their identity as
a member of a victimized sub-group. The dramatic and powerful energy built up and released by "Born in the U.S.A." can

spotlight the formation of a victimized sub-group, precisely according to the script of multiculturalism. And so the politics of multiculturalism seemed to automatically apply: now that you are identified as a member of the victimized sub-group, you know what to do. You know your friends—you know, the people who are also victims of the same mistreatment you have suffered. And you know the enemy—you know, those people who are happily benefiting from your mistreatment. No common ground here, just winners and losers, both looking to the government for help. The government can either preserve the status quo or enforce a new legal order. There is no neutral third option—either way, the government takes a side in this battle. In the multicultural wars, the grim logic of Schmitt's politics of friend and enemy makes sense of the situation. If we permit multiculturalism to be our guide, liberal democracy was never really about an impartial and fair government seeking the peaceful compromises that advance the good of the entire country. That's all empty rhetoric. Politics can only be about winners and losers, with each citizen's very life at stake.

Schmitt anticipated, largely by accident, where the multiculturalism trend could be headed. If your sub-group can't get satisfaction from the government, you don't lie down and take it. Starting a rebellion or a civil war can win respect. Maybe your sub-group can secede to form a new independent country. Say, to an American this is starting to sound familiar. How was the U.S.A. born? Right—Englishman versus Englishman in a war of rebellion. And how was it reborn in the fires of a second civil war? Yes, that episode in democracy cannot be forgotten either. Maybe Schmitt's political theory applies to the history of democracy as well as its future. Has anyone else become convinced that liberalism has to resolve the problem of multiculturalism? Distinguished American historian and political philosopher Arthur Schlesinger, Jr. regarded the multicultural wars as the death-march of democracy towards destruction. His 1990 book *The Disuniting of America: Reflections on a Multicultural Society* argues that the only way to avoid the fractious wars of each sub-group against the rest is to demand assimilation to a common culture, with a homogeneous identity as an American first and nothing else second. If you are born (or naturalized) in the U.S.A., Schlesinger says, then you had better stop seeking some special privilege or special treatment for your sub-group. If everyone is obsessed with what is best for his or her sub-group, no one is looking out for what is best for the entire country. Being born in the U.S.A. means that your primary identity is being American. Unless this principle is the guiding principle of politics, critics of multiculturalism concluded, there is no way for democratic politics to do what is best for the U.S.A.

Where is liberal theory supposed to go now? If the liberal respect for individual rights goes in the direction of cosmopolitanism, then people must suppress their identities as members of some particular sub-group. In the long run, nationalism could get submerged by international democracy. If the liberal respect for individual rights alternatively goes in the direction of multiculturalism, then people become mostly identified with their sub-groups. In the long run, nationalism could get disabled by intercultural struggles. Schmitt and Schlesinger recommend homogeneity—if a country's citizens see themselves as sharing a common culture and sharing a common destiny, then politics works (it works as a fighting weapon for Schmitt, as a peaceful tonic for Schlesinger). Should liberal theory renounce diversity and pluralism, as well as nationalism?

Perhaps it is too soon to surrender the idea that democracy was the kind of politics that could successfully combine pluralism and nationalism. There ought to be something special about being born, no matter who you are, in the U.S.A. Isn't that why so many immigrants have struggled so hard to start new lives and families here? These hard questions should make us step back and reflect on the diverse interpretations of "Born in the U.S.A." and liberal democracy.

Unity Born from Diversity

We have looked at some alternative interpretations of Springsteen's "Born in the U.S.A." and their implications. We then looked at some alternative interpretations of liberal democracy and their problems. Parallels between these two trains of thought emerged: similarities between the possible meanings of "Born in the U.S.A." and the possible destinies of liberal democracy are now visible. For example, "Born in the U.S.A." can be understood as a plea of sympathy for the suffering and tragic fate of one of America's sub-groups, the Vietnam generation. Similarly, liberal democracy can be understood as driven by victimized sub-groups, each forced to fight for its own identity and survival. From a different angle, we can view "Born in the U.S.A." as a cry of patriotism for the pride and hopeful destiny of the American nation, the "greatest country in the world," as its citizens are wont to remind themselves. Similarly, liberal democracy can be understood as powered by the nationalistic patriotism of all citizens, permitting the democratic process to focus on what is best for the whole country rather than on the narrow agendas of its sub-groups. Alternatively, taking a darker worrisome perspective, we can read into the "Born in the U.S.A." phenomenon a surging tide of angry nationalism that revolves around identifying "us real Americans" against "those un-Americans" in a potentially deadly conflict. Similarly, democracy might reach its full maturation only when the homogeneous majority asserts its rightful dominance over all competition, compelling assimilation or extermination.

We cannot here decide which of these interpretations is correct; in a way, they are all more like inviting questions, rather than definitive answers. And Springsteen was never a poet to give his listeners definitive answers, relieving from them any effort to think for themselves. Like earlier poets of democracy before him, such as Walt Whitman, Woody Guthrie, Hank Williams, and John Lennon, Springsteen throws the burden of figuring out your country back on you. Citizens of democracies, unlike any other type of citizen, are supposed to be able to handle this. If the people are supposed to rule, instead of kings or aristocrats, then they had better be able to figure out their country's problems. Brains count more than brawn when you are part of democracy.

While not much of a poet or songwriter himself, America's greatest philosopher of democracy, John Dewey (1859–1952) celebrated the capacity of Americans to think about their common problems. His greatest book about democracy, *The Public and Its Problems* (1927), still stands as the most profound defense of citizen participation in governing. Published at a time of wavering confidence in democracy, thrown in the face of communists and fascists and monarchists and militarists, this book explains how democracy must work if it is ever to succeed. Dewey confronts the problem of pluralism and multiculturalism directly. He declared that the entire point of democratic government, unlike any other form of government, is intelligently to manage diversity. If it can't manage the inevitable conflicts between a country's sub-groups with peaceful compromises, then democracy deserves to be discarded as useless.

Why isn't assimilation and homogeneity the answer? Because democracy is ultimately supposed to be about freedom from oppression—if you want to enjoy the culture of democracy, you have to embrace the liberty of everyone to live freely. If you instead want the freedom to live your way, and to not have to live with someone else living life quite differently, then that sort of freedom is not democratic and you don't want to live in a democracy. All sorts of alternative non-democratic totalitarianisms and dictatorships can fulfill their promise that you wouldn't have to suffer from diversity under their rule—you can live just with people just like you! Their offer may be tempting, because of the high price each person must pay for democracy: you must eventually compromise, for the good of the whole democracy, with people whose beliefs or fashions or lifestyles turn you off.

No wonder we spontaneously organize into sub-groups of unified identity, Dewey pointed out. The simple sociological explanation for so many voluntary associations and organizations and identity groups that proliferate across the democratic landscape is because people need each other. We group together into communities for common causes, when we can benefit from group effort. All of these co-operative communities—Dewey calls then "publics"—compete with each other for their own particular interests. Think companies, but in the civil sphere, not the economic sphere, where the "business" of democratic living gets done. Now, from this sociological explanation of what democratic culture is like, how does Dewey explain where democratic politics comes in?

Remember how democracy involves (1) liberty; (2) diversity; (3) publics; and (4) competition. Competition can lead to violence, naturally. Here Dewey offers a vision of democracy directly contradictory to Schmitt's. Yes, politics is about managing conflict between competitive sub-groups. But in a real democracy, still ultimately committed to freedom from oppression, that competition cannot be permitted to escalate into actual violence. Any political system that permits inter-group conflict to escalate into violence has completely abandoned its responsibility to govern, and any democracy that permits inter-group violence has forgotten its duty to protect all citizens from oppression. Democracy must manage conflict peacefully—and every democratic citizen knows this and is committed to this responsibility. Any actual democratic country, of course, may harbor plenty of non-democratic citizens, who would eagerly use violence for partisan goals, or would gladly elect any politi-cian who promised that their particular lifestyle would become the law of the land. Any type of political system reasonably aims to govern a population of citizens who conform to that political type, and so any democracy reasonably wants to govern only democratic citizens. Democratic citizens, regardless of their sub-group identity, simultaneously identify themselves as citizens of a common democracy. That's where the needed cohesiveness is found. Genuinely democratic citizens are capable of (1) respect-ing the liberty of all citizens; (2) respecting the diversity found across their democratic culture; (3) forming and managing publics that advance their interests; (4) competing with other publics without resorting to oppression or outright violence. The citizens are ready to be members of a democratic community in the wide sense: a "great community" of which each citizen is proud to be a member.

If you see where Dewey is going, the separate pieces of democracy are now easily put together. A democratic citizen will always have a double identity, a double loyalty. Loyalty to one's communal sub-groups, yes; but also loyalty to the idea of democracy itself and to one's country that tries to be a democ-ratic community. Democratic politics is about that difficult com-promise. Sure, I can fight for the interests of my sub-group even if that harms many other sub-groups and maybe the good of the country as a whole. But that is not the democratic way. It is always true that sometimes I have to think like a victimized member of a suffering sub-group—I just can't stand by and watch my livelihood and my way of life die a slow death from neglect. But sometimes I have to think like a citizen of the coun-try, too—I must try to imagine a way that my life can change for the better in some way that also contributes to the welfare of many others too, maybe for the good of the whole country.

Democracy as a political system is about seeking smart and creative compromises between conflicting sub-groups so every-one can somehow benefit. But democracy is ultimately about a personal system of internal thinking inside each citizen's head. The thoughtful citizen has to imagine, personally, a future when his or her own welfare is improved by some larger change in the system that is better for others at the same time. A person who really cares about the country, who is loyal to the country, can try to do that. This is not utopian dreaming – democratic citizens have been doing this for centuries. The social and political progress made by democracies is the cumulative work of millions of ordinary people. As democracies begin to cooperate together for global benefit, a cosmopolitan level of community emerges as well, so that people can feel a loyalty to the global community too.

Yes, you should be proud to be born (or naturalized) in the U.S.A. Your American pride, Dewey tells us, should be properly placed in the ideals of democracy for which this country was born and still lives. Your suffering and struggles and even defeats are an essential part of this American story that we are all helping to tell together. America is a great poem, as Whitman declared; America is a dramatic narrative of all the stories of the American people woven together. If you can sympathize with Springsteen's narrative of a real American experience, your loyalty to the U.S.A. is entirely justified. It matters where you were born, and being born in the U.S.A. is a huge responsibility. Citizens who try to live up that responsibility deserve to be proud Americans.

5

On the Cover of the *Rolling Stone*: Revolution in the U.S.A.

DOUG ANDERSON and RUSSELL ANDERSON

Singer-songwriter Richard Shindell often introduces performances of his song "Che Guevara T-Shirt" with a story of the
irony of the t-shirts.[1] Che the great anti-capitalist revolutionary
has had his name and image thoroughly co-opted by the shirt
makers not for revolutionary purposes but to make money for
the company owners—the capitalists.

This is not a new story. Herbert Marcuse (1898–1979), immigrant to the U.S. and well known neo-Marxist and critical theo-
rist of the 1960s, argued that in the contemporary capitalist
world there is no escaping such co-optation. We are made "one-
dimensional" by capitalism's single-minded orientation toward
greed and growth.

Canned Revolutions

The upshot is that there can be no genuine revolution or cultural revision from within the system—the genuine revolution-
aries, à la Che Guevara, must operate from outside it to make
significant changes. To ground a revolution, contemporary society would have to allow for a "new subject"—a new kind of person—who is not manipulated by the web of political and
economic power. But, Marcuse says, in the present situation the

---

[1] Shindell also notes that his own song isn't directly about the irony but is a
love song about a young woman wearing the shirt. Yet, the young man who
cannot resist the woman ends up in prison for pursuing her because he is an
illegal immigrant to the U.S.; so at another level the irony does appear.

58   *Doug Anderson and Russell Anderson*

"power and efficiency of the system, the thorough assimilation of mind with fact, of thought with required behavior, of aspirations with reality, militate against the emergence of a new Subject."[2] For Marcuse, the *illusion* of freedom for revolution is perhaps the most dangerous and pernicious feature of the industrialized capitalism of the twentieth century: "The totalitarian tendencies of the one-dimensional society render the traditional ways and means of protest ineffective—perhaps even dangerous because they present the illusion of popular sovereignty" (p. 256).

In similar fashion, another member of Marcuse's philosophical cohort, Theodor Adorno (1903–1969), argued specifically that American art—especially popular music—was thoroughly co-opted by capitalism, a feature of our general commodity fetishism. He argued, for example, that jazz was music *sold* to democracy and therefore was artistically at the bottom of the barrel. To be capitalistically popular or "pop," is, for Adorno, a mark of debasement and aesthetic inferiority. Adorno argued that such music and art become tools of dominance and oppression—they can be used to manipulate the "desires" of the masses and can thus be used to control political orientation.

Adorno's addendum to Marcuse's concern for one-dimensionality is important because it suggests that the one place where one might think one could find revolutionary freedom—the arts—has also been co-opted. Marcuse was himself tempted by the suggestion that the "aesthetic dimension still retains a freedom of expression which enables the writer and artist to call men and things by their name—to name the otherwise unnameable" (p. 252). But he came to side with Adorno, arguing that the popular arts have simply become "an omnipresent ingredient of the administered society" (p. 239); they help create a society in which we have become "possessed by our own images." (p. 250).

We use Bob Seger's "Like a Rock" and the Band's "The Weight" to sell Fords and Chevys. Our co-opting actions are blatant and profoundly rude, and yet we act as if nothing important has happened. In this cultural milieu, Bruce Springsteen's work fares no better; from the standpoint of philosophers like Marcuse and Adorno, he would be neither an important artist

---

[2] Marcuse, *One-Dimensional Man* (Boston: Beacon Press, 1964), p. 252.

nor a revolutionary thinker—he is just another Jersey boy in the employ of the economic-political junta of the U.S. innocently selling "America" back to those who suffer under its manipulative activities.

Is Springsteen Co-opted?

We know that Springsteen has critical things to say about American culture. From "Factory" to *Tom Joad* and *Magic* we find him offering critiques of our industrial practices and our government's decisions. In his youth he flew "the flag of piracy" and "broke all the rules"; he told tales out of school about being born in the U.S.A. Perhaps we could go even further. The whole of Springsteen's body of work, even when it is celebratory, reveals our own dissatisfactions with the drudgery of our labor, with the aimlessness of our acquistiveness, and with the Hollywood imagery of our political bureaucracy.

Yet, from the perspective of Marcuse and Adorno, Springsteen and the rest of us are deluded if we believe these criticisms make any difference or if we believe Springsteen's music is genuine art. Allowing Springsteen—or Tupac or Eminem—to "critique" our culture is merely a sop to Cerberus and has no revolutionary pay-off. After all, we are not even free to "choose" Springsteen; we are sold music-candy by Columbia Records and the rest of the corporations as they control the production of the music—they "release" things for us to listen to. More importantly, they control the distribution of the sounds—why else would they be so fundamentally committed to the legal control of the internet? This new venue not only threatens their profits, it threatens their control and manipulation of the market.

Can Springsteen, or any other American artists, survive Marcuse's critique—his analysis of all of us as beings co-opted and controlled by an industrial-political structure that has grown so efficient as to be immune to any internal critiques? Let's take a look at the "bad news" first and then see if Springsteen can offer an alternative reading of his own practice.

Gonna Buy Five Copies for My Mother

In the November 1st 2007 issue of *Rolling Stone*, Springsteen is interviewed by Executive Editor Joe Levy in an article entitled

"Bruce Springsteen's Restless Heart." Of course his image graces the cover—again—together with his well-worn Fender. Turn the page and one encounters a two-page spread photo of a Chevy Malibu. As we'll see, the issue is top heavy with Chevys—are we to suppose this is an accident given Springsteen's endless talk of Chevys and Camaros and his claim in "Pink Cadillac" that his "love is bigger than a Honda, it's bigger than a Subaru"?[3]

For those who don't remember and for those who never knew, *Rolling Stone* started as an "underground" magazine— it was anti-war and anti-establishment. It was counter-cultural, poor, and rife with criticisms of big business and the U.S. government. To be sure, the recent issue includes an article venting against the "hucksterism" of capitalist-turned-politician Mitt Romney, an article documenting the doom of global warming, and a two-page ad by The Gap which says that the next generation can change the world in part by purchasing its "Red" trademark t-shirts. The ad implies that some of the purchase money will go to the "Global fund to support programs which provide HIV/AIDS prevention, care, and treatment, including ARV medicine, in Africa." There is no suggestion that a direct contribution to the fund might be even more useful and efficient.

All of these efforts at political correctness are nevertheless surrounded and underwritten by a host of famous folks selling everything from cars to televisions to whiskey. Perhaps the most heady evidence on behalf of the outlook of Marcuse and Adorno is a twelve-month calendar inserted into the issue in which famous musicians pimp their "favorite" Chevrolets. It's interesting that they each became Chevy fans for this issue. For someone like me, who took thirty years off as a reader of *Rolling Stone*, the response is a stoned out, "Huh"? Where'd the magazine go, man? Jake Dorman of Farmington, Connecticut, agrees with me at least in part. That's because the previous issue of *Rolling Stone* had included a retrospective on Hunter S. Thompson that was, of course, promoting a new book about Thompson's life and was put together by some former employees of *Rolling Stone*.

---

[3] Springsteen, "Pink Cadillac," www.brucespringsteen.net/songs/PinkCadillac .html, 2007 Sony BMG Music Entertainment.

Dorman's response to the magazine concerning that issue was published on page 10 of this one: "I enjoyed your article on Hunter, but maybe it's time you stopped dwelling on the past and tried to make *RS* relevant by hiring writers who are as revolutionary as Thompson." Relevant? Revolutionary? Man, this thing is about sales, subscriptions, and the bottom line—no money, no revolution. Hey, why not make a Hunter S. Thompson t-shirt to go with Che Guevara? Probably been done, dude—check out the t-shirts and rock 'n' roll memorabilia at the back of the issue!

It gets worse. The issue includes a review of the Eagles' dual CD *Long Road Out of Eden*. In the review we find out what many had already found out: that the Eagles "have chosen Wal-Mart as the album's exclusive retailer." The ghost of Thompson might be asking in irony, "Where was Wal-Mart when I needed them?" But note the reviewer's subsequent line: "There is the inevitable contradiction in buying a record that attacks corporate greed and blind consumerism in songs like 'Do Something' and 'Frail Grasp of the Big Picture' from a superchain with a bleak record on employee rights and health care."

That Hegelian word "contradiction" was itself co-opted by Marx and Marcuse. Hey, man, do your remember *Steal This Book*? I think we're gettin' ripped off again! Do you think? The revolutionary mag with the glossy ads is selling you the "critical" CD retailed in Wal-Mart. Marcuse's point: no one *hears* the critique or the revolution; there's no revolution and no critique. There is only an image being sold to wealthy Americans who indeed have a frail grasp of the big picture!

And now Springsteen. He's on the cover of *Rolling Stone*. Good for them—good for him. Coincidentally, his new album *Magic* has just appeared and, if you turn to the "Charts" on page 102, you'll find it at "Number 1" in the "Top 40 Albums." It's ahead of Soulja Boy and Rascal Flatts. Good for them—good for him—good for Columbia Records. Another week at that spot earns someone something. So, here's the philosophical question again: can Bruce Springsteen, who is again on the cover of *Rolling Stone*, be an effective social critic and a genuine artist? Can he be any sort of revolutionary? Marcuse and Adorno say "no"—their analysis of the current system says there is no way out unless one is all the way out. The greed and growth of American capitalism have wrapped up the commodity known to us as Bruce Springsteen and sold it to America. He is de-fused, de-clawed, and has no aesthetic edge. As the reviewer noted, this is just the "inevitable contradiction" of American capitalism.

Socratic Revolution?

Is there better news? We think Springsteen answers the question asked above honestly and autonomously. He thinks that even as he is sold to us, he has the opportunity to speak to us from his restless heart, to admit if and when he *has been* co-opted, and to risk succeeding or failing as a genuine artist. This is Springsteen's residual and resistant American populist politics, and it survives the Marcusean critique because he doesn't buy the premises Marcuse and Adorno are selling. He thinks there is a mid-world between sheer autonomy and sheer co-optation.; the "inevitable contradiction" is for him not a foreclosure on his freedom but a living tension with which he freely struggles.

The ambiguity of Springsteen's response to the U.S. is the crucial first step in his response to the charge of co-optation in Marcuse's account of the one dimensional man. For Marcuse, one is either outside the system as a free revolutionary or inside the system as a co-opted slave of economic and political manipulation. One is either in the Matrix or out—there can be no Neos or Trinitys who work both sides at once. The ambiguities Springsteen proclaims in song *must* for Marcuse be themselves co-opted outlooks since Springsteen still operates within the American capitalist system working for Columbia Records. Springsteen's own worldview holds no such necessity—unlike Marx and Marcuse, and like Socrates and John Dewey, he projects a political theory of possibility and risk. Let us return to his interview with *Rolling Stone* with this in mind.

Springsteen claims his music is in an ongoing dialogue with his audience. Both in particular performances and by way of his recordings he sees himself in a transactional situation—there is a process of mutual influence and suggestion. He has always seen his music as engaged in this transactional process, even before he became well known:

> It comes down to trying to make people happy, feel less lonely, but also being a conduit for a dialogue about the events of the day, the issues that impact people's lives, personal, social, and political

and religious. That's how I always saw the job of our band. That was my service. At this point, I'm in the middle of a very long conversation with my audience. (*Rolling Stone*, p. 52)

It's interesting that he thinks of it as work. Pop music is not often described as a "service industry" but Springsteen sees himself that way or, perhaps more accurately, as engaging in a kind of public service. Most importantly, this description leads into a different conception of what it means to be a revolutionary than the one presented by Marcuse. Springsteen's revolutionary must both give voice to a perspective and must *listen to* the voices of other perspectives around him. The cultural changes to be effected in this way must always be in transition; one does not simply step out of a capitalistic world into a socialistic or communistic world. The conversation is where it's at for Springsteen's revolutionary—in this much we might call him a Socratic revolutionary. And herein lies the importance of ambiguity.

Art for Freedom's Sake

From earlier songs like "Factory" and "Born in the U.S.A." to the present "Radio Nowhere," "Magic," and "Long Walk Home," Springsteen has exercised a steady voice of concern for and complaint against various aspects of American culture. At the same time, there is much about our culture that his music celebrates. He is a spokesman for the America that can laugh at itself, critique itself, and can work to right itself. But he is a staunch critic of the America that is insular, exclusionary, dogmatic, unrelentingly narrow and afraid to grow. The Socratic revolutionary Springsteen invokes stands in the middle of this ambiguous relationship to America and engenders conversation through his art. Springsteen buys the suggestion that a free artist is in a unique position to alter a culture—not as a propagandist for any side, but as a revealer of cultural practices and as an imaginer of alternatives.

The initial evidence supporting Springsteen's freedom as a revolutionary artist is his ability to listen. When he shifted gears after *Born to Run* and recorded things like *Lucky Town* and *The Ghost of Tom Joad*, his audience talked back. He heard applause from the intellectuals in the audience for his down-to-earth reflections on personal life and political damage. Those inspired by the energy of Springsteen's social realism of the American northeast talked back in other ways. Springsteen recalls the many times he's heard someone say, "I liked the old Bruce better . . . ." Even as he listened to the critical voices, he refused to sacrifice his artistic vision of the moment to imitate the sound many of his fans had fallen in love with. His freedom was exercised in his willingness to write and perform songs that were *not* the old Bruce, even when his audience resisted.

"Listening," for a Socratic, does not mean "agreeing with." He stuck with his own vision and left it to others to follow him or not. His freedom was exercised in his willingness to shift from stadium concerts to singing solo in small theaters around the world. It was exercised in his pursuit of music history and of satisfying the folk dimension in his heart when he turned to the originary work of Woody Guthrie and Pete Seeger, two models of the American Socratic revolutionary. In short, Springsteen was in conversation but he was not driven by his audience—or his producers—even as he listened to them. The Marcusean artist, after all, should have ridden the wave of "Born to Run" for *all* it was worth not just *some* of it—Springsteen is not Bon Jovi.

As a Socratic revolutionary, Springsteen does not engage in conversation aimlessly. He has a pretty clear underlying "takes" on worldly affairs. For example, he is not in favor of the current war in Iraq. But for the most part he does not hit us over the head with these takes; he allows them to work their ways into his songs. If we think back to his issues with Viet Nam, we don't find him singing Country Joe McDonald's "I-Feel-Like-I'm-Fixin'-to-Die-Rag." He is more subtle; he works through a variety of experiences; he makes it possible for us not just to choose sides but to reflect on what the sides have to say. His songs are neither broadsides nor pipedreams empty of social relevance. Springsteen's revolutionary art is to use his music in conversation with his listeners to open spaces of reflection on the issues at hand.

> It's not like a one-on-one dialogue. It's more what you feel back from them. You create a space together. You are involved in an act of imagination together imagining the life you want to live, the kind of country you want to live in, the kind of place you want to leave to your children.

In "Born in the U.S.A.," for example, especially in the version released on *18 Tracks*, we are in a space where we hear both our underlying appreciation of being American and, emphatically, the serious problems we have trying to be Americans. Like Socrates, Springsteen draws no hard and fast conclusions; instead he gets us to take hard looks in certain directions. We enter the space of reflection with him and, confronted with the actualities of our own lives, are led to consider our past and our possibilities. Unlike the Marcusean revolutionary who sees us as dominated and manipulated and himself as utterly free, Springsteen sees us as like him—a bit manipulated, a bit adrift, and a bit free, but each with our own limited tools for social revision and reconstruction. This is his populism. We can imagine other ways of living and we can take small steps in the direction of those other ways.

The Best Policy

There is, however, a Marcusean moment in Springsteen's revolutionary activity in the need for self-awareness and self-reflection. One needs a hardcore honesty to have a sense of when one is being manipulated by a bureaucracy, an economy, or a social habit and to know when one has sinned against others, the world, or oneself. This kind of honesty pervades Springsteen's work from "4th of July, Asbury Park," to "Pink Cadillac," to "Radio Nowhere." When we enter a reflective space with him, we must bring our own honesty—this is the bone marrow truth in Springsteen's work that awakens us and drives us when we enter into conversations with him. It is only in this temper of brute honesty that we can see ourselves.

> My songs, they're all about American identity and your own identity and the masks behind the masks, both for the country and for yourself. And trying to hold onto what's worthwhile, what makes it a place that's special, because I still believe that it is.

For Marcuse, it's masks all the way down and nothing is worthwhile. For Springsteen, as for Socrates, there is no specific end-in-view but the unmasking makes a difference. American life at its best is an ongoing process of revision, an ongoing revolution.

As Springsteen puts it: "It'll be a lifelong journey by the time that I'm done" (p. 52).

The Socratic revolutionary Springsteen embodies is not a prophet. He may critique our ways of living and reveal the possibility of dire consequences, but he does not aim to speak for God. Unlike the Marxist revolutionary, Springsteen offers no promise of a communist utopia—he is not a member of some isolated intelligentsia. Like Socrates, he is a working person's revolutionary. He knows that we first have to "get by." He has a resilient faith in the American way of self-transformation that, he thinks, even the worst arrogance and demagoguery cannot fully undermine: "The American idea still has enormous power in its best manifestation. And ten George Bushes cannot bring that down—a hundred cannot bring that idea down" (p. 54).

Springsteen's Revolution

Springsteen, as Socratic revolutionary, does not allow us to end the democratic idea of change through conversation, persuasion, and imagination. Just as Socrates refused to leave Athens, Springsteen is unlikely move to Canada. For him, as for his heroes Woody Guthrie, Bob Dylan, James Brown, and Martin Luther King, art is a liberator, not as propaganda, but as a site of reflection on where we've been, who we are, and where we might go. There will always be some darkness, some suffering, and some dysfunction. And we must be watchful of our own co-optation by anyone. But that is precisely what calls out the Socratic revolutionary. It will call out the resistance of "Growin' Up": "when they said, 'Sit down' I stood up."[4] It will call out commitment: "no retreat, no surrender."[5] And it will call out a wise sympathy: "So receive me brother with your faithless kiss, or will we leave each other alone like this, On the streets of Philadelphia."[6]

---

[4] Springsteen, "Growin' Up," www.brucespringsteen.net/songs/GrowinUp .html, 2007 Sony BMG Music Entertainment.
[5] Springsteen, "No Surrender," www.brucespringsteen.net/songs/NoSurrender .html, 2007 Sony BMG Music Entertainment.
[6] Springsteen, "Streets of Philadelphia," www.brucespringsteen.net/songs/ StreetsofPhiladelphia.html, 2007 Sony BMG Music Entertainment.

Springsteen has understood the basics of Marcuse's one-dimensionality, and he has seen enough social damage to sleep with one eye open. But he also understands Socrates's down-to-earth ways of confronting the workers of the world. Revolution is not a game for intellectuals whose lives are disconnected from the life of labor. Revolution is just another form of work—it's a job requiring practice, repetition, sweat, and suffering. This is why one doesn't see a bad Springsteen concert. He's committed to the conversation, he has lived enough to sympathize and empathize with his audience, and he *respects* that audience. He knows, contra Marcuse, that for them, as for himself, the revolutionary task of "growing up" is one's own personal job of work.

II

When We Were Wild and Innocent

6

Blinded by the Subterranean Homesick Muse: The Poet as Virtuous and Virtuoso

RANDALL E. AUXIER

Bruce Springsteen is a poet, a very good one. But poets and philosophers have been on bad terms in the Western world for at least 2,500 years. In the *Republic*, Plato refers to the quarrel between poets and philosophers as "ancient," so it may be a lot older, but if Plato didn't start the fire, he has certainly been stoking it for the last two and a half millennia.

Why? Well, Plato declared poets to be a pack of liars and excluded them from his ideal city, the city to be ruled by a *philosopher* king. Plato thought that poets cannot be trusted because they say just anything they damn well please, and they say it so prettily that the mass of people *believes* them. And you just can't expect the masses to choose the True over what seems Beautiful, and, having chosen what pleases their fancy, they'll *also* claim it's the truth. That's why many religious people today (not all) like to believe in the Bible. It pleases them to do so and it makes them feel like they know something divine. And people are, by and large, both gullible and frightened of the unknown—I don't exempt myself from this, of course.

In Plato's day, people treated the epics of Homer the way today's fundamentalists treat the Bible. And on that account, Plato had a low opinion of the intelligence and judgment of ordinary people; the Greeks called them the *hoi polloi*, the teeming and chattering unwashed masses.

In ancient Athens the trouble was all these damned poets going around with their clever words, invoking various Muses as their guides, to sanction their authority, and then telling scandalous stories about the behavior of the gods. These stories

make the gods seem less admirable—and less moral—than ordinary human beings. It was sort of like watching the celestial
divines take turns on the Jerry Springer Show. The behavior of
the God of Abraham in the Bible is a close parallel.[1] And the
people ate it up. In our day, it's television invoking corporate
sponsors and then depicting our leaders as, well, people who
seem less admirable than we are ourselves. And *we* eat it up. The
more things change, the more they stay the same. What can be
done? Plato suggested that any city or community that wishes to
keep its own soul from rotting simply has to *ban* such people.

He also explained why the poets lie—it's because they don't
really *see* the truth. They *think* they do, but they believe the
world of the senses is reality, matter in motion, and so they use
their imaginations (which depend on the senses), instead of the
power of reason, to create their songs. Their words become a
verbal *copy* of the physical world, and when these words are
nicely arranged, people recognize their own sensory and emotional experiences in them, and they are pleased, or angered, or
saddened—or (and here's the point) they feel whatever the
poets *want* them to feel. Because the people *feel* it strongly,
they only *see* what the poets want them to see. That would be
fine, Plato thought, if poets *knew* anything, but they don't—they
make things up, and with the encouragement of applause, poets
become convinced that they are speaking the truth, even though
they really know they're making it up.

I'm sure that more than a few readers here have noticed what
a problem television is, especially to uncritical people. The mass
audience sees an image on CNN or Fox News, and they forget
about the corporate powers that sponsor those images, and also
edit and select and manufacture them—to serve a number of
interests, mainly financial. But the TV viewer thinks he has a

---

[1] I wonder how many people know that the Bible is simply filled with poetry.
Pick up a Bible. Now turn to *Genesis* 3:14, where God is pronouncing the
curses on the serpent, the man, the woman, and the earth. You'll notice that
the indentations and line breaks are different here. That usually means you're
reading poetry. God's curse is a poem. Now thumb through the book. You'll
see this pattern a lot. Almost the whole book of *Isaiah* and about half of
Jeremiah, for example, are written in verse. The New Testament has less
poetry, but it is not exempt. See *Revelation*, Chapters 18 and 19, for a couple
of long poems.

truth, because he thinks he saw something with his own eyes. What's actually happening is that the images seen stir *feelings* in the viewer, and the feelings then dictate the opinions a viewer forms about the images he has seen. In time, he sees only what accords with the habits of feeling that have developed while watching the canned images. Springsteen recently adapted an old maxim to this situation when he says "believe none of what you hear, and less of what you see" in the song "Magic."

How many of us would be tempted, if made king, simply to ban the TVs? Or perhaps many others among us would seek to control the images ourselves for some higher purpose? We don't want to serve ourselves or control others, we just don't want them to be misled, right? Well, Plato isn't interested in controlling the poets either. He suggests that we offer them a laurel and invite them to go to a different city, one that is already corrupt, to ply their trade. Plato is sort of a "Poetry NIMBY."

I may sound sympathetic to Plato up to this point. I like Plato as well as the next philosopher, but on this matter I am not in sympathy with him. I think he's a dangerous elitist, and I don't like people who think better of themselves and their own abilities than those of their fellows. Blame it on my working-class family origins, or call it a democratic disposition, or call it plain common sense. I can't stand elitists. Psychologically speaking, poetry is a threat to philosophy because philosophers want *their own* stories about "reason" and "truth" to be believed, but they don't tell the stories well enough to bring applause from the masses, let alone conviction. And so, while people pay good poets a lot of money to sing their songs, they ignore the "truths" of philosophy, and they think of philosophers as daft and unaccountable dreamers. That pisses off the philosophers. Philosophers, in general, secretly harbor the conceit that they'd all be better leaders than the ones chosen by the people. There are a lot of crypto-totalitarian personalities studying philosophy, and Plato is their leader.[2] Be extremely wary of anyone who

---

[2] For an example, take a look at Stanley Rosen's essay "The Quarrel between Philosophy and Poetry," in *The Quarrel Between Philosophy and Poetry: Studies in Ancient Thought* (New York: Routledge, 1988), pp. 1–26. Rosen belongs to a school of philosophers called the "Straussians," who are students and followers of a Plato scholar named Leo Strauss (1899–1973). This bunch is elitist in the extreme, and to my thinking, a collection of crypto-totalitarians.

likes Plato too much. That person really wants to be *obeyed*, not argued with.

So what of it? I want to see whether I can, as a chastened philosopher (whose *cats* won't even obey him), invite the poets back into the city and see what they *know*—about Beauty, about Goodness, and about Truth. I have a feeling that poets *do* know something more than the world of the senses, and I think we should begin the reconciliation by examining their Muses—the deliverers of the Beauty, Goodness and Truth that the poets "know." We might as well start with the scariest and most potent poets alive.

A Grudge Match

There's a certain type of song that only the virtuoso poet-song-writer can pull off. It may even seem to be a genre unto itself. Some examples everyone knows are Don McLean's "American Pie," Bob Dylan's "Subterranean Homesick Blues" and of course, Bruce Springsteen's "Blinded by the Light." There are certainly others by lesser-known virtuoso songwriters, such as "When I Go" by Dave Carter, and "The Bishop and the Ghost of the Nazarene" by Jonathan Byrd, and "Stained Glass" by Danny Schmidt.[3] Astonishing, impossible songs! The songs I mention here are all in the domain of white-boy folk music, but other styles of music have their own close equivalents. I'm not speaking of the merely clever poetizing of the better then average song-writerly song, I am speaking of the completely over-the-top, testosterone-laden, swashbuckling wordsmithery that only a *young man* (or a man with a young Muse) would even dare to attempt. This is a sowing of lyrical wild oats in the far-flung back forty of the human imagination, and only the chosen few reap a harvest *there*. That field, when plowed, is dangerous to the soul and the mind, a place on the edge of sanity itself.

There are numerous studies by people, both amateurs and professionals, who spend their precious energies trying to puzzle out all the references and allusions in these songs, and I'm

---

[3] Do yourself a favor. Google these songs. Don't just read the words, listen to them, and add these three songwriters to your iTunes inventory. I'm not kidding. You don't know what you're missing.

not saying that is total a waste of time. It can be fun, but it's mainly beside the point. What is this sort of swaggering of the poets?

As far as I know, the song genre doesn't have a contemporary name (I'll try to name it before the end of this essay), but this type of song has been around for a very long time, longer than recorded history. The ancient Greeks apparently called it "dithyramb," although that *name* is not Greek and came into their language from some mysterious place beyond history. In the days of Plato, the dithyramb was a kind of ecstatic song sung to the god of wine, Dionysus. But Dionysus was a late arrival in the Greek pantheon, a young god as gods go, and the dithyramb is much older than he is. It was originally sung to the goddess, not a god.

In the dithyramb, the singers would face off against one another and have poetizing contests. It probably looked like a scene from *Eight Mile*. It's still alive. But men have apparently been doing this sort of song for a long time—for about as long as there have been women. And that may be a great part of the point. We will get to that. Some men have a gift for the spontaneous demands of the contest, but most men can't do it at all. The contest is one way that, among poets, the men can be separated from the boys, the virtuosos from the merely virtuous. If you'll excuse the image (and it is the first of many you'll have to excuse), the dithyramb is a poetic licking contest, and the guy with the trickiest tongue wins.

And how do poets know who wins? In a sense, everyone just *knows*, when it's over, and it's like a poetry slam in which the audience decides, but pushing it off on the audience only defers the deeper question. Grant that the audience just *knows* who won; how? This is not a rational process of developing criteria and measuring each contestant against some objective standard. In truth, the poets are comparing Muses, and they are *not* saying "I love my Muse more than you love yours," they are saying the converse: "my Muse loves *me* more than yours loves *you*, and I can prove it, you pantywaist . . . watch this":

> . . . Madman drummer bummers and Indians in the summer with a teenage diplomat, in the dumps with the mumps as the adolescent pumps his head into his hat . . .

It may seem juvenile, but I have to propose a grudge-match:
Dylan and Springsteen. Whom do the Muses love the most?
Picture Bob and Bruce, in concert, at The Meadowlands. We are
all in a circle, no lyric sheets allowed. Oh, and Weird Al
Yankovic is the Master of Ceremonies.

The Tenth Muse

A Pause. The reader of a feminist bent may already have had
more than enough of all this boyishness. Yes, yes, I know. We
all talk too much and say too little—as Gertrude once put it to
a long-winded man, "more matter, less art." But you *like*
Springsteen, right? And you can tolerate (or perhaps secretly
enjoy?) *his* constant objectifications and eroticizations and
romanticizations of the "fairer sex"? If you really *don't* want to
be put on a pedestal and sung to by an impassioned man, why
don't you listen to (and read about) someone else? I think you
do want that, and that you do want to be adored, and you do
want a man who would die for you—or at least a woman who
would, which is why you *also* like the Indigo Girls. Amy Ray is
Bruce Springsteen in drag, or vice versa, because when erotic
desire gets that intense, frankly, it doesn't matter who is doing
whom.

I think that is why Plato (who was something akin to gay)
called Sappho, the poetess from Lesbos (who was either a les-
bian, or not, or poly-amorous and omni-sexual, or not, depending upon which expert you ask and when, and what sort of
mood you're in when you hear the answer . . .), anyway, Plato
called Sappho the "Tenth Muse." We will spend some time on
the other nine Muses shortly, but for now, be aware that Plato
didn't say this because Sappho was a *woman*, he said it because
she was so very good at poetry that it seemed divine to him (if
not sufficiently divine to win her a place in his ideal city). In the
ancient world, the idea that a woman should be poetic came as
no surprise at all—it was *expected*. In the world before history,
everyone understood that women can do *directly* what men can
do only *derivatively*—whether that is creating words or creating
babies, both of which were seen as pretty magical back then
(and still are by anyone with any sense).

The simple point is that when a woman could do the poetizing thing, this was regarded as entirely natural. *Of course*

women have the power of the word. That's why they ruled the whole world for about ten thousand years before recorded history.[4] What is surprising, to the ancients, is when a *man* can do anything creative at all. And then as now, no *real* man would be stupid enough to take credit for the achievement—he credits the woman who loves him, his inspiration, his Muse. None of this happens without the blessing and power of the woman in charge, and the man receives the words as a gift, just as he receives children. All the Muses are female. How absurd would it be to have a male Muse? But feminine authority, creativity, and generosity do not begin or end with just the Muses.

For example, Socrates wasn't called the wisest man in Athens because some *dude* told him so. It was a woman, the Oracle at Delphi—and she added an interesting left-handed compliment. If Socrates was wise, it was because he recognized the full extent of his personal ignorance. Just the sort of thing I hear from the women in my life, minus the part about being wise. Socrates took that oracular observation as a blessing anyway. Only once did he become so full of himself as to claim he really knew anything, and the only thing he claimed to know was *love*—eros. He had reason to regret having said that afterwards, but that's another story.[5]

So if you my dear feminist would rather throw away the key to your chastity belt than entrust it to a man, I can't blame you.

---

[4] Since the middle of the nineteenth century, archaeologists have increasingly been unable to avoid the conclusion that human civilization is about ten thousand years older than recorded history. The archaeological record also increasingly indicates a widespread likelihood that women were the leaders of these complex civilizations. To learn about this, I recommend that you begin with the writings of the Swiss classicist Johann Jakob Bachofen (1815–1887), and move from there to the Cambridge classicist Jane Ellen Harrison (1850–1928). Their writings are easily available. The best recent writer is, in my opinion, the Lithuanian archaeologist Marija Gimbutas (1921–1994), who was a better archeologist than an interpreter of what she found, but she is still a very responsible interpreter. Unfortunately, there is a lot of total crap out there about this "pre-history," like Riane Eisler's popular book *The Chalice and the Blade*. She has the audacity to call the careful, qualified language of responsible scholars "quaint," but Riane, sweetie, it is that careful language that separates women like Harrison and Gimbutas from girls like you.
[5] If you are intrigued, I told the story in my own way in "Chef, Socrates, and the Sage of Love," in *South Park and Philosophy: Bigger, Longer, and More Penetrating*, edited by Richard Hanley (Chicago: Open Court, 2007).

Men are pigs. But we're all pigs for *you*, baby, and I'll need to ask you to read a different chapter. But I will grant you one thing for sure: the idea that there are only nine Muses, with just one Mother, is definitely a *male* invention. Men get nervous when too many women start generating too much of that delectable energy, and when men get nervous, they start counting things. "Nine of you and no more!" said Herodotus. In truth there are infinitely many Muses, as many as there are actual women and *possible* women. Please don't be too harsh with us when we are frightened. If you only understood what you *do* to us, it would scare you *too*.

The Early Rounds: History, Tragedy, Comedy, and the Stars

You'll have to wait for the main event between Dylan and Springsteen while we warm up. How did it come to this, the battle royal between the two titans of the white-man dithyramb?

Well, in the early eliminations we saw some able poets. For example, in the eastern semi-finals, Michael Stipe did "The End of the World as We Know It," and Billy Joel sang "We Didn't Start the Fire," but the audience knew that these were not the purest and most powerful deliverances of the Muses. Still, Stipe and Joel made it *to* the semis by backing up their poetic claims with "Fall on Me" and "Only the Good Die Young," which are pretty impressive pieces of rhyme, if not quite the pinnacle. But their weakness is exposed when we consider that it is not so difficult to turn *actual history* into rhyme. Any able wordsmith can do it. The Muse of history is Clio, and she isn't the Queen Mother of the Muses. The problem with history is that, well, it's over. Her songs, the ones she inspires without help from other Muses, may serve as a clever record of past experience, but they don't burst into the future. The Muses together do not only sing of what *was*, they sing of what *is* and *will be again.* To make it into the finals, the offering must transcend the past, and that is why Billy and Michael were eliminated in the Urban White-boy Division.

And they were eliminated by Paul Simon, when he did "Sounds of Silence." He had set them up for the take-down with "Fifty Ways to Leave Your Lover." But when Simon came up against Springsteen in the regional finals, he pulled out his best,

"You Can Call Me Al": "A man walks down the street, says 'why am I short of attention? Got a short little span of attention and oh my nights are so long' . . ." It was good, but Bruce won by a nose with "Spirit in the Night": "We'll pick up Hazy Davy and Killer Joe / And I'll take you out to where the gypsy angels go / They're built like light and they dance like spirits in the night . . ." Clearly a whole gathering of Muses, no?

Paul Simon's primary Muse is named Melpomene, the Muse of tragedy. If you think about it you'll see that the vast majority of Paul's lovely words depend on the sense of tragedy and loss—even when he is chipper enough to be singing about the color film in his Nikon camera, he still just worries that his mother will take it away from him. Bruce is not so limited. Your mother is not going to take your film, Paul. Chill. It makes me wonder if the "mother and child reunion," the one that was "only a motion away," actually ever occurred. Paul left us all hanging on the outcome. Maybe Mama Pajama just spit on the ground and sent the boy to the house of detention. Paul has issues, but he's a grand poet. I am not sure he *wants* to be loved by his Muse. He seems to be doing straight time in *her* house of detention, and she's a Nun with a big ruler for his hands. Where's the radical priest when you need him?

Bruce, on the other hand, shows that he has the favor of Clio in songs such as "Youngstown" and "Nebraska," and he is on better than formal terms with Melpomene in songs like "Streets of Philadelphia" and "Reno." Yes, history and tragedy are there, and they are not cruel nuns. They like Bruce and he likes them. The audience just knows.

But speaking of Melpomene, word has it that Robert Johnson and Muddy Waters are scheduled for the finals in the Delta Blues Division down at the crossroads in Mississippi; the Devil himself is making the calls there, since they have both already cashed in their mortal chips. And it's down to Jimmie Rogers and A.P. Carter in the Dead Hillbilly Division, but there are rumors that Carter lifted some of his lines from his kinfolk, and then someone's daddy came looking for him with a shotgun. Hank Williams and some Honky Tonk Angels (hopefully not too many for a pinhead) are the judges in that one.

When it comes to blues and country and hillbilly music, this is a collaborative effort between Melpomene and Thalia, the Muse of comedy and nature poetry. Bruce leaves the nature poetry to John Denver and other wimps who change their names,[6] but he *does* do comedy. Bruce doesn't write "ha-ha" funny songs, but he does write songs made from funny stories, and his favorite comic trope is irony.[7] A good example of Thalia's efforts with Bruce would be "57 Channels (And Nothin' On)," in which Bruce also calls on the help of Urania, the Muse of the celestial sky. In that tune he buys a satellite dish, points it at the stars, and "A message came back from the great beyond / There's 57 channels and nothing on." He finally shoots the TV, a tribute to Elvis. You'll find simply countless lines about the sky, the stars, the sun and moon, and the "great beyond" in Springsteen's poetry. He and Urania are pretty tight, and Bruce doesn't like the way "the Giants of Science spend their days and nights" trying to control her skies and count everything (see "Santa Ana" from *Tracks* if that bit of lyric evades your memory).

Sam Houston's Ghost

However those contests may unfold in the great beyond, what we will have at the Meadowlands is a truly impressive contest for the (temporarily) living. But this is like the Super Bowl—you have to endure a lot of commentary before kick-off, but the game will be worth it. Probably. Never trust a philosopher.

This may come as a surprise, but maybe not. Texas has its very own Muse, and all songwriters have to pay homage to her. It's true that whatever Texans can't *buy* they will simply steal, whether it's oil, culture, Iraq, or Texas itself, and their Muse is no different. They stole their Muse from Mexico, but the Mexicans had already stolen her from the Spanish, and the Spanish stole her from the eastern Mediterranean in the Middle Ages. Her name is Calliope, the very one who crashes to the ground in "Blinded by the Light." Calliope is a *big* woman, pear shaped, fertile, Texas-sized; she likes gravy and greasy bar-b-cue and she ain't satisfied with a short poem or a little tally-whacker (that's what they call it in Texas, in *polite* company). That is why

---

[6] I suppose you're all well aware that Bob Dylan's name used to be "Zimmerman."

[7] If you want to hear the purest deliverance of Thalia in the "ha-ha" category, download "Title of the Song" by the group Da Vinci's Notebook, from their album *The Life and Times of Mike Fanning*.

Townes Van Zandt couldn't write a short song. He was from Texas. I don't know about his tally-whacker, but I do know that Calliope liked him better than he liked her—she wouldn't leave him alone, couldn't get enough of him. Townes was supposed to face Steve Earle in the finals of the Drunk and Drugged Cowboys Division of our contest, but he died. Calliope crushed his skinny ass. Steve Earle wasn't willing to let the thing go, so he has been trying to die ever since then, just so he can get his match. Some people, especially Right-wing politicians and the corporate powers of Nashville's Music Row wish Steve well in his quest for the other side. But I don't. I like him right where he is, and Townes can wait.[8]

All of Calliope's boys know that they stole her from Mexico (see "Pancho and Lefty" from Townes's catalogue), and they'll tell you so if you ask them. Bruce learned the story. He had to. He kept on singing about Spanish girls (definitely an obsession of his) until one day the big ole woman said "you have to write about Texas, that's where I live; and as for your little ditty about Go-cart Mozart, I don't care for it; I was *not* sneezing and wheezing when you tripped me, and I am not a silicone sister, these are *real* . . . so you *owe* me." Bruce gave her an epic, "Galveston Bay," and then told the story of her kidnapping in "Santa Ana." Penance done. Bruce has always been a good, pious Catholic.[9]

---

[8] Actually, the event really did occur, sort of. Check out the CD *Steve Earle, Townes Van Zandt, Guy Clark: Together at the Bluebird Cafe.* It sounded like Steve and Townes were so very intoxicated that night that they could barely perform at all, but it is such an amazing gathering of true Texas poets that it is worth a listen. Guy Clark was, as far as I could tell, more or less sober, but it's not like he was unfamiliar with the rule requiring strong drink. Nobody won that night, however, because Calliope didn't show up at all—the Muses have a pact, ever since the whole Dixie Chicks debacle: they don't cross the city line in Nashville any more, although they will visit some of the more depressing towns on the outskirts. As Guy Clark wryly observed, alluding to Townes Van Zandt as "William Butler Yeats in jeans": "There ain't no money in poetry / That's what sets the poet free / And I've had all the freedom I can stand." (See Clark's "Cold Dog Soup.")

[9] A certain *type* of Catholic, that is—Springsteen calls himself "lapsed," but as Stan Friedman notes in a recent review, although Springsteen's "words certainly are not scripture, many of us have used their dense layers of meaning to help reflect on our own faith. No one should be surprised. Springsteen's theology has been the subject of numerous magazine articles, books, and even

Canadian Border Five Miles from Here

There are some pretty poets north of the border. Leonard Cohen won the Shivering Canucks Division, when Gordon Lightfoot made the supreme mistake of singing "Wreck of the Edmund Fitzgerald" in the final round. The audience fell asleep, and anyone could see that this wasn't Clio's best work. Cohen had advanced to the finals with a victory over Joni Mitchell (the Canadians are so damned egalitarian that they let women into these things). But Cohen got to go first, and proved the *better* woman by singing (or *attempting* to sing, which is about all he *can* do, but that never stopped Dylan either) "Joan of Arc." In that astonishing procession of lyric, Cohen actually has the audacity to depict the fire, yes, the *fire*, as Joan's amorous suitor. The fire stalks her all of her (short) life and then "marries" her at the stake, and *consummates* that desire by *consuming* her body—and with some coaxing, she *wants* it. *Holy shit!* That is what I said the first time I heard the song. Love'll do that to you if you aren't careful. The "Joan" reference wasn't lost on Joni, and she decided to forfeit. Discretion is the better part of valor. Good call Joni. Leonard is a little bit unstable.

Then Cohen clinched the deal over Lightfoot in the finals with "Hallelujah," which I know you've heard. This is an impossible song, but it isn't the same sort of song as "Blinded by the Light." It's a hymn. Cohen works with all the Muses, and it's a good thing Springsteen doesn't have to compete with him (due to the immigration restrictions the Canadian government, adopted in 2002 to keep all *thinking* Americans from overcrowding Toronto in search of safety and genuine civil liberties). But Leonard's favorite Muses are Erato and Polyhymnia. Erato, as you might guess, gives her boys erotic poetry and marriage songs. "Joan of Arc" is principally hers. Polyhymnia, as you might also guess, is responsible for hymns—sacred song of all kinds, and she worked together with Erato on Cohen's "Hallelujah."

---

seminars. Churches work his songs into their liturgies. Biblical allusions populate all his albums, with some cuts being influenced by authors such as Flannery O'Connor." Springsteen is indeed a Flannery O'Connor sort of Catholic. And Friedman's entire review of *Magic* is very perceptive, and right on the money in my view. See it at http://www.christianitytoday.com/music/glimpses/2007/magic.html.

Bruce knows Erato and Polyhymnia very well indeed, as any Springsteen fan can attest. Religious imagery shows up in almost every Springsteen song, and when he *gets* religious, it's almost always about some woman. My current favorite is "I'll Work for Your Love," from the new CD *Magic*, in which Bruce takes the Ecstasy of Saint Theresa and turns it into a seduction song for a bar maid who catches his eye. "I watch the bones in your back like the stations of the cross," says he. This tune may be the best collaboration of Erato and Polyhymnia since "Hallelujah," but with the added help of Thalia. Where Cohen's song is so over-the-top that it borders on giving way to simultaneous joy and despair (if that is even possible, which I wouldn't have believed until I heard the song), Springsteen's tune displays ironic wit— he surely snickers at himself as he says "I watch your hands smooth the front of your blouse and seven drops of blood fall."[10] It's too much; it's funny.

Dancing in the Light

We are down to just two Muses now, so the *pièce de résistance* can't be far away. Their names are Euterpe and Terpsichore. They are performing Muses, the ones who descend on the performers and the audience and create the magic in the music (that's Euterpe's part) and the ecstatic dance (that's Terpsichore's part). The contest is not just about the words, it's also about the delivery, the energy, the communication between the poet and the crowd. Some artists specialize in just this part of the poetic process—performing other people's songs and doing it so well as to enchant us all. Undoubtedly, in recent times, the darling of Terpsichore and Euterpe was Elvis Presley. He wasn't much of a songwriter (he did-n't suck, it just wasn't his gift). When Elvis sang and danced, we all wanted him, women *and* men. There wasn't a dry seat in the house. How can one man possess that much erotic energy? Euterpe and Terpsichore wore Elvis out, and us too.

---

[10] Stan Friedman thinks this may be a veiled reference to *Leviticus* 16:19. That looks right to me, and is reinforced by an earlier verse: "The dust of civilizations . . . Slip off of your fingers / And come driftin' down like rain." See Friedman's review cited above. I don't know what Bruce reads, but he certainly *once* read the Bible and the *Lives of the Saints*. It's all over his music.

Plato held such poets in special contempt. The Greeks had a name for poets who performed other people's songs: "rhapsodes." In contrast to the poets who create their own poems, who are simply *deceived* about whether they know anything, the rhapsode just sits around cultivating his own vanity, and hasn't the moral fiber to realize that he's just a wanna-be. Plato wrote a whole dialogue about the pretensions of the rhapsodes, called *Ion* (that's the rhapsode's name, and he was sort of the Elvis Presley, or more likely the Michael Bolton, of ancient Athens). Plato was hell-bent on making this type of poet look as bad as possible, so he depicts Ion as a total fool and a hopeless poser who really wants to be a military leader, but hasn't either the courage or the knowledge to do anything except *act.* It sort of reminds me of Ronald Reagan's service in the Second World War—and as President.

Obviously Terpsichore and Euterpe also love Bruce. They have given him a sense of the power of performance that exceeds most of the rhapsodes, if not quite coming up to the level of Elvis. And Bruce is no rhapsode, he's a real poet. Of particular note for our purposes is that Terpsichore and Euterpe have a very uneven relationship with Dylan. More often than not audiences come away from a Dylan show disappointed. I have never heard anyone say that about a Springsteen concert. Dylan does not love or respect his audience, and he does not want to be loved by the Muses of performance, although sometimes they take hold of him whether he wants to be taken or not. Clearly Dylan knows these Muses, but he's a ragged clown, and while the reels of *rhyme* may be skipping, Dylan himself is standing stark still, hiding under a hat, behind dark glasses, chasing shadows, just like he said. I wouldn't pay it any mind.[11] Meanwhile Bruce is dancing in the *light,* and not too badly for a white boy (even the Muses can't wholly counteract the genetic stiffness of a northern European heritage—which is why I have come to question whether Elvis was really white), and he's dancing with *Courtney Cox,* who looks like the embodiment of Terpsichore to *me.* What a babe.

---

[11] I am *not* alluding to the infamous "booing" incident at Newport when Bob pulled out the electric guitar. Not only is that all blown out of proportion, but Bob was right. Folk music had become maudlin. It was definitely time for a little electricity.

The Poetic Virtue

You can see that the fightin' words are starting up at the Meadowlands. Both Dylan and Springsteen are virtuosos. They are, at least some of the time, loved by *all* of the Muses. That is what *makes* a poet a virtuoso. But that isn't enough. What makes a poet virtuous? The words "virtuous" and "virtuoso" obviously come from the same root. It's the Latin "virtutem," which means moral strength, manliness, potency, excellence. The word "virile" comes from the same root, "vir," which means both a man and a hero. "Virtuouso" comes into English from Italian as the man possessing the greatest skill, especially in music. I don't suppose I have to point out that the word "music" comes from "muse," but I just did anyway. This "virtue" is literally a certain relationship between a potent man and his Muses.

The virtuous poet is something akin to *chivalrous* in his response to the Muses. He loves and yearns for them, he would die for them willingly, and he sees them everywhere and in everything. I say this is akin to chivalry, and not chivalry itself, because the yearning isn't chaste—not in the least. The virtuous poet is an amorous type, and nothing is off limits—he wants all the Muses at once, if he can persuade them—a *ménage à neuf* (*dix*, if you include the poetic member, but every poet has a *dix*, while only the best can get a *neuf*—sort of gives a new sense the line "I can't get e*neuf* of your love . . ."). And indeed, that *neuftette* is what creates songs of the sort we find in "Blinded by the Light" and "Subterranean Homesick Blues." And that is the name I'm proposing for this sort of song—the Ménage à Neuf. It's a special kind of song, needless to say.

How does it come about? Obviously I'm just guessing. I have never written any such song. The best my imagination can come up with is this: imagine a bar, the poet's meat market. It's simply packed with young men on the make. But there are exactly nine women. You already know their names. Now, in such a bar, the odds of going home with just one of them are not high, even for a pretty smooth talker. They are not coy, not chaste; they want to go home with someone in this joint, but they are picky. You'll have to do better than "do you come here often," or "your place or mine?" if you want any company tonight. I am way out of my league. I'll be lucky even to get my face slapped. And these women are all very different. Clio is bookish, Urania is pretty spacey, Calliope just ordered an extra helping of gravy, Terpsichore won't sit still, and Euterpe keeps trying to sing with the band. It's bedlam in here.

Now imagine some young buck strolls in and he leaves with *all* of them, while the rest of us have to settle for Rosie Palm and her Five Sisters (at least for tonight—we'll be back).[12] On a night like that, dressed to the nines and *for* the nine, you could get blinded by the light, because this affair isn't done in the darkness. Or you could go seriously subterranean, because all these women, even Urania, come from underground, Gaia's cave, and they're always homesick. What can a poet say to woo them *all?* What impossible pick-up line can he invent? I mean all of these women are beautiful—well, there are eight beautiful babes and one big ol' mama from Texas who will be a lot of fun in the sack.

There is a secret to it. The poet asks their Mother. She owns this bar, and it's only by her good graces that any aspiring poet even gains entrance. You see, poets don't just make up their words—they "remember" them. The Mother of the Muses is named Mnemosyne. In English we still use (or misuse) her name when we speak of "mnemonic devices," meaning memory aids. Her name means "memory," of course, and if there is a single master key to the poetic art, it is the art of memory. And my clue that this must be what's going on is that the song that flows from the Ménage à Neuf is so devilishly hard to *remember.* It doesn't follow chronology or history, it is so replete with extra rhymes and metrical tricks that if you want to learn such a song, even as a second rate rhapsode, you'll have to spend days and weeks on it. And Springsteen and Dylan not only *learned* such songs, they wrote them. All nine Muses will go home with a poet if and only if he knows how to woo their Mother—to cultivate memory. And I don't mean simply his personal memory. The poet has to tap into the collective memory of the human race, and to see in it all the configurations of the present and the future, what was, is, and will be again.

It requires a gift, but the gift is worthless without the discipline to use it, to become worthy of it. The two things the

---

[12] If you don't know what I'm talking about, listen to the tune Jackson Browne put on his live album *Running on Empty,* called "Rosie." If you still don't understand the nature of this lament, I can't help you.

virtuous poet *knows* are: (1) that his creations are not his own, that he must approach them with gratitude and humility, because they can be taken from him at any time; and (2) that if he doesn't work with his own memory and the memory of the race, he will never create anything worthwhile. The virtuous poet is grounded and disciplined, appreciative and humble to his Muses, if not toward the rest of us. That is why all good poets read widely, and among the things they study most intently are the lyrics and musical moves of their fellow songwriters.

You Can't Tell the Players Without a Program

The main event is here. A hush falls over the Meadowlands. A young poet who expects to be a contender announces his arrival on the public scene with a piece of almost impossible poetry, a Ménage à Neuf, as proof that he has gotten the permission of Mnemosyne to enter the contest. And he saves that gift for the finals. Dylan has a lot of great bits, but he knows which song is his true Ménage à Neuf. He was so brash as to have Allen Ginsberg and Bob Neuwirth write out some of the poster-boards and stand behind him at a distance as he flipped them to the ground in the video for "Subterranean Homesick Blues"—the whole idea of a music video was quite possibly his creation. Those poster-boards are the very gauntlet. And Springsteen is there to pick it up. The winner gets to call Woody Guthrie his daddy.

Dylan doesn't think any white man's Muses love him more. These "niners" (I am tired of typing the whole French phrase, so we'll call these songs "niners" for short) are punctuated with astonishing internal rhymes—where the poet of ordinary virtue settles for a nice rhyme or partial rhyme at the end of the line, Dylan says:

> Get sick, get well, hang around a ink well
> Ring bell, hard to tell if anything is goin' to sell
> Try hard, get barred, get back, write Braille
> Get jailed, jump bail, join the army, if you fail.

The audience says "oooh." And Bruce answers:

And some fleshpot mascot was tied into a lover's knot with
  a whatnot in her hand
Now young Scott with a slingshot finally found a tender spot
  and throws his lover in the sand
And some bloodshot forget-me-not whispers daddy's within
  earshot save the buckshot turn up the band.

Very fancy. Dylan edges ahead by a nose for economy and
meter on the "internal rhyme" round. All poets know that using
fewer words is better, and resorting to proper names for an
internal rhyme is a sign of weakness. Now Bruce goes first:

Some silicone sister with her manager's mister told me I got
  what it takes
She said I'll turn you on sonny, to something strong if you
  play that song with the funky break.

In this round we add alliteration to internal rhyme. Bob impa-
tiently answers:

Maggie comes fleet foot, face full of black soot
Talkin' that the heat put, plants in the bed but
The phone's tapped anyway, Maggie says that many say
They must bust in early May, orders from the D.A.

Note that he uses the proper name for meter, not rhyme. But this
one has internal rhyme, alliteration, assonance, consonance.
Notice how he gradually transformed the rhyme from "foot" to
"but" by interposing "soot" and "put." Masterful. Bob is trying to
cut the contest short—skip ahead to the heavy stuff. "Top that,
asshole," he seems to say. Bruce says:

Some brimstone baritone anti-cyclone rolling stone preacher
  from the east
He says: "Dethrone the dictaphone, hit it in its funny bone,
  that's where they expect it least"
And some new-mown chaperone, standin' in the corner all
  alone watchin' the young girls dance
And some fresh-sown moonstone was messin' with his
  frozen zone to remind him of the feeling of romance.

And the whole audience knows Bruce is referring to Bob as the moonstone, and he is suggesting that Bob will be courting Rosie Palm tonight while Bruce goes home with all the choice trim. So Thalia really likes the part about the funny bone, and she always liked Bruce better than Bob anyway, and Terpsichore didn't fail to notice the part about the young girls dancing, which Bob can't do. So together they hatch a plan. Clearly this was going to be stand-off, a stalemate, a draw. Dylan is the more accomplished poet, but Bruce has the heart. He's a scrapper. Don McLean's people are off sulking in a coffee-house, singing Roy Orbison songs, but at the Meadowlands the crowd could only say "ooooh," and look from Bob to Bruce, Bruce to Bob, and it just didn't look like anyone was going to give an inch.

You know their stories. Year after year, song after song, the Muses kept delivering the goods to both Bob and Bruce. But time has told the story. After about fifteen years, something happened to Dylan. The Muses left. The songs started looking lame. It became undeniable when Dylan thought he had been born again. For heaven's sake Bob, you were chosen *in utero* for a special life. Why don't you just appreciate it?

Things were looking a little rough for Bruce too, during the days of *Lucky Town* and *Human Touch*, but he never lost his faith, like Dylan did. In1995, with *The Ghost of Tom Joad*, it was clear to those who were listening that Bruce's Muses were *all* still with him, even if that was one of Melpomene's albums—and they still are. In 2007 Bruce wrote:

> I'm rollin' through town, a lost cowboy at sundown
> Got my monkey on a leash, got my ear tuned to the ground
> My faith's been torn asunder, tell me is that rollin' thunder
> Or just the sinkin' sound of somethin' righteous goin' under?

It isn't a niner, but it's at least a fiver, and it's been a long time since Dylan wrote anything comparable.[13] Back at the Meadowlands, Thalia and Terpsichore have whispered something in the ear of our emcee, Weird Al Yankovic (Thalia plays

---

[13] I will say that Dylan's last release, *Modern Times*, is pretty good. I don't think the Muses are coming back, but they threw him a bone or two on that one.

in the sandbox with him sometimes, as you know): "Al, sweetie, we want you to prance right out between Bruce and Bob, and this is what we want you to say, and be sure to say it just like Bob would." Al doesn't need to be told twice:

Rise to vote, sir
Do geese see God?
"Do nine men interpret?" "Nine men," I nod
Rats live on no evil star
Won't lovers revolt now?
Race fast, safe car
Pa's a sap
Ma is as selfless as I am
May a moody baby doom a yam? . . .

And he goes on and on like that, ending with the poetically impossible:

Go hang a salami, I'm a lasagna hog

. . . all to the tune of "Subterranean Homesick Blues." You might overlook it at first, but study those lyrics very closely. The whole song is written in palindromes—the same backwards as forwards. Weird Al named the song, well, what else? "Bob." Who's the ragged clown now, Bob? The crowd at the Meadowlands gets the point. Bob doesn't know what he's talking about. No wonder the Muses left him to his own right hand. He treats them like they were his personal bitches, and they got tired of it. Taken down and bested by a geek, the Clown Prince of Pop. Anybody can do *that* trick, Bobby, even Weird Al.[14] You just

---

[14] I was at an Arlo Guthrie show once, in Oklahoma, and he was telling tales on Dylan. Among many very funny stories he had, one was about a "vacation" he had taken with Dylan and some third songwriter—I think it was Ian Tyson—and they all rented a cabin off in the woods upstate to write songs. Arlo compared it to fishing for songs, and complained that he had been fishing downstream from Dylan all his life, and the trouble is that Dylan catches them all, and he never even throws the little ones back. And Arlo actually *can* call Woody Guthrie "daddy." I share this anecdote because I have been hard on Dylan here, and it must be obvious to all of you psychologist types that I know good and well he's the best. Writing tribute songs in the basic style of "Subterranean Homesick Blues" has become something of a sport among his admirers. I recommend that you check out Dave Carter's "Don't Tread on Me,"

take yourself *so* seriously. Have a little *fun* for god's sake! And probably Bob has a small tally-whacker and never wrote a kind word about Texas. But pride goeth before the Fall, and I don't think Bruce ever gave in to pride. I'll bet a fiddle of gold that Bruce is a sensitive lover and would never do a quickie with a Muse (or two). Just my suspicion, but I'd wager. But there is a reason why, today, Bruce's voice is regarded as a moral guide, while Dylan wields no moral authority at all. Just a good song-writer, or at least, he used to be.

That leaves only one thread hanging. Why are the philoso-phers so peevish about the poets? It's simple. There is no Muse for philosophy; it's boring, and the philosophers are just jealous, and they don't stand a chance in that oh-so-excellent bar. But I could also point out that Plato started as a poet, a pretty good one, apparently. But not the best. And his ego wouldn't take it, and we've all been paying the price ever since. Plato was just a philosophy geek, and I suppose he's had his revenge, but I won't be booking any flights to his city. I'd rather go to Asbury Park.

---

and Jonathan Byrd's "Cocaine Kid." Tonight was just Bruce's night, and he had the home field advantage. Across the East River, the story would have been otherwise. The audience really does matter.

7

Racing in the Street: Freedom, Feminism, and Collateral Damage

DOUG ANDERSON

Stories of fast cars tell us much about twentieth-century American culture—especially the culture of men but also, indirectly, about the culture of women.

NASCAR, perhaps the largest sports organization in twenty-first century America, grew out of fast cars carrying moonshine around the North Carolina hills; as George Jones used to sing it, "phew, white lightnin'." Neal Cassady as Dean Moriarty in *On the Road* and as himself with the Merry Pranksters, drove madly across the U.S. hauling Jack Kerouac, Ken Kesey, and the Grateful Dead, if for no other reason than to reveal to us both our finitude and the possibility of a transient joy in that finitude. And in the mainstream we heard the Beach Boys' "Shut Down" and "Little Deuce Coupe," and Jan and Dean's "Dead Man's Curve." It's telling that we inaugurated this century with the bastardized reincarnation of James Dean in Vin Diesel's "Dom," in *The Fast and the Furious*. The culture of American boys is underwritten with this subtext of fast cars as compensation for whatever else is lacking in our lives.

The stories of fast cars reveal two tales of American freedom—one for men and one for women. And there is no doubt that Bruce Springsteen is a man's man. Especially the young fiery, pre-reflective Springsteen: the Springsteen of "Thunder Road," "Born to Run," and "Racing in the Street." I am experientially convinced that it is precisely the drive to freedom and a kind of authenticity that the personae of these songs bring home to us—to "we American boys."

The male protagonists in these Springsteen songs seem to have a dim sense that their quest involves a domination—a damaging domination—of the women around them. But they seem to see this incidentally and as through a glass darkly. In "Racing in the Street" there is even a hint at a shot of redemption for this sin—but only a hint. Whatever it is they are aware of, the men do not seem to recognize the underlying philosophical difference that allows them to remain in their state of addiction to the systematic mistreatment of women: that is, the difference between what freedom has meant to men in the U.S. and what it has meant to women in the U.S.

In her explosively popular song of 1988, "Fast Car," Tracy Chapman provides us with some insight into this difference. She poetically expresses what feminists such as Margaret Fuller (1810–1850), Charlotte Perkins Gilman (1860–1935), and Martha Nussbaum (born in 1947) have been trying for years to articulate philosophically. In the U.S., what one conceives to be the primary mode of freedom sought depends on whether one is a man or a woman. Fuller comes at this by attending to the oppressive strategies of free men in the nineteenth century. Gilman explores how men have constructed social behaviors that are systematically damaging to women and, ultimately, to men as well. And Nussbaum, more recently, focuses on how women can address the damaging social structures.

Racing in the Street: A Man's Freedom

Since the originating days of the American Revolution, Americans have sought what philosophers call "negative freedom." We want freedom *from* political constraint on our actions and beliefs—we want to be free to choose our religious beliefs, we want to be free to speak our minds, and we want to be free to hang out with whomever we wish. Just read "The Declaration of Independence" and the "Bill of Rights." The condition of being free to do these things is a fundamental freedom from constraint. This is the freedom of Jefferson, of Andy Jackson, of Andrew Carnegie, of Friedrich von Hayek and Milton Friedman, of Ronald Reagan, John Wayne, and philosopher Robert Nozick. It is the freedom of modernity and the Enlightenment—negative freedom.

Springsteen's nose for the desire of negative freedom is exceedingly accurate: "Hey, what else can we do now / roll down the window and let the wind blow back your hair / Well the night's busting open, these two lanes will take us anywhere."[1] The promised land for Springsteen's heroes, as for Chuck Berry's, is no particular place to go. It is "anywhere," sheer open possibility, and the point is that in this promised land we are unconstrained, uncontrolled; we can in fact go anywhere. No self-respecting American male in his heart can deny the lure of Springsteen's call of the wild. Even—or especially—those of us walled up in our ordinary experiences and daily routines recognize that when the time is right we would love to go racing in the street. The throb of Springsteen's Fender, as the throb of the engines in his imaginary fast cars, takes us into ourselves and back out into imaginary streets of freedom, of roads going "anywhere."

The call of negative freedom, after all, has a cash value for our lifestyles. We call it variously personal freedom, autonomy, independence, or being "left alone." It's all about seeing the world as a horizon of possibility. Henry Thoreau (1817–1862) gave it its best name; he called it "wildness" and suggested that somehow this wildness would preserve the world. If we can achieve wildness, we can learn to be alive and not among the living dead or the quietly desperate. We all recognize the "need" to work, to get a job, to earn a living, to make a wage—but at the same time we are experientially sensitive to the oppressive weight this "need" brings to our lives. Springsteen's hero confronts us with two options: we can come home from work and die "little by little, piece by piece" or we can "wash up, and go racing in the street" (p. 342). Racing puts us back in the game of negative freedom making inroads on the world of duty and responsibility. If we are any good at it, we can compete; we blow off the competition in the first heat, we set them up and then we shut them down, and on good nights we blow 'em right out of their seats (pp. 339–341).

The move to racing opens us to a possibility, to a competition for the ownership of wildness and possibility, to be awake and alive. This is the American male's way—as Gilman points out, we American men make even education a competitive

---

[1] *Bruce Springsteen Complete* (New York: Columbia Pictures Publications, 1986), p. 463.

enterprise—scoring grades to score money, to score negative freedom where no one can tell us what to do. The hero of "Racing in the Street," together with his partner Sonny, wins; he only runs for the money and he cashes in. He beats the "dude from L.A." and drives off with his "little girl" as a prize. The hero and Sonny make enough to travel freely, and like the mythic pool shark, they seem to live without work; they ride from town to town with no strings attached.

Springsteen's hero, like Thoreau's, in achieving the pinnacle of negative freedom has achieved the ultimate status of out-lawry. As Thoreau notes, his ordinary townsmen finally achieve a sense of freedom and elevation when they recall their youthful wildness and have a "reminiscence of a previous state of existence, when even they were foresters and outlaws."[2] Why else would we American males make heroes out of Hell's Angels? Why would we aging doctors, lawyers, and accountants ignore the reality of Altamont and spend fifty to a hundred thousand dollars on Harleys and go riding in the streets? We laud and envy the outlaw for his freedom. After all, Springsteen's hero could easily have gone to race driving school and worked his way up the circuit to become a multi-millionaire salesman–race driver for Nextel, Anheuser-Busch, or Sprint. But the hero of negative freedom would then be told what to do—he would have to speak properly in television interviews and wear the appropriate sponsor's hat in the winner's circle—he would be owned. The hero of negative freedom must race in the streets—anywhere from back roads to interstates.

The curious and dark thing about male freedom is that often, when it is achieved, the hero doesn't know what to do with it. This is at least one reading of a "rebel without a cause." This was precisely Margaret Fuller's complaint about men in the 1840s. She didn't want men to help women earn their freedom because they had for the most part squandered their own. The "man" of the nineteenth century, she says, exercises his "freedom" to enslave others and "to pamper his appetites and his indolence through the misery of his fellow beings."[3] Men get free from their external constraints and then become aimless;

---

[2] Thoreau, *The Portable Thoreau* (New York: Penguin, 1982), p. 594.
[3] Fuller, *Woman in the Nineteenth Century* (New York: Oxford University Press, 1994), p. 12.

they buy boats, guitars, televisions, video games, and fast cars—things for the most part undesirable to women.

"Fast Car": A Woman's Freedom

Gilman argued that women's brains had been socially damaged by years of domination in educational systems constructed and run by men. Martha Nussbaum agrees in general and pushes a bit further. Like Gilman, she sees in women tremendous abilities for learning, creating, producing, governing, and so forth. But by way of our political construction of the "family" as male dominated, we have routinely repressed and constrained these abilities.[4] Women, recognizing the suppression of their abilities, thus begin to see freedom in a different light than do men—they think of it as enabling them to bring their abilities to bear on the world around them. They think of it as genuinely flourishing as a human being, according to Nussbaum.

To be clear, this is not to say that women who agree with Fuller, Gilman, and Nussbaum reject negative freedom; they understand that to exercise their capabilities they must be free from external constraints, especially those induced by a "man's world." However, their vision of freedom does not end with being "free from"—they see before them a positive freedom, the possibility of bringing their own identities to life. They want to show that they can be great poets, teachers, CEOs, race car drivers, and so forth. Like Spinoza, they see that working in league with their environment—not living in isolation from it—is the road to forming an identity. In absence of constraint, they can empower themselves to flourish—they can "be someone."

Tracy Chapman's "Fast Car" reveals this difference between men and women in the U.S. As a woman, the song's protagonist begins with "nothing to lose" and, at the same time, with "nothing to prove." The latter claim could be misleading. It's not that she doesn't want to "be someone," as we find out later in the song. Rather, she's pointing out that she is not driven by an insecure ego, and in claiming to have "nothing to prove" she is

---

[4] See, for example, "Love, Care, and Women's Dignity: The Family as Privileged Community," in P. Alperson, ed., *Diversity and Community* (Oxford: Blackwell, 2002).

establishing this difference between herself and the insecure "fast car" man of the song. The car, having it and driving it fast, is his attempt to "be someone"—as the hero of Springsteen's "Thunder Road" points out: "all the redemption I can offer, girl, is beneath this dirty hood." Chapman's heroine, recognizing that it's a man's world, sees the fast car as a way out of nowhere. "Maybe we can make a deal," she says, "maybe together we can get somewhere."[5] She's the one offering redemption. The game isn't love, it's the road to freedom. The heroine reveals her ideal to be just the inverse of Springsteen's "Racing in the Street" hero. Her "plan" is that they will cross the border *into* the city—not to the open road—to find freedom in order to become someone. It's a place to find work and to begin to show her abilities.

Chapman's heroine gives us the background of "starting from zero." She tells the familiar family story that Nussbaum routinely documents. Her "old man's got a problem." He's an alcoholic who is unwilling to work and who has let his body get old before its time. Her mother has left, and now she has quit school, feeling the traditional pressure for a woman to "help" her shiftless father. Underwriting her story is a systematic family structure in which women must care for the men. When the mother "fails" and leaves, the burden of care falls to the daughter. This inheritance leads to the occlusion of *her* abilities; she recognizes the trap but doesn't fully see the next trap that is set for her. Like the woman in "Racing in the Street," who switches from the Camaro from L.A. to our hero's car, Chapman's heroine sees her boyfriend's fast car as a way to her own freedom. The male spin on this is that it's "her choice." But this misses the point to which Fuller, Gilman, and Nussbaum direct us—we men have created and maintained a social structure in which women are often directed to find themselves *through* a man. It's a dead end but most other options are simply not available. And what Springsteen and Chapman both reveal is that despite changes, this structure remains substantially in place in American culture in the twenty-first century. Misogyny is no stranger in contemporary music and film.

---

[5] Tracy Chapman, "Fast Car," www.about-tracy-chapman.net/debutalbum_lyrics.htm#fastcar.

Chapman's heroine recalls the feeling that enticed Mary in "Thunder Road" and Wendy in "Born to Run." She remembers the fast car with "speed so fast I felt like I was drunk," and she remembers the feeling of his arm around her shoulder providing the comfort to believe she "could be someone." But, as Nussbaum argues, failure was built into the structure of the solution. The boyfriend and his fast car want to be free from drudgery, responsibility, and constraint—he seeks only negative freedom. When the fast car fails to deliver, there is always a bottle to replace it as the locus of freedom. The heroine must come to realize, as she does, that she seeks a different kind of freedom and that seeking this freedom through men and fast cars is a dead end. Even when she gets a job and he does not, she hopes "things will get better / You'll find work and I'll get promoted." But like Springsteen's power drive hero, the boyfriend hangs with his friends more than with his kids, and like her father he stays out drinking. As soon as she sees this, Chapman's heroine shifts gears.

Like Fuller, Gilman, and Nussbaum, Chapman's heroine finally awakens; ironically her freedom does come *through* a man, but only by way of rejecting him. She feels the constraint and oppression, and her first genuine act on her own behalf is to send her fast car man on his way. She leaves him to his own aimless freedom: "So take your fast car and keep on driving." She even threatens the ultimate end of the Dixie Chicks's famous "Earl": "You leave tonight or live and die this way." She recognizes the need to be free from the constraints placed on her by the man's ineptitude and attitude, but she sees beyond negative freedom to her own empowerment. When she's free from him, she will not dead end—she will find a way to put her abilities to work to be someone. She will find a meaning for her own identity, her own way of being.

A Fork in the Road

In both songs we see not only the two visions of American freedom but also the very apparent collateral damage that attends the male's negative freedom. Think of the few lines given over to the woman ("my baby") in "Racing in the Street." As with Chapman's heroine, she is trying to find her way to herself through an alpha male whose most important aim in life is racing in the street. Treated clearly as a commodity—a prize—she moves to the cars of the "winners" enacting a bizarre form of upward social mobility. It's difficult to tell this story occurs in 1970 instead of in the world of *The Iliad*—a world in which Helen of Troy is treated openly as a commodity and in which Agamemnon sacrifices his daughter for his own success. Springsteen's heroine next appears while crying on her daddy's front porch, another casualty of the family structure Nussbaum describes. The racing hero, we suspect, thinks she's crying because he is off racing. But she's angry and acts as if she wished she hadn't been born—this sounds more like the frustration of being locked into her oppressed life than it does a concern over the hero. Moreover, as the hero begins to acknowledge his age and his sins, he notices, seemingly for the first time, the "wrinkles around [his] baby's eyes"; he also notices that she cries herself to sleep at night. Again, because she asks "Baby, did you make it all right?" he supposes she's worried about him. But the perfunctory question again veils another possibility—the questions she's asking about her own life that she does not, or dares not, raise with him. What are *her* possibilities hanging out with an aging street racer?

Apparently motivated by these recognitions, the hero, again apparently without consultation, decides he and his "baby" will "ride to the sea" to relinquish their sins and seek some form of redemption. One must wonder about *her* attitude as she sits in the passenger side awaiting *his* version of salvation. But even as he drives toward redemption, he cannot get over his quest for negative freedom, because "summer's here and the time is right for racing in the street."

Springsteen and Chapman confront us with an interesting existential question: which freedom is more valuable, and which should we pursue? In our American circumstances, the man's negative freedom is clearly and persistently dialectically coupled with the oppression of women. From a straightforward consideration of justice, Nussbaum and Chapman seem right: something must be done to curtail and, ultimately, to end the collateral damage. The call for justice must trump the call of the wild.

If Fuller is right, however, the damage of negative freedom is not limited to women. It's one thing to see Springsteen's own life as an outcome of the drive to man's freedom; it's another to consider the lives of the majority of us who just manage to get along or who end up drunk, desolate, lonely, and with a sense of cultural alienation that stays with us to the end. Springsteen is no street racing hero. So we are led to question the value of negative freedom as an end in itself; unless it is instrumental to some positive form of freedom that can engender self-worth through the exercise of our abilities, it hardly seems worth pursuing. The woman's account of freedom seems to make a good deal more sense than its alternative.

Yet perhaps the freedom question is not so easily answered. If our histories and cultural habits have led women to pursue their version of positive freedom, it seems relevant to suggest that the same habits and histories have led ordinary men to search for their negative freedom. That is, there is something about our lives in America that drives the call of the wild. Choosing to race in the street to keep alive is not just a random decision. It is a response to unsatisfying experiences and conditions. In short, "being someone" may not be all it's cracked up to be. The collateral damage for women is underwritten by other damages in men's lives. I don't offer this as a Marxist or Freudian story of excuse, but, given the causal case we make on one side, we must be careful not to ignore men's experiences— they too should be felt, heard, and addressed. Doing this is, in part, the basis of the power of Springsteen's work. Perhaps it's better, then, to think of the two freedom stories together; it may be that addressing the inadequacies of "being someone" as a man who is born in the U.S.A. is a prerequisite for bringing the collateral damage to an end so that women may more easily be able to achieve an empowering freedom.

Some feminists might be able to accept this conclusion— Fuller, for instance, certainly hints at the economic and social conditions of men's failures. And Gilman clearly argues that the dependence of women on men built into our cultural habits is as harmful to men as it is to women. But acknowledging this possibility will not alter the primacy of positive freedom, especially for someone like Tracy Chapman. Until one has experienced the freedom to be someone, it does not make sense to ask her to question whether "being someone" is worth it. I suspect Chapman is suggesting to all of us "freedom seekers," whatever our romantic attachments, that we must seek it in something other than fast cars. Or, at the least, we must demand that our fast cars bring with them local aims and purposes that can give genuine meaning to life.

8

An Everlasting Kiss: The Seduction of Wendy

RANDALL E. AUXIER

Bruce Springsteen's female characters are composites of women we all know, archetypes—but they all seem to be boxed in and smothered, by parents, by conventional expectations, by working class economics, by their own fears. The message to one and all that Bruce brings them is "together we can break this trap." Especially prominent among the objects of his desire is "Mary," who shows up in about ten songs. But Sandy, Linda, Rosalita, and their many sisters, all receive this message: you can be rescued from your disapproving parents and uninspiring jobs. Even if you aren't so young anymore, you will be taken away to a place where love will be wild and real, to the river, to thunder road, or at least the boardwalk. It's a sort of fairy tale. And that's the point.

Dreams and Visions

Many of us not only grew up with Springsteen, we grew up *on* Springsteen. He has always had an almost magical power over those who were in the frightening transition between childhood and adulthood, the time when we are on the threshold of responsibility, when we are old enough to see what became of our parents and young enough to believe that it need not happen to us. And Bruce knows a secret about us. We may be growing up, but secretly we still want someone to read to us in bed at night, to fill our imaginations with possibilities and hopes. To remain on the path we are following results in broken backs, broken wills, and broken hearts. We see it in our parents.

This moment of awakening is a doorway, or more likely, a window, and Bruce appears there at bedtime telling us stories about places we haven't been and things we haven't done, but still might go and do if we don't wait too long. Yet, we are too cool for the same old fairy tales—now we need more than just directions to Highway 9, we want suicide machines to take us there, because the crocodile that swallowed the clock is turning us all into pirates. It's a death trap. We need to flip a Never Bird to that whole dying town on our way to, well, wherever we're going—second star on the right and straight on until morning. So I think Bruce is a rebel *with* a cause, and the cause is keeping the dreams and visions alive, and not *quite* growing up—at least not if that means killing off the madness in his soul.

Bruce is Peter Pan. And he knows it. That is why he sings his most passionate seduction song to Wendy. Some people will have forgotten, and younger ones would not know, that NBC did a famous live broadcast of the play version of Peter Pan in 1960, starring Mary Martin as Peter, and it was so popular and beloved that it was repeated (with much publicity) in 1963, 1966, and notably, 1973, about the same time Springsteen was writing "Born to Run." Kids of Bruce's generation grew up with the play on television, as well as with the 1953 Walt Disney animated movie version.

One thing that has always been fascinating about Peter Pan is that tantalizing relationship between Peter and Wendy. If you have never read J.M. Barrie's classic book, but have settled for just the stage version or the many movies based on it, there is probably something about Peter Pan that you don't know: the play may be about Peter, but the book is about Wendy. (The play was first produced in 1904, but Barrie did not write it into a full book until 1911.) It begins with Wendy and ends with her, describing a girl who has an issue with her mother, Mrs. Darling. Mrs. Darling's position as the center of attention is threatened by Wendy's birth. As Barrie describes Mrs. Darling:

> She was a lovely lady, with a romantic mind and such a sweet
> mocking mouth. Her romantic mind was like the tiny boxes, one
> within the other, that come from the puzzling East, however many
> you discover there is always one more; and her sweet mocking

mouth had one kiss on it that Wendy could never get, though there it was, perfectly conspicuous in the right-hand corner. (p. 7)[1]

You'll want to pay attention to that kiss, the one Wendy can't get from her mother. It's important. Barrie makes it clear that Mr. Darling can't get the kiss either, and eventually he forgets about it or pretends it isn't there. But Wendy sees it and she wants it. Mrs. Darling doesn't know it, but by withholding the kiss she is creating Peter Pan in Wendy's imagination, and the more she strives to control Wendy's "dreams and visions," the stronger Peter becomes. Here is what Mrs. Darling does to Wendy:

> Mrs. Darling first heard of Peter when she was tidying up her children's minds. It is the nightly custom of every good mother after her children are asleep to rummage in their minds and put things straight for next morning, repacking into their proper places the many articles that have wandered during the day. If you could keep awake (but of course you can't) you would see your own mother doing this, and you would find it very interesting to watch her. It is quite like tidying up drawers. You would see her on her knees, I expect, lingering humorously over some of your contents, wondering where on earth you had picked this thing up, making discoveries sweet and not so sweet, pressing this to her cheek as if it were as nice as a kitten, and hurriedly stowing that out of sight. When you wake in the morning, the naughtiness and evil passions with which you went to bed have been folded up small and placed at the bottom of your mind and on the top, beautifully aired, are spread out your prettier thoughts, ready for you to put on. (p. 9)

Is this a children's story? I suppose that if the (aptly named) Brothers Grimm are telling children's stories, so is J.M. Barrie. But this is dark stuff, the sort of thing that could keep Freud busy for a lifetime. Even from watching the sanitized play or the movies of Peter Pan we can tell that the children aren't happy, that they want to escape, to fly away, but we are never told precisely why. Taking a gander at what Barrie says above, it becomes a little clearer. If Bruce wants to "guard" Wendy's

---

[1] *Peter Pan* is available free on-line from the Guttenberg Project: http://www.gutenberg.org/catalog/world/readfile?fk_files=34649&pageno=6. All my quotes from the book are taken from this source.

"dreams and visions," I think I know why she *needs* a guardian. Maybe we all do.

Barrie enters the darkest corridors of childhood, parenthood, and adolescent struggle, and in that place he finds the character Wendy. Scholars agree that while the name "Wendy" can nowadays be a diminutive for "Gwendolyn," it appears that J.M. Barrie simply made up the name "Wendy." There were no "Wendys" before Peter Pan, even if there's a Wendy's on every third street corner now, serving up gigantic slabs of beef tallow to clog our arteries and dull our minds. But Barrie's Wendy is *all* women—as they *wish to be*, not as they *must be* to satisfy a world that will brand them as tramps if they don't comb their hair in the rearview mirror. But Bruce can see that Wendy doesn't want to be one of those girls, she is different— the object of his passion, the mother of lost boys, the May Queen who returns to Neverland in spring to clean the winter's mess.

Falling for Wendy

Every boy who has so much as a sliver of imagination falls in love with Wendy as soon as he first hears the story of Peter Pan. Those boys who have a romantic turn of mind never get over it. Bruce never got over it. I can tell. Neither did I. That is why "Born to Run" affected me (and millions like me) so profoundly.

The mansions of glory and suicide machines may have drawn in the boys on the football team and the ones in shop class, but the romantics demurred until the first line of the second verse: "Wendy let me in, I wanna be your friend." He's singing to *Wendy*, we all gasped. "Let me in?" we asked. "Where?" But romantics all know, and Bruce knows that we know: Let me in the *nursery window*. Peter Pan appears at the window, and he can't come in unless Wendy opens it. And Wendy always does, because that is what Wendy really wants.

This is all quite conscious on Bruce's part. He didn't pull the name "Wendy" randomly from a hat or ask to be "let in" just because it was cold outside. He knows who he's after. And as I imagine it, Bruce must have asked himself "who is the girl every romantic boy wants to steal . . . no, not steal, she has to *choose* it . . . to liberate?" That girl has had many names: Persephone, Helen of Troy, Rapunzel, Juliet, Becky Thatcher, and for boys of the twentieth century, her name is Wendy. We have always loved her and we always will.

I think all the boys, including those destined to be gay, fall for Wendy (even if a few just want to *be* Wendy, which is fine by me and Bruce). Most of us recover, which is to say, we eventually grow up. But while we're still boys, rescuing Wendy is our very calling. Sometimes she is trapped in Kansas on her aunt and uncle's farm, until a cyclone takes her to Oz. But the Tin Man and the Scarecrow and the Cowardly Lion, those romantic dreamers, all love her, whether in Kansas or Oz. Sometimes she lives on the bluffs above the Mississippi River in Missouri and is lost in Injun Joe's cave. Sometimes Wendy is the Pretty Woman trapped in a life of prostitution until Richard Gere shows up to bring her the fairy tale. But sometimes Wendy is stuck in a toxic, rusting hole in New Jersey. For every Wendy there is a Peter Pan. Sometimes he's made of tin, sometimes he arrives in a big black limousine, and sometimes he's just a scared and lonely rider. What is always true of every Peter Pan is that he hasn't really grown up, and he doesn't plan to do so. He's the man-child, the *puer aeternus*, as C.G. Jung called him, the eternal son. He leads with his heart, not his head, and he deals with the fallout of doing so, regardless of the cost. The lost boy loves Wendy and *only* Wendy—well, it might be more accurate to say that he loves *every* Wendy.

For you girls reading this (and I do mean *girls*, since I'm not attempting to address the *woman* in you), I am well aware that your perspective is being left out of this. To this complaint I have only two things to say. First, I'm a boy, so I can't easily pretend to understand how Bruce's song affects you. Second, I have something else for you to read. I recommend Hope Edelman's essay on losing her virginity to Bruce Springsteen's music called "Bruce Springsteen and the Story of Us."[2]

And here we come to a point that bears some investigation. If it were just *me*, I'd be too embarrassed to proceed with this, but over and over I hear from men and women across generations that this damnable song, "Born to Run," reaches down into a place inside of us, grips the vitals of our souls, and tugs until

---

[2] In *Racing in the Street: The Bruce Springsteen Reader*, edited by June Skinner Sawyers (New York: Penguin, 2004), pp. 196–210.

it loosens the scar tissue and frees an almost uncontrollable pent-up passion. We yearn and pine for something that seems lost, we want out, we want it back, whatever *it* is. Finally, as the *words* fail, as the *music* reaches a screaming crescendo and then falls down in a chromatic scale that touches every single note and into a vortex of anarchy (that is where Wendy is, at the bottom of that musical hole), Bruce counts off and we learn that the highway is *jammed* with broken heroes, just like us, on a "last chance power drive"—and I don't know in my intellect *what that is*, but my heart knows, and I don't care if I lose my mind, I'm headed there, with Wendy, and if it costs me my very life I'll die with her on the street in an everlasting kiss. And somehow, at the moment we feel it, this doesn't even sound stupid.

It may seem anti-climactic, but when I recover my full-grown wits, I would like to know, frankly, how does Bruce *do* that to me—and to half the people I know or ever knew? And why do I pity the boys who don't see it, who don't share it? Don't they love Wendy? Cynical, pathetic bastards. Bean counters. Senators and sons of senators. They have *no* imagination. They don't believe in fairies. Screw them.

The Wild and the Innocent

Most philosophers are uncomfortable with discussing imagination—they discuss it, but they don't like it much. It has been thought to be just the opposite of "reason," and philosophers *like* reason. Imagination is unruly, it deceives us, it likes to play tricks on us, and it doesn't want to be pinned down to just one orderly way of doing things. Thus, it is not surprising that most philosophers in the Western world have, since the days of Plato, belittled and condemned imagination—most, but not all.

Robert Pirsig's lonely rider in *Zen and the Art of Motorcycle Maintenance* discovers, with great effort, this same conspiracy to kill imagination, and while it may cost the rider his sanity, he resolves not to give in to the pressure to "grow up" and be rational. Pirsig's narrator's alter ego, Phaedrus, is overwrought to say the least, but it isn't a bad idea to read this character as Peter Pan, and the lonely rider as a grown up Peter Pan trying to remember what his younger self once knew.

For a small handful of devoted ponderers, the power to create images before our minds has seemed like the grandest and finest mystery of all. They admit that imagination is the servant of our emotions and passions (it's hard to argue with *that*), and they readily confess that in serving these fiery masters, imagination also further inflames them. But, some of them have countered: given that we humans are such emotional and passionate beings, it seems strange to neglect the topic, or to demote the powers of consciousness which spring from and serve our passions to the level of mere annoyances and obstacles to the "serious" work of the mind.

Perhaps the most notorious defender of imagination was an Italian philosopher named Giambattista Vico (1668–1744). Most professional philosophers have heard of him, but only the most intrepid among them will dare to study his ideas. Studying Vico could cost you your sanity. His masterwork, *The New Science* (1744) is one of the wildest rides you could ever take.[3] This is the philosophical equivalent of a moonshot. Why?

Vico was a fairly ordinary and respectable philosopher until he became (dangerously) curious about the origin of human law. Being a thorough sort of inquirer, he dug around in ancient books until one day it occurred to him that he couldn't really escape the conclusion that law—and religion, and science, and just about everything else—comes from myth, and the bad news is that we *made up* the myths. This can be troubling to the sorts of people who want "truth" and "knowledge" and "morality" to be something *more* than just our collective imagination. But Vico was fearless. Twenty years of study followed this disturbing realization before he discovered the "master key" of his new science: what he called the "imaginative universal." You know this idea by a different and more familiar name, the "archetype." The notion is so much a part of our parlance and culture today that you may not have realized that someone somewhere along the way had to come up with this idea. Vico was the guy who first saw it and named it. People thought he was crazy. Many still think that.

---

[3] I don't advise you to take this ride alone. There is a nice English translation of *The New Science* by Thomas G. Bergin and Max H. Fisch (Ithaca: Cornell University Press, 1968), but I recommend that you first consult a slightly tamer guidebook. Get Donald Phillip Verene's *Vico's Science of Imagination* (Ithaca: Cornell University Press, 1981). Think of it as a safety net when you're walking the wire.

What did Vico discover? It's so simple that it is hard to believe the idea wasn't obvious all along. But it wasn't, not to grown up minds. From the time of Plato, people on the Western side of the world had been working without surcease to discredit myth and to prove that reason was the legitimate root of all human knowledge—even God was rational, they said. God didn't *imagine* the world into existence, He spat out mathematical formulas, and here we all are. These laborers were so successful that the Western world finally forgot that there was ever an important constructive connection between myth and reason, even though the connection was plain to see in Plato's own works. When they demoted myth to the status of falsehood and lies, they made human imagination the liar. In short, we all forgot the childhood of the human race and tried to pretend that reason was its own self-sufficient creator. But Vico was determined to help us remember our childhood.

He argued that imagination has a logic all its own, more basic and far richer than what we call "logic" today. When we think, Vico said, our operating platform is made of these "imaginative universals." You can't think at all without them, but you can't grasp them with reason; you have to grasp them in the way that you understand fables and fairy tales. It sounds wild to an adult, but any innocent child can do it, as Vico pointed out.

Darkness on the Edge of Town

There are lots of examples of imaginative universals—every myth is packed with them, but let me isolate just one imaginative universal to help you along. Vico says that in mythic imagination, a *city* is actually an *altar to the gods*. Cities are not *like* altars, they *are* altars. We *create* cities *as* altars, and the whole idea of a city comes back to that. If you dig deep enough, you'll just *see* it. But let me offer a few analogies to help you.

Traditional villages of indigenous people are organized around certain crucial places. They have a heart, which is usually marked with a consecrated totemic symbol. In modern cities, the area is called "downtown." As for the totemic symbol, I happen to live along the Mississippi, and it is pretty difficult to miss the Arch as one approaches St. Louis, or the Pyramid as one approaches Memphis. What the hell are those? They don't always put them downtown, but these totemic symbols still mark the meaning of the place, its heart. There is a giant statue of Vulcan in Birmingham, and a giant Jesus overlooking Rio de Janeiro, a huge obelisk in downtown Buenos Aires, and the Eiffel Tower in Paris, a Space Needle in Seattle and another in San Antonio, and even Mary of the Mountain overlooking Butte, Montana. Washington D.C. is simply nothing *but* totemic symbols. In Atlantic City, it's the Boardwalk, where Madame Marie used to tell fortunes better than the cops.

Traditional villages have a place where decisions are made, a place where the elders meet. It is the "head" of the village. In modern cities, that is city hall. It may be downtown, it may be somewhere else, but this is the place where the decision-makers are supposed to consult the wisdom of the ages. This is where the "law" is kept. It is like the chancel area in a church or synagogue or mosque where the sacred writing is kept. The sacred writing of a city is its law and its *history*. That's why you expect to find statues and portraits of past leaders throughout the place—these are the ancestors, and wherever we keep their images or their possessions, we do so because we know we cannot forget the ancestors without also forgetting the law.

Traditional villages have places, usually a dark place on the edge of town, where the dead are buried. We still consecrate the ground and fill it with symbols, creating a "necropolis," a "city of the dead" that mirrors in form and structure the city of the living, with its own heart, head, and sacred writing.[4] And finally, traditional villages all have a place where the refuse of collective human life is deposited—archaeologists love digging around these places. In modern cities, this is called the dump. It may be the necessities of communal living that determine the need for such places, but it is the human imagination that separates and sanctifies them as the proper altar to the gods. Your house is organized in a similar fashion, a microcosm of the city, an altar within an altar.

---

[4] If you're saying to yourself "wait a minute, the old cemetery is downtown," you are showing your lack of historical sense. We don't do things that way, and you know it. The cemetery *was* on the edge of town, until later the town grew up around it, which is why the houses around the cemetery are newer than the cemetery. It's true that the burial ground is often the churchyard itself. This requires a longer story than I can tell here, but it's an interesting one for another time.

If your city lacks a consecrated heart, or if it doesn't properly respect its own law, or its ancestors, or if it treats itself as though it were simply one huge dump, the sacred order is upset. The city is an altar, and you don't want to defile it. The child in you already knows this. The grown-up will have to remember it, which is hard. But remembering this piece of poetic wisdom is the only way you'll ever really know *why* we want our cities to be beautiful and prosperous and orderly and safe and bustling with life—such cities make the gods happy when they are. This is also why we want a winning sports team; it proves the favor of the gods upon our city. And you already know this. But if you treat your city like we have treated, say, Newark or Camden, you soil not only your own nest, but you defile your altar to the gods. Don't be surprised if the sports teams can't win. This is part of the reason Bruce's songs about the hopelessness of the dying city and the desire to find a better place strike us so deeply. We simply *know* that to live in a death trap is a suicide rap. We have to get out while we're young.

Obviously Wendy is also an imaginative universal, as is Peter Pan, and Captain Hook, and the Crocodile who swallowed the clock, and Neverland itself. There are many thousands of imaginative universals, all of them deep and rich in imaginative content. Poets, like Bruce Springsteen, write with them. These images can morph and change into infinitely many forms, but when they have been packaged well, we grasp them—not with our rational minds, but with our memories. Vico says that memory *is* imagination, and it is far more important than rational thinking. Vico also points out that the education of children deeply depends on these mythic stories and their archetypal characters. He says that if we fail to teach our children the fables of the race when their imaginations are strong, in childhood, they will have nothing to *think about* as their imaginations wane in adulthood. I fear that northern New Jersey has a lot of people whose parents didn't tell them stories, or more likely, the leaders and the wealthy people of these dying towns just don't believe in fairies.

But it is also pretty hard to listen to Vico. He seems like a hopeless romantic man-child who taps at the window of the mind's nursery, not a serious scientist of thought. And his (ironically titled) *New Science* reads like a description of Neverland.

The pirates don't like it. Before you get all indignant about this, consider at least one of their arguments.

Captain Hook

René Descartes (1596–1650) was probably the most unrelenting critic of imagination who ever lived; he was ingenious, and he looked just like Captain Hook. He had lots of very impressive rational arguments, but one was especially effective at proving that there was a great difference between *thinking* about something and *imagining* it.[5] He instructed us to *think* about a figure with exactly a thousand sides of equal length. He called this a "chiliagon." There's nothing unclear about this concept, and it would be easy to verify, mathematically or empirically, whether any given object in our senses or our minds was or was not a chiliagon. You could, for instance, ploddingly count the sides, but the best way is to measure just one side, multiply by 1000, compare the result with the area of the entire figure (arrived at by another precise formula), and thereby determine whether the figure has exactly one thousand sides. The object in your senses will perfectly match the concept in your mind.

But now, try to *imagine* a chiliagon. You quickly discover that you sort of can't do it. You can imagine a figure with a lot of sides, but you can't tell whether it has exactly a thousand, or maybe 999 or 1,001, or just a lot. Why, Descartes wants to know, can't you get a determinate and clear idea with your imagination, when you can do it *so easily* with your reasoning? There *must* be a difference between imagination and reasoning, he concludes, and you would do well to trust your reasoning, your "thinking" and *not* your imaginings, at least if you want knowledge. And Captain Hook wants knowledge.

Famously, Descartes then insisted that "I *think*, therefore I am," is the safest bit of knowledge anyone can have. And this is pretty much the opposite of "I imagine, therefore I am." This is very convincing. It is so clever that it pitilessly turns children into pirates. It is so convincing that it seems to deal a near fatal blow to Peter Pan, while Descartes and the rest of the pirates

---

[5] This comes from Descartes's "Sixth Meditation," in *Meditations on First Philosophy*.

capture Wendy and condemn us all to a life of running from the crocodile. Western philosophy grew up, and growing up means counting and measuring everything until imagination simply dies, the light goes out and no one claps for Tinker Bell. Such are the leading men of Newark, and maybe your hometown too, and maybe your nation. Bruce shows us the situation in "Born to Run" and a hundred other songs. And that's where Wendy is being held by the pirates.

The Crocodile

If we want to rescue Wendy, we have to find the flaw in Captain Hook's plan. There always is one. Descartes's argument, for all its ingenuity, cannot explain the *origin* of reason. In the world he lived in, the seventeenth century, people were happy to believe that God gave us reason when He created us. That was their favorite fairy tale, and they believed it so hard that it seemed like they hadn't even made it up. Reason didn't *have* a worldly origin, only a divine one, they said over and over. They weren't entirely wrong, but inside their cold-blooded logic was a ticking time-bomb.

Vico told us that if we didn't pay attention to history, we would have no account of reason and how we *became* rational. Reason, he insisted, also came from myth, and developed over time. In fact, he said, *reason* is a "modification" of the mind. You know how to modify a car? Well, it's like that with the mind, it just takes longer in the shop. You can't buy an after market package for modifying the mind, you have to weld each part from raw materials—you even have to mine and refine the metals yourself, first the Iron, then the Bronze, then the steel. It's a long story, as long as history itself, but the short version can be seen in this point: you can *imagine* without reasoning, but you can't *reason* without imagining. At the very least you have to *remember* the chiliagon long enough to *think* about it, and memory is not a kind of *reasoning*, it's a kind of *imagination*—which is why it is so unreliable and variable from one person to the next. And Descartes did not discover his argument about the chiliagon using reason, he made it up—that is, he imagined it before he could put it into logical and mathematical order. Vico did what he could, but people believed Descartes anyway.

Yet, as the human race "grew up," it kept encountering more and more evidence that the world was very old, that many civilizations had existed for thousands of years and had gotten on quite well on the strength of fairy tales. And then they finally noticed that their *own* civilization was based on myths too, like Adam and Eve. There was mist on the beach of reason. Soon there came terrible fights between pirates and lost boys when the romantic poets showed up in the late eighteenth century. The lost boys took down a lot of pirates, but they didn't get Captain Hook. Then about 1859 Charlie Darwin came screaming down the boulevard. He was driving a hemi-powered drone called *The Origin of Species*, with a crocodile riding shotgun, spouting a new fairy tale about the human race that the pirates couldn't live with and couldn't live without. The tale was told in a way they couldn't resist, full of facts and figures and slimy creatures that crawled out of Greasy Lake and took over Jungleland. Crocodiles, are very old, you know. They haven't evolved in any serious way since the Triassic (that's about 220 million years ago). Crocs don't evolve because they don't *need* to—a perfect predator, a time machine you never have to wind up. For them, the Energizer Bunny isn't even much of a snack. That's a pretty scary clock.

Charlie and the crocodile said humans weren't always rational, that our race has a natural history, that our myths came long before our reasonings, and that time is very real. Vico had warned us, but pirates are very proud and they never listen. Now they're in a hell of a fix, and Wendy is up for grabs. That's when Bruce comes in the window.

The Kiss

And so what about that everlasting kiss? In Barrie's final chapter, "When Wendy Grew Up," Mrs. Darling is adopting lost boys and sending them off to school, but Peter wants nothing to do with that. He perches in the nursery window and listens to Mrs. Darling's plea that he be adopted also. He doesn't budge, but Wendy can't stand to see him go away. This is the moment when Bruce sings his song to Wendy. Peter says that she should come with him:

"Well, then, come with me to the little house."
"May I, mummy?" [Wendy says to Mrs. Darling.]

"Certainly not. I have got you home again, and I mean to keep you."

"But he does so need a mother."

"So do you, my love."

"Oh, all right," Peter said, as if he had asked her from politeness merely; but Mrs. Darling saw his mouth twitch, and she made this handsome offer: to let Wendy go to him for a week every year to do his spring cleaning. Wendy would have preferred a more permanent arrangement; and it seemed to her that spring would be long in coming; but this promise sent Peter away quite gay again. He had no sense of time, and was so full of adventures that all I have told you about him is only a halfpenny-worth of them. I suppose it was because Wendy knew this that her last words to him were these rather plaintive ones:

"You won't forget me, Peter, will you, before spring cleaning time comes?"

Of course Peter promised; and then he flew away. He took Mrs. Darling's kiss with him. The kiss that had been for no one else, Peter took quite easily. Funny. But she seemed satisfied. (pp. 124–25)

I'm not saying Bruce read *Peter Pan* and *consciously* noticed the importance of the kiss, but whether it was from study or simply a powerful imagination, Bruce built the kiss into the climax of his most passionate song. Anyone can see that the song is *about* the everlasting kiss, and about being willing to die for it. In the moment that our lonely rider offers that everlasting kiss to Wendy, he teaches her to fly, to find Neverland, the place with no time where the kiss *can* last forever, and in that embrace is both death and life.

This is no chaste offer. Wendy will have to wrap her legs around the velvet rims and strap her hands across the engines. (What sorts of rims are made of velvet anyway? I want to *see* those rims, Bruce. Get back to me on this, will you?) The price of that deal the rider offers is nothing short of *motherhood*. But in motherhood is the everlasting cycle of life and death. Wendy *has* to grow up. But Peter does not. He's always losing his shadow. His is not the curse, and every Wendy knows that. It isn't fair; it's just the way things are. But we can live with the sadness. The madness of love is worth it.

And where did the lonely rider *get* this catastrophic kiss? He took it from Wendy's mother, *quite easily*. And how did he manage that? Barrie helps us out a little bit. When Peter first appears, Mrs. Darling is asleep by the fire in her children's nursery, dreaming. It is she, not Wendy, who first sees Peter Pan. This is what Barrie says:

> The dream by itself would have been a trifle, but while she was dreaming the window of the nursery blew open, and a boy did drop on the floor. He was accompanied by a strange light, no bigger than your fist, which darted about the room like a living thing and I think it must have been this light that wakened Mrs. Darling.
>
> She started up with a cry, and saw the boy, and somehow she knew at once that he was Peter Pan. If you or I or Wendy had been there we should have seen that he was very like Mrs. Darling's kiss. He was a lovely boy, clad in skeleton leaves and the juices that ooze out of trees but the most entrancing thing about him was that he had all his first teeth. When he saw she was a grown-up, he gnashed the little pearls at her. (p. 12)

I have to ask you now to use your imaginations. Remember, the city *is* an altar. Peter Pan *is* the kiss. Barrie understands this, and so does Bruce, and so do you, when your insides catch fire at the climactic line in "Born to Run." But I have to ask you to make one more imaginative connection. Mrs. Darling *is* Wendy, when she grew up. It is complicated and a little scary, but Barrie helps us cope with it. On the night when Peter steals her children, this is the scene in the nursery:

> Then Mrs. Darling had come in, wearing her white evening-gown. She had dressed early because Wendy so loved to see her in her evening-gown, with the necklace George had given her. She was wearing Wendy's bracelet on her arm; she had asked for the loan of it. Wendy loved to lend her bracelet to her mother. (p. 14)

The suggestion of a loving and symbolic bond between the father, the mother, and the daughter is reassuring. And in spite of the threat Peter poses to her happiness, "Mrs. Darling never upbraided Peter; there was something in the right-hand corner of her mouth that wanted her not to call Peter names" (p. 14).

It's easy to forget that the entirety of "Born to Run" is one side of a single conversation with Wendy. What a stroke of

poetic genius. Bruce rewrote the seduction of Wendy by Peter
Pan in language we could all remember, from childhood. Our
lonely rider is trying to make Wendy believe that he *has* the kiss,
no, that he *is* the kiss. And he isn't lying. She is hesitating. Who
can blame her? It's crazy. In the song, we never get her answer.
But we already *know* the answer. She will go with him for a time
and then she will grow up. And he won't. But the kiss will last
forever, and she always *will have been*, and always *will be*
Wendy. And by the way, I think that the strangely enchanting
glockenspiel in "Born to Run" *is* Tinkerbell, and I think Bruce
did that on purpose. But what can I say? I believe in fairies. If
you don't, I am quite content to let the crocodile have you.

III

The Dark Edges

9

Driving with Springsteen into the Darkness at the Edge of the World

JAMES COUCH

Come along with me on a ride with Bruce Springsteen. It's understandable why the Boss incorporates numerous images of driving, cars and the road into his songs. Standing out as prominently as a smiling chrome grill, these things represent youth, America, and freedom, but they also provide insight into individual human existence.

Eagerly jumping behind the wheel to be confined in two tons of metal, shaped and fashioned by human hands, we speed, swerve, and stall on the many highways and byways of life—generally lost, looking for that one glorious scenic outlook just around the next bend, and as we try to forget the fact that all roads have the same destination, really "nobody's kiddin' nobody as to where it goes."

Springsteen knows this and gives his listeners a subtle reminder of the ambiguity and uncertainty surrounding modern human life.

Powershifting on the Rattlesnake Speedway

So, rather than cruising during the day, being able to see and be seen as we travel with top down and sun high in the sky, this will be a ride that starts at dusk. We will drive as the shadows lengthen, the light fades, all the while being assured that darkness will overtake us. This will not be a drive on the smooth shocks and plush cushions of a pink Cadillac, rather it will be a speeding suicide machine, an unfinished heap hurling us along the lunar landscape of an unfamiliar highway in search of an elusive border that marks the line between the struggle, suffering, guilt, and death found in each of our lives and an unknown land of potential. What we hope lies just across that line are the things that compel most of us to press on—happiness , love, stability, and even the prospect of becoming a better person, someone who is more genuine and authentic, someone who has found home, peace and rest.

Springsteen in numerous songs invokes the atmosphere and feelings that accompany the *situations* usually heard in the heartache of country tunes or the pangs of despair in the blues—real life. Telling us stories of individuals who have been tried and tested, relating the successes as well as the failures, the songs of Springsteen show us to ourselves as if our own lives were being displayed at a roadside carnival. The existential trip he invites us on is one where we may occasionally see the shapes and distant lights of cities and towns, but more often than not the only things we will see are abandoned mansions, fading factories, closed mills and ghosts that all lie at the edge of the world. His lyrics help us connect with other people through the things we all share, but just as importantly they help us to distinguish ourselves from those same people. Like the attempt to tune in a radio station, we fade in and out, oscillating between stations as we turn the knobs of the self. And we must keep in mind that even as his songs invite us to travel together, ultimately the only travel companions we have are ourselves- scared and lonely riders-each alone.

For any and all singers and songwriters that truly affect us, the Boss being no exception, they must literally and figuratively strike a chord of resonance that reverberates into the very core of our being. Not only does this cause our feet to tap in time and lips to take on the shape of the words, but occasionally these become only external signs of something happening internally. Opening the eyes via the ears, we are stirred to see both the world and ourselves differently. Most of the time this means unexpectedly finding ourselves with shared feelings, associations, and situations, but occasionally we are exposed to just how paradoxically we are isolated from everyone else. Going a bit further, we can say that we sometimes gain a deeper understanding of ourselves through the unique variations we individually find in the shared themes owed to singing of the human condition.

This may be why I could easily agree with many others who have heard and enjoyed the song "State Trooper." We all hope we are not going to be stopped by the police as we are speeding home at night, yet I would need to insist that such a common fear brings with it a deeper sense of foreboding and anxiety concerning my existence. In other words, even as I, like everyone else, continue to look in the rear view mirror and scan the horizon for any signs of the law, I nevertheless must still catch a glimpse of *myself*. That trembling person reflected in the mirror is me and it is I who must face the uncertainty of life and the certainty of death. This is an existential theme, and Springsteen sprays it on his music like a dotted line down the asphalt, and it is one that we will attempt to follow by means of what one existential philosopher, Karl Jaspers, has termed ultimate or boundary situations.

It is necessary to locate a few land marks so as not to go too far astray in traveling the existential turnpike within Springsteen's music. As a result we will begin with further exploring what is meant by the "ultimate situation," determining in what ways it bears on the individual. From there we will look at Karl Jaspers and his thought. Once the first leg of the trip is completed, we will then look at the specific boundaries of death, suffering, struggle and guilt. Having done that, we will have prepared ourselves for turning completely off the road in order to see what is over the edge of this rattlesnake speedway.

Strange Creepin' on the Spooky Turnpike

Ultimate situations are those moments when we are brought to ourselves by being shown the very limits of our existence. These times expose life's oppositional character, its uncertainty and lack of permanence, but in doing so they offer the choices that, when chosen, come to define us. Because these boundary situations are uncomfortable and disturbing we may be tempted to allow ourselves to "go tripping cross that thin line" and "go driftin' off into some foreign lands" where the unsettled feelings can be dismissed or covered over; on the other hand, because life is unstable, things could be different—we still could realize those unique dreams or possibilities only discovered in the darkness on the edge of town.

We can here set what Jaspers has to say about our human state before us:

> We are always in situations. Situations change, opportunities arise. If they are missed they never return. I myself can work to change the situation. But there are situations which remain essentially the same even if their momentary aspect changes and their shattering force is obscured: I must die, I must suffer, I must struggle, I am subject to chance, I involve myself inexorably in guilt. We call these fundamental situations of our existence ultimate situations. That is to say, they are situations which we cannot evade or change.[1]

He continues by telling us of the way we usually act in facing such certainties:

> In our day-to-day lives we often evade them, by closing our eyes and living as if they did not exist. We forget that we must die, forget our guilt, and forget that we are at the mercy of chance. We face only concrete situations and master them to our profit, we react to them by planning and acting in the world, under the impulsion of our practical interests. But to ultimate situations we react either by obfuscation or, if we really apprehend them, by despair and rebirth: we become ourselves by a change in our consciousness of being. (*Way to Wisdom*, p. 20)

So many of Springsteen's songs expose the hope and desire of crossing boundaries, limits and lines that hold the promise of something better that lies just beyond. These hopes and desires arise out of the various situations people find themselves in. Though we constantly remain in some situation or another, there are certain situations that are not affected by our many attempts to control and influence the outcome. Differing from the common situations in which we act toward practical, everyday concerns, we attempt to evade those situations that bring to light our helplessness and weakness regarding those things we cherish most. Unfortunately the situations that bring our powerlessness to our attention only differ in their particulars, and continually resurface.

---

[1] Karl Jaspers, *Way to Wisdom* (New Haven: Yale University Press, 1951), pp. 19–20.

Consequently, songs that tell the stories of love lost, incarceration, and death indicate the persistent quest for a place other than where we are now—a place "somewhere across the border, where pain and memory have been stilled," but through such songs we are also made aware of the very limited character of our existence. It is as if we are surrounded by a river of trouble "six foot high and risin'." Once the waters of this river come into view, we notice that "what once seemed black and white turns to so many shades of grey," and we ultimately notice that we are sinking slowly into the deep, black water of doubt. And it is precisely this precariousness that presents us with questions over what we think we know about ourselves and the world. As a result, such a situation not only provides an opportunity for song, but it is also the source from which philosophy springs.

As I mentioned earlier, the situations that are capable of bringing to our attention both the frailty and conditioned nature of human existence, along with our own unique and authentic possibilities, were termed "ultimate situations" by Jaspers. Jaspers was born in the town of Oldenburg, Germany in 1883 and lived through the perilous times of the First and Second World Wars. Living when he did, Jaspers was unavoidably caught in the political turbulence of the time and lived long enough, dying in 1969, for the drastic changes in the political and philosophical thought of the early and mid-twentieth century to take center stage in his work. Even as he attempted to make sense of the world, the existentialism he developed early on in his career remained a constant.

Jaspers began his career studying law, and then turned toward medicine and psychology, before giving way to philosophy and political concerns. Of the several important philosophical figures that bear on his thinking, Immanuel Kant (1724–1804) casts an especially long shadow. Jaspers's move from science to more philosophical concerns was in large part motivated by his desire to reinterpret Kantian thought in ways that were less formal and optimistic regarding the extent of human knowledge. It was in this move that Jaspers came to focus on the limits of knowledge, freedom and the possibilities of a more authentic life. Helping him make this move across the border were two additional thinkers many have heard of, especially in regard to existentialism, namely, Kierkegaard and Nietzsche.

Both the Danish thinker Søren Kierkegaard (1813–1855) and the German Friedrich Nietzsche (1844–1900) introduced a considerable disturbance to traditional philosophy through their severe criticism and denial of absolute certainty, but it was their insistence on the freedom found in the potentiality of the individual that was decisive for Jaspers. Jaspers likewise recognized his time, as Kierkegaard and Nietzsche did previously with their own, as one in which there was an undue confidence in our human capacities, specifically reason as it is applied to the sciences and technology. Related to this is the ever increasing demand by society for conformity, this was again something all three experienced as a loss of individuality. Kierkegaard saw it as a profound separation and inauthentic relation to God, Nietzsche saw a glorification of the mediocrity of the "herd," while Jaspers found the frightening conformity and willingness to be led into disastrous, even murderous political conflict to be a decisive loss of humanity. Jaspers by being married to Gertrude, a Jewish woman he deeply loved, felt first hand the precariousness of life and witnessed how so many were pulled into unthinking agreement with Nazi designs. We can easily understand Springsteen's words in this respect as indicating one distinct existential possibility Jaspers was well aware of, "Fear's a powerful thing, It can turn your heart black you can trust, It'll take your God filled soul, And fill it with devils and dust."

Jaspers's philosophy is called "*Existenz*-philosophy." What he means by *Existenz* comes from Kierkegaard, and considers the "who" that each of us is in inwardly comprehending ourselves. This is not merely our organic life, as a living thing in a certain place and time, it is not who we are in abstract reflection, nor is it something spiritual, as that which tries to include our experiences, culture and life. *Existenz* is who we are to ourselves—limited and exposed, authentic and free—standing before the all, "Transcendence." The haziness of this idea is intentional, because even though it is the basis for our specific historical existence it can not be captured by a concept and is only made actual by being truly self-aware. Resulting from these ideas is the notion that *Existenz* is a possibility we each individually possess as human beings, no other thing has this as a possibility, and unfortunately it may never be realized, and if it is, it is only momentary, ultimately fading back into something inauthentic. Nevertheless this mode of existing is a possibility for overcoming any number of names or labels we might give to ourselves- poor, rich, banker, mechanic, thief, con, husband, wife, and so on. So, in the end this mode of existing can be considered the possibility of coming back to ourselves.

With this in mind we can think of Jaspers's philosophy as trying to bring *Existenz* to light, relate it to itself and expose its possibilities. Since *Existenz* is something that each person must be brought to on his or her own, speaking about it is ambiguous and filled with the risk of misunderstanding. But this is necessary in order that a person's reason can be brought to its limits and that is how a person can gain the impression of that something just across the border. And this is precisely what becomes possible in an ultimate situation.

So, if we return to the different types of ultimate situations, death, suffering, struggle, guilt, and take the time to elaborate on them in respect to Springsteen's songs, a more precise picture of the road we are traveling will emerge.

Rubbernecking at Death on the Highway

We can begin with death. Death is an interesting place to start, since death is an end, and an end shared by all living things. But because "all things die, and that's a fact" we can't, in the course of living, help forgetting this objective inevitability. Death always lies at a distant, indeterminate time and remains inconsequential in the general state of things. Death hits home only when it directly confronts us, and this can happen when a loved one dies or when one is confronted by one's own death. In either case there's a recognition of loss, whether a loss of being able to communicate and be with the person you love or the loss of one's appearance in the world of the living. Narrowing these ideas to an even finer point, we can say that there is a sense of horror at the prospect of not being, whether it is a person who is loved or yourself.

Existentialists see that the prospect of non-being and the feelings that accompany it, anguish, dread, unease, come out of the misty perception that the world and even the self rest on nothing, there is no absolute basis or ground. It is as if we, driving through our lives, have set the cruise control, but occasionally we are stirred from our road-induced stupor and become aware that the tires of the car are not hitting the pavement, we are actually driving over a bottomless gorge, suspended over nothing, supported by nothing. This realization assuredly brings about a wreck on the highway, but a necessary one if we are ever to overcome merely cruising through life and reach the "salvation" of *Existenz*.

It's easy to imagine through the song "Wreck on the Highway" someone who has come across death, and been thrown upon the unwanted prospect of no longer being with his girlfriend or young wife. Death has knocked on the soul like a state trooper knocking at the door. As a fellow existentialist notes, "To exist as a human being means to be exposed to Nothingness." And the salvation that occurs from this exposure is being able to live in the truth—the truth of never finding the world to have stable ground. "The bottomless character of the world must become revealed to us, if we are to win through to the truth of the world."[2] All the tales of those who have been confronted by death speak of people who have had the ground drop out from under them; and this is no less true for those who have lost their jobs and livelihoods. In both cases the heroes go sinkin' down, and this is not limited to Youngstown, although it may be worse there these days.

Reacting to death can be done in any number of ways, yet there seem to be certain basic tendencies that are capable of being classified in one of two forms. One all too common tendency is to deny death the fullness of its potentiality. The song "Across the Border" expresses one reaction to death. In this song Bruce sings of a land not so far away where "pain and memory have been stilled," and in this land across the border are flowers and pastures and clear waters, "and in your arms 'neath the open skies / I'll kiss the sorrow from your eyes."

Here we have a picture of the Promised Land, and what would heaven be without the one you love? Unfortunately, thinking that life will continue after death is but one side of a several-sided problem. This life becomes a simple phase to endure until the afterlife. Similarly, even if heaven is not a consideration, but life is understood as holding nothing permanent, everything fades and passes away, a sense of assurance is created, while simultaneously encouraging apathetic dealings with the world. And still if one were to develop a hunger or exces-

---

[2] Jaspers, *Philosophie* (Berlin: Springer-Verlag, 1932), p. 469.

sive zeal for life in its many temporary instances, what has been overlooked is the ambiguity of life in addition to death. To preserve death's character as a boundary situation there is a continual risk that must be taken. The risk is not truly being oneself, the self to be gained is the one able to remain in the open and uncertainty of existence. You must be able to retain the suspense found in death and non-being. "Despair is the font from which we draw the assurance of being. It is the nature of our sense of being that to be means to have looked upon the face of death."[3]

The Never-ending Stretch of Badlands

One of the alluring qualities in the songs of Springsteen is the ability to relate the common and not so common sufferings people face. Whether singing of the hardship of a job or the loss of it, the struggle to find and keep love, or simply the dissatisfaction with life, he presents us with the inevitability of suffering. Living in the badlands of the world means suffering; we constantly come up against painful obstacles that block the way to happiness. The constant back-breaking work we do and the continued pressure to get the job right lead to suffering—this along with our constant dissatisfaction fuels the drive to get rich, to control more, to somehow get over the hill, are the badlands we hope to make good. These barriers are erected by the combination of our aspirations and our physical state. Examples like sickness, bad luck, and, more often than not, other people, each mark a limit to existence that no one can escape, as Bruce says "hunger is a powerful thing."

Although misery loves company, we all must realize that suffering is both unavoidable and definitively ours. As a boundary situation suffering cannot be thought of as something that can be by-passed. Though we do have some success in avoiding and overcoming certain pains and sufferings, there still must be the acknowledgment that suffering is certain and just as importantly, forges who we are. According to Jaspers, there must again be a risk and an oscillation between poles. We must risk being happy in our suffering and adjust our alignment between

---

[3] Karl Jaspers, *Philosophy*, Volume II (Chicago: University of Chicago Press, 1970), p. 199.

passively accepting life's hardships and actively fighting an unwinnable battle. Traveling in this way allows each of us to see our suffering as inherently bound to us and not simply occurring from a toss of the dice. From such a heightened perspective we may come to see the suffering of others as part of our own suffering. As a result we may come to be possessed by the ghost of Tom Joad and feel ourselves there when and where ever there is a fight against blood and hatred.

Real World, Real Struggle

From suffering the next turn is struggle. As opposed to death and suffering, both of which occur without any specific doings on our part, struggle, as well as guilt, comes about due to the actions we take. Yet here again we find a certain inevitability, for we cannot help causing these situations by living in the real world. We struggle against the world, against other people, in addition to ourselves. In all of this our struggles can either be violent or loving. Violent struggle is easily recognized, for this happens when our existence is threatened and threatens another's existence—there simply is not enough space for us to co-exist. When this happens we may very well end up like Johnny 99, either dead or wishing we were. Loving struggle, on the other hand, is a nonviolent fight, it is the attempt to manifest who we truly are to another person. Of course achieving this goal is rare and momentary, but if achieved, we have opened ourselves to another to such an extent that he or she catches a glimpse of who we really are. As Bruce puts it, "I'm searchin' for one clear moment of love and truth / I still got a little faith / But what I need is some proof tonight / I'm lookin' for it in your eyes."

How can we not imagine in Springsteen's mournful and beckoning cries to the women that have kept him searching in the night that these cries are the cries of a loving struggle?

The Inevitability of the Price You Pay

The last situation we all have come up against is guilt. Here again we confront certain consequences because we live and must act in the world. And when these consequences reveal the exploitive character of living, we find guilt. Just as in other situations that bring our limits in view, revealing an ambiguity, guilt does the same. There are things we should feel guilty about, because we could have acted differently and avoided the consequences. But there's also guilt that cannot be escaped. In the song "Darkness on the Edge of Town," Bruce says:

> Everybody's got a secret Sonny,
> Something that they just can't face,
> Some folks spend their whole lives trying to keep it,
> They carry it with them every step that they take,
> Till some day they just cut it loose,
> Cut it loose or let it drag 'em down.

And in "The Price You Pay," we find these words:

> You make up your mind, you choose the chance you take,
> You ride to where the highway ends and the desert breaks,
> Out on to an open road you ride until day
> You learn to sleep at night with the price you pay.

These Springsteen songs bring the situation of guilt into the foreground. With the realization that both money and a wife have been lost, there is also the realization that these things might have been avoidable, but our hero has to race, and because the Trestles have such a strong pull. Sooner or later his actions were going to incur a price to pay—guilt. Yet, as we hear the claim in the first song, "Everybody's got a secret, Sonny," we come to suspect that there is inevitability in making choices, and because of this there is also an unavoidable guilt. Such guilt keeps us struggling to "learn to sleep at night." The question quickly becomes, "What are we to do?" Jaspers provides an answer, but we are still caught at the border, "It is not a matter of guiltlessness any more, but of really avoiding whatever guilt I can avoid, so as to come to the profound, intrinsic, unavoidable guilt- without coming to rest there either" (p. 217). In other words, we are "fallen," but can help ourselves only by falling in a more concerned way.

Reason to Believe When There's None

Has your car at this point swerved off the road? Has it begun to sputter and stall? Have you driven into a tunnel with no headlights? Or have you reached a tollbooth with no change, stuck between the edge of town and the vast expanse beyond? If so, good, but now put your foot down, let the spinning tires get traction, close your eyes and let the car jump the guard rails into the unknown. This is a leap of faith and for Jaspers a leap of *philosophic* (rather than religious) faith. Running up against the limits should cause you to think there is infinitely more, something unfathomable, and becoming aware of this is becoming aware of the Transcendent.

Saying "yes" or "no" to this "something" is done in complete freedom, and there are no good reasons from which you can make a decision; it is something only you as an individual can do. If you catch a whiff, whether as sweet fragrance or something less appealing, of God, then you are getting the idea. What Jaspers is proposing is that the Transcendent is Being with a capital B, and it is that out of which all things, including us, spring forth. However, unlike the God of Sunday school, the Transcendent cannot be known; it is that impenetrable mystery on the other side of the border.

So when Bruce rightly puzzles over how people find a reason to believe as their faithful dogs die, their fiancés leave them at the altar, and spouses take the money and run, we can suggest that these people have found themselves in an ultimate situation and it's entirely up to them, as it is for all of us who face such situations, whether the car is gunned, setting the street on fire as their tires spin, and they continue to drive all night.

10
Thunder Road

GARY L. HERSTEIN

The Screen Door Slams, Mary's Dress Waves

In the beginning is the Event. Not the word, the event. Well, there's also a Chevy hanging around out back, but we'll have to wait before we get to it. Anyway, not the word: the word seems fixed and definite, knowable somehow in its own right. But the word must be spoken before it becomes a word, much less "the" word. The word is parasitic upon the act of speaking—equally the act of hearing—and any *act* is itself a kind of event.

And not was, but *is*—the event is still here; we still hear it. Even having passed, its passage still lingers with us; a taste on the tongue, a scent on the breeze, a song we can't quite recall. Or perhaps, a song we can't quite forget.

An event is not an object—a thing—that is somehow just passively waiting there for the word to name it. The screen door and Mary's dress do not, in the ordinary account of "things," stand together as a single "object." But they do comprise a single event, or at least, the beginning of an event.

And when, exactly, did that event begin? With the slamming of the screen door? The waving of Mary's dress? Are those two actions concurrent, playing simultaneously the one upon the other with Mary's dress waving even as the screen door slams? Does each stroke of the lyric inform the other, the one with image and the other with sound? Or are they serially related parts of a larger whole, the slamming of the door *and then* the waving of the dress? This last demands some caution: just because the language used is sequential does not license us to

assume that the event itself was. What we have here is a narrative, and narrative—like language itself—is necessarily serial.
Yet the events themselves need not be, and we *get* that in the
song; there is no "and then" in the opening event. How is it that
linearly connected words can so effectively convey the simul-
taneity and the overlapping of realities?

Bruce Springsteen is not simply a musician, he is a storyteller.
The Irish—who have the insufferable habit of inventing words
that nobody can either say or spell for ideas that already have
perfectly ordinary English terms—call such a person a
"Seanachie" ("SHAWN-a-key").

A Seanachie does not simply relate a story to others; such a
person creates an *experience*, a notable event that goes beyond
the mere words and rhythms of which it is composed. Such an
event becomes in its turn the active creation of an entire world.
That world is not merely imaginative in character. The materials
the Seanachie creatively shapes are the events of *this* world,
molded so as to redefine and re-create *this* world as something
new. Bruce Springsteen is a Seanachie.

Philosophers, on the other hand, have the insufferable habit
of tossing around unpronounceable foreign terms (and the Irish
agree, they are foreign) that already have perfectly ordinary
English words, because it is otherwise too hard to look erudite.
Philosophers also like to use the word "erudite" a lot. Unless
they are French, in which case everything they say is in a foreign language. Or unless they are Alfred North Whitehead.

Ghosts in the Eyes . . .

Alfred North Whitehead (1861–1946) had the insufferable habit of
being brilliant. (On the other hand, the insufferable habit of
always calling him by all three of his names belongs to those
lesser luminaries who are trapped by events into interpreting his
works. However, a really clever person could almost certainly
blame that on Whitehead also. Note, in addition, that like everyone else, we still get to call him by just his last name when we
get tired.) He was also English—I mean, *really* English, and not
just speaking the language—which might otherwise make him
automatically insufferable to the Irish. Except that Whitehead, in
addition to all of his other intolerable character flaws, was such
an absolutely decent fellow that it was impossible not to like him.

Moreover, Whitehead understood the value of rhythm, of poetry, of the art of the Seanachie. This despite the fact that he was educated and worked most of his life as a mathematician.

Despite . . . or because? Might it be the case that being sensitive to the multiplex relatedness of reality, while expressed in different forms, is equally essential to both the mathematician and the Seanachie? (Edward Rothstein—who is neither dead nor sufficiently insufferable to merit a middle name—explicitly connects the creative energies of mathematics and music in his delightful *Emblems of Mind.*) In any case, here is yet another respect in which Whitehead—regardless of his failure to be Irish—is a philosopher that one is hard pressed to dislike.

Unless, of course, you're another philosopher. In *that* case you have to deal with the fact that not only was Whitehead *way* smarter than you, but he constantly exercised the insufferable habit of not only inventing words, but inventing words for ideas that nobody had yet invented any terms at all for. What makes this utterly unendurable is the fact that he had really good reasons for doing so.

You see, according to Whitehead, the fundamental structure of reality is not the object, the "thing," but the *event.* And here the Seanachie is likely to pay attention as well, and with good reason. Because words—words by themselves, naked and unassociated—tend to be linked in our minds with "objects." But if Whitehead was right, then objects are not the primary "stuff" of reality. Objects are just shadows, lingering characters of the *passage* of reality, but not reality itself. They are just ghosts in our eyes. What are real are events. And events call for a different sort of characterization than mere chimerical "objects," a characterization that is built upon words but not reducible to them. Events call for narrative.

And narrative needs a Seanachie.

Across the Porch . . .

But we digress, and "Thunder Road" presses further questions in upon us. We spoke before as though we had already isolated the opening event, but have we really done so? "Mary's dress waves," . . . but is it perhaps the case that "the" event began even earlier, when Mary first heard the unmentioned roar of the unnamed narrator's unidentified car's engine in the drive (a roar that will echo forward in time—but we'll talk about the Chevy in a moment)?

What about the solo harmonica that preceded the declaration of both the screen door and the dress ("both" assuming they aren't actually one event)? It actualized the setting for the words, announced the hunger and the longing they expressed, *placed* them in a context that can no longer be *dis*placed by mere speech. What about the silence that preceded *that*? The intense, hanging anticipation of an emptiness that isn't empty, because it is filled with an as yet undefined expectation of what is to come, of the event that is yet to happen? Are those all separate events, or are they separate angles on the same event, perspectives of the one event implied by the acts of narration and interpretation themselves, all extended and extending back through time?

And if so, how far back? Ralph Waldo Emerson (1803–1882), who was himself a Seanachie (albeit, one crippled by the lack of an electric guitar—Thomas Edison, the lazy sod, stopped at the light bulb) essayed this question about the meaning of events in his work "Self Reliance." How much of that "monstrous corpse" of memory (as Emerson called it) must we drag along with us in order to understand the events before us? Or in order to understand the event that *is* "us"?

Is it still before us? Has it already passed us by?

While the Radio Plays . . .

Even as the slamming of the screen door still echoes in our ears, the narrator, the Seanachie, redefines what had been definite with a vision—like a *vision* Mary dances—and a radio. The concreteness of sound insinuates itself into the tenuousness of imagination, and together they reach out to us with a promise of the desperately familiar, the desperate *because* familiar. (The longing of that opening harmonica still isolates us in a hollow, echoing world.)

The story continues with Roy Orbison, "singing for the lonely."

And what could be more familiar? We know exactly what song is playing on the radio, we can hear the words behind Springsteen's own, see the shadowy image of sideburns and dark glasses just off to the side. The narrative *creates* all of this for us, it does not merely point to something that is already there. Indeed, we can say more than just this. Narrative is not simply a way of evoking the familiar; it is typically how we *make* the familiar in the first place.

Paul Ricoeur (1913–2005) argued that it is through narrative that we discover our sense of both time and self by our variously making the temporality of experience in the stories we tell and the ways we tell them. Ricoeur—who evidently had no middle name worth mentioning—is French and recently deceased. This latter is commonly the only good thing an American will find to say about a Frenchman, even one who spent a great deal of his time teaching at the University of Chicago. But Ricoeur had the decidedly anti-French habit of expressing himself with engaging care and substantial clarity, despite the considerable subtlety of some of the ideas he dealt with. In response to this insufferably unGallic behavior on his part, when it came time to reward Ricoeur for his contributions to philosophy with a special book about *his* philosophy, other philosophers mostly ignored Ricoeur's investigations into the topic of time and narrative (which Ricoeur cleverly squirreled away in a three volume work entitled *Time and Narrative.*) But that's a different story . . .

Ricoeur's story—the one about time and narrative, rather than the one about *Time and Narrative*—is that even when we engage in very complex, non-sequential stories—stories that break the simple time-line of the "and then" presentation of events—our narratives continue to implicitly embed us in that very same "and then" structure of time as an irreducible part of the world around us. But it is not just a story about the world. It is a story about the story-tellers, and how the story-tellers render the structures of events intelligible by means of the narratives that they tell and that we listen to. In essence, Ricoeur is posing the claim that we orient ourselves in the outer world by orienting ourselves inwardly through narrative. Said another way, we discover ourselves in the stories we tell.

Narrative is, of course, storytelling. But that storytelling comes about in many ways. The "how" of our storytelling is itself an event, and the "how" of such events is never neutral to the "what" or the "why" of any given act of storytelling, any more than narrative at large is neutral in our overarching grasp of events *per se*. And here again our themes—narrative and event (the Chevy is still idling in the drive, this is not a carbon neutral song)—begin cautiously to approach each other like a pair of fencers on the strip with the points of their swords in line: still too far apart to pounce upon one another, but much too close together for even a pretense of ease.

Facing Myself Alone Again . . .

Sometimes the confrontation of narrative and event is too intense, too painful to be borne. The image of the fencers on the strip stays with us, for such a competition is what the Greeks (who didn't even have *last* names, much less middle ones) called an "agon," from which we get the perfectly serviceable English word "agony." Mary understands the agony of the confrontation of narrative and event, for she has retold her story to herself in such a way that all she can do now is to crucify her would-be lovers and "throw roses in the rain."

There's nothing about this that is unfamiliar. We recognize it in ourselves as instantly as we recognized Roy Orbison. We can run away from, or at least run back inside to avoid, the stories we tell. We can hide from the revealing mirror of narrative, but only by enshrouding that mirror with another narrative. And that narrative will only hide the first by telling yet another familiar truth.

The familiar is the familial, the family resemblance, the like-us but still different-from-us. We acknowledge our families and even love them, though often enough only because we have to. In no small part, we also hate them for the mirror and the memory they hold up to us, the echo of ourselves we find in them, like the sound of a harmonica we can't quite get out of our heads. And so we recognize ourselves in the voice of the narrator even as we still remain ourselves; other, not the same, yet familiar.

The Seanachie brings us face to face with the unfaceable chasm of loneliness in his distant vocals, and we identify ourselves in it as our *selves* incarnate. But the recognition is not just in the words—the words as text, as written—but in the voice that is saying those words, the incarnation of that voice. We hear the brittle, distant ache, and feel it echoing alone and true in our own hollow emptiness. The voice gives a body to those words, one that we know and identify in our own experiences. But what exactly *is* that "self" we find there, even as we redefine our self within the vague horizons of this ongoing narrative? Is it anything *beyond* the narrative itself?

Mary recognizes herself in the Seanachie's narrative, but unlike all the other boys she sent away, this one stops her in the story of her self: she *knows* why he is here. There is the fear, of course; is it too late to rewrite this story?

Young Anymore?

No small part of that story is that we're just not that young anymore. The narrator says as much to Mary. But it is no longer just a story about Mary at this point (not that it was ever just that). Because, God knows, *I* haven't been that young for a long time now—what about you? Indeed, the narratives I have and tell are all replete with the stories of the opportunities that have repeatedly presented themselves to me to reach for something more. Those events and the stories around them so often point to the same narrative of missed chances that I wonder if I was ever *that* young.

Such opportunities—events in their own rights—present themselves all the time, to you, to me, and then slip by unnoticed. To notice such events, such living possibilities in their passage, would be to narrate them, make them a story in a life, whether yours or mine, and tell that story aloud. And then once those opportunities are past, all that we have left *is* the story, and the endings to *those* stories have no heroes. Perhaps the hope is that if we do not sing the songs about such stories, then the gnawing tooth of familiar desperation won't bite so hard. But it is a fool's hope, and a fool's story. For the narration is still there, just shifted to another line and another lyric, a different bar of the song that we *are* singing.

And now it's clear that it is not just Mary's dress that is waving. It is the spirit that has abandoned the narrative of hope, because it's too painful a story to tell. You, me, we are not that young anymore; there aren't any happy endings to be found in the stories that remain to us. Go ahead, hold the song up to your life, and see your reflection. You know what Mary and the narrator are up against here. You know because you've made the same compromises, rewritten the endings to your various subplots to fit the storyline given you, edited your narrative to redefine the events of your life. Go ahead and look into that mirror: how has your story changed with time, with age, with failure, with the first eight lines of the song? I know how mine changed, the first time I heard it.

Hey! You're Alright!

I don't want to seem maudlin, but a philosophical event in the near future requires a narrative now. It could be anyone's but I'm most familiar with my own. The voice changes, but the story continues . . .

In any event, I know exactly where I was; I can still see the room as though I were sitting in it now. Although you and I can thank whatever powers we believe in that neither of us is there now. In my case, it was an apartment in a horseshoe shaped complex that catered to graduate students in Central Los Angeles; and I've seen cheerier motels that charged by the hour. (Easy here! we don't know each other well enough for you to make assumptions about where I have been in my life!)—

If you know or ever meet people who are academics, you can engage in a game of pointless torment by asking them to recall the worst place they ever lived while they were graduate students. (Or if they are "adjuncts," where they are living now— never mind, it's a long story.) Most of them will have to think the matter through for a moment (this is the entertaining part, watching the grimaces that play across their faces), because the competition for the *worst* place, amongst all the variously horri- ble places in which they have lived, will probably be fierce. Is the contortion act, the visceral squirming accompanied by the occasional inarticulate mewl, part of the narrative, the story of *that* awful place? Or is it part of the event itself, the reality of living there, still being dragged along, yet another monstrous corpse of memory?

—I was not in graduate school myself at that time, although I was arguably in one of the worst "places" I have ever been. I had, by that time, spent the previous four years running; not back inside, but away from the stories that had defined me. My running had carried me into the Army, off to Germany, and back again to California. In one sense, I was far from home. The distance between me and it was considerably greater than the distance between Los Angeles (where I was) and San Diego (where I'd begun). On the other hand, four years and ten or fifteen thousand miles is not really all *that* far—especially when you discover it has not taken you anywhere at all. I'd left home five days after graduating from high school, a scared and lonely kid knowing only that the path my life was on didn't even end in a bus accident. Rather, where I was going—where I already was—was more like a flat tire just outside of Fresno. Not even in any danger, just stuck in long walking distance from the middle of nowhere.

(Yeah, yeah, I know—everybody in Fresno is now going to rise up in one voice to denounce my snarky reference to their fine city. Blah, blah, blah, Fresno has *so* grown up. Blah, blah, blah, Fresno has a Macy's. . . . Oh, except Macy's went bankrupt . . . never mind.)

The point is, I tried to run away from who and what I was by radically altering every external circumstance in my life. I changed everything but my name, severed as many of my connections with my past as I could touch, and still found myself with that monstrous corpse hung about my neck, dragged along with me through military and civilian life, a story I could not untell, the narrative of me.

So there I was, the most dramatic rewrite I could attempt a monumental failure, the same scared and lonely kid I'd always been, sitting in the apartment of a couple of friends (who *were* grad students—that's why their place was so horrible) and the guy says to me, "You've got to listen to this."

And the first song from the phonograph was *Thunder Road*.

Redemption . . .

Speaking of narrative, when did the narrative change here? What I mean is, when did the narrator's voice—not in the song, but *here*—become so personal that it was no longer about an abstract "us" and "we," but concretely about me and you? Do you recall? Or did it really change at all? Was this narrative ever about anything, or rather *anyone*, else?

The only path into narrative is through narrative, just as the only general characterization of an event is with other events. This essay is its own narrative, and its own mirror of events. Welcome to the funhouse—does this make you look fat or thin? (How do I look—to you, I mean?)

So there I was, and the harmonica begins. I sat, I listened; the song played, the song ended. Transfixed by the event that had just transpired, I had no words other than those that had just been given me. The Seanachie had spoken. And I knew at that moment, knew in a way I could not express other than by replaying the song, that I was not alone. Whatever other true stories might be told about me, I was not alone.

Mary knew it as well. There was no hope for forgiveness or understanding, but there was a shot at redemption, formulated in the blank spaces behind the dirty hood of the narrator's car. It is here at last that the Chevy makes its unnamed appearance. And don't you already know that it *is* a Chevy—V8, of course—that he's talking about? No offense to the House That Henry Built, but what else would it, could *she* be? (And you know his car is a "she" as well, don't you?)

How can this be? How can the image be that specific and so clearly set out when it is not even mentioned? The word "Chevrolet" only shows up later in the song, as the burnt out skeleton frames—those monstrous corpses—dragged about by all the boys that Mary has sent away.

But perhaps we're cheating here. Instead of taking the song in its own terms and as it stands by itself, we've already reached out to the shadows, to the *Darkness on the Edge of Town*, and pulled back from that album the '69 with the 396? You already know the song I'm referring to, perhaps you're saying to your-self, "Yes, that must be it."

Let's suppose that that is what has happened here. Does it matter? Is there any such thing as taking the song, or any narra-tive, "as it stands by itself" or "in its own terms"? Do such phrases possess even the *possibility* of intelligibility? Or might it rather be the case that narrative is the kind of thing that never stands by itself, never has its own terms, but only exists in terms that have no meanings unless they stand with others?

Are we *cheating* when we see the Chevy behind that dirty hood? Or is it that we are *finally* understanding the narrative when we see the Chevy there?

Magic in the Night . . .

Narrative is a form of understanding. The structural forms avail-able to narrative vastly outrun what is possible within the usual comprehension of scientific understanding. This means that narrative can neither be reduced to, nor limited by, the structures of observational description or formal logical connection that are the principal strengths of the modes of discourse used in science. This is not a criticism of science; it is simply a fact—a "true story," if you will.

But among other things, this means that narrative can run backwards in time. A story—which is never really fully written to begin with—can and must be reflectively *re*written by what comes after any particular instance of its telling. To illustrate this, let me tell you a story . . .

In 1980, some two-plus years after I had first encountered *Thunder Road*, Bruce Springsteen came through Los Angeles on the mandatory promotional tour for the recently released dual-LP album, *The River*. Now, while it's true that the record companies always require artists to tour as a promotional device to sell recordings, phrasing things as I just did ("mandatory promotional tour") generally serves only to mislead in its simplistic factual accuracy. I do not know whether record companies are merely parasitic or just simply stupid (probably some combination of both), but I am certain that Bruce Springsteen does not tour because he has recorded an album. I think he records albums so that he can go out on tour.

Anyone who has seen Bruce Springsteen live in concert knows what I am talking about. Anyone who has not seen Bruce Springsteen live in concert needs to send me a name and address, care of this publisher, because I want a list of all the people in the world that I am cooler than.

Words cannot begin to capture the experience, which is why it is necessary to resort to narrative. The show nominally started a half-hour late—at 8:30 rather than the scheduled eight o'clock. But this delay was a matter of no consequence. Bruce and the E Street Band came out, and but for a half-hour break somewhere in the middle, put on a full-out, no-stops show that went on until well past one o'clock in the morning. There were no warm-up groups; no follow-up performances. Just Bruce Springsteen and the E Street Band.

Beyond the fact that I checked my watch as I was leaving the Los Angeles Sports Arena, I don't quite recall when it ended. I'm not altogether sure *that* it ended. I remember Bruce Springsteen and Jackson Browne jamming away on stage long after the concert was "finished." I know I must have finally walked out of the Sports Arena, because I'd remember if I'd been wheeled out on a gurney. Altogether, it was a once in a lifetime event.

But that's not the story I want to tell you now.

During that concert, the band played Springsteen's song "Factory." I had, by the time of this concert, collected all of Springsteen's albums to that date. And like any fan with a modicum of decency, I had memorized all of the songs and lyrics until I could recite them backwards standing on my head. And I can't stand on my head.

So along comes this song. And as with most of his songs, Springsteen was leading into it with a riff about his family life, growing up, watching his dad go off to the grinding labor of the factory only to come home exhausted and an inch less human than when he left. Almost as soon as he started talking, everyone in the audience knew what song was coming and settled into their seats in preparation for it.

Except me. I was squirming in my seat in what began as sharp discomfort and quickly twisted itself into outright pain. For while Springsteen was talking, Clarence Clemens and (most likely) Max Weinberg were doing a percussion set behind him—Clemens with a tambourine, Weinberg on drums—and the whole thing had gone egregiously wrong. (By the bye, I say "most likely" because (1) it was almost twenty-eight years ago, and (2) I was *wincing*.) Somehow or other, as well-practiced and professional a group of musicians as they are and were, they had completely bollocksed the whole thing. Instead of working together, they were on two completely different and opposed rhythm sets, fighting each other in the most brutally antiphonal act of stubbornness you could ever imagine seeing and hearing on stage. One of them *had* to shift gears, and get on the same program as the other, but neither of them was budging. It was like listening to fingernails raking down a blackboard; like a dentist's drill on tooth enamel. It was like listening to Bartók. Meanwhile, Springsteen just kept talking on and on, drawing out the agony of the whole process to unendurable lengths.

At last Springsteen came in on the song itself. But really there could be no "at last" here, because whichever side of the equation Springsteen entered, all that could happen is to make the other side wrong. But even worse than that, he didn't come in on one side or the other tug-o'-war. Instead, he came in on a third point, one destructively situated between the other two, adding to the insufferable chaos . . .

And transforming it into a unified whole.

I was utterly thunderstruck; what I had just witnessed seemed an absolute impossibility. There was no way one could take such a bald-faced contradiction of sounds and resolve the contradiction by *adding* a third and different line to it, creating in the event a single aesthetically complete totality, a single narrative. Yet the fact was there before me, indisputable and manifest. It completely rewrote the previous story and reinvented it; a future narrating backwards into what was past and redefining that past in its original telling. It was magic.

Pulling Out of Here . . . to Win?

Such is the work of narrative: not every resolution of conflicting parts is achieved by *eliminating* the conflict. A fractured collection of events can be repaired not simply by removing the failed pieces. It can also be made whole by *adding* another piece to the original structure, a piece that retells the story as a complete and functionally integrated totality. The event of adding to the narrative alters the narrative of the event, and the two retell and reread themselves in one another.

Thus, for example, at the end of the day (or just the end of the song) it must be recognized that *Thunder Road* is not a cheerful tune. It is not a happy or an upbeat one, and it is certainly not "victorious." If you're a fan, you already know this; you've not been taken in by the studio cut of the song. If you are not a fan:

1. Why aren't you? And

2. Why are you reading a bunch of philosophers to learn about Springsteen?

But if you are a fan, then you've heard some of the other versions of this song, the ones that were originally pirated from tapes covertly made in club performances. You probably first heard one of these versions on a copy of a copy of a . . . on a cassette player of your own. It was almost inaudible it was so

scratchy. But you recognized the voice and you knew the song
. . . no, that's not right. You knew the *words*. The *song* was something you were hearing again for the first time. Anyway, by now
you own a CD version, because the record companies gave up
fighting the inevitable and just made an official copy, and you
bought it because it was Springsteen. And on this copy—let's just
assume it's the CD—you hear Bruce, the Seanachie . . .

. . . and no one else. There is no E Street Band accompanying this version. Just Springsteen, his harmonica and his guitar—
and very little of these last two. To all intents and purposes, he
is singing *a capella*, a lone voice confronting not the howling
chaos of the unknown road, but the empty silence of absolute
despair and loss. There is no Mary dancing across a porch like
a vision; there is no porch; there is no redemption. There's no
triumphal rise of the sax and the keyboard at the end, nor a full-
throated pounding of guitars and glockenspiel. There is nothing
at the end but the hollow emptiness of inconsolable desolation.
This dusty beach road ends nowhere but at a headstone. And it
is all in his voice.

The words are not enough. The story is not a story until it is
told; the event cannot be made known until it is made incarnate
by the Seanachie. The words by themselves are nothing: not the
brittle, sharp pang of hope or loss; not the gray chalky weight
of despair; nothing, just nothing. You can read the lyric to
Thunder Road—or, for that matter, you can read the words in
this chapter—but in the end you cannot know if the narrator is
singing or weeping until you hear the voice that goes with those
words.

Case the Promised Land

So is that it? Is that all we are left with? A meaningless froth of
vacuous words and voiceless events? Are we all just born to run
down this unknowable highway? Tripping over ourselves and
each other trying to find the words to this song, a voice for this
narrative we call our life, lost amongst irreconcilable and contradictory rhythms that stubbornly refuse to listen or yield? The
only answer we can give here is, "yes."

And because of this, we are free.

The events of this world do not wait exclusively upon the
Seanachie as singer or musician for their telling—or, more

importantly, for their constructive *re*telling. Springsteen brings out his guitar and lends the Seanachie's voice to our narratives, because that's the kind of story-teller that *he* is. How those story-telling events come to be constructively embedded in our own narratives is a creative addition that *we* have to make; it is not given to us in the songs on the CD anymore than the songs Springsteen sings can be found in just the words on the album jacket.

Because the only voice we can give to our narrative is ultimately our own; Bruce is just one of the background vocals. The creative making of the narrative of this world, of our world, your world and mine, is a task yet to be attempted, present to us only in so far as it is still in the making. It is not a fact already accomplished. Maybe I am that young, after all.

But now it is time for me to depart as the narrator of this tale. You alone remain; you and your narrative. And I say again, you are free. Because you are the Seanachie, and you are free to choose your narrative. The words might already be there, but it stands to you to compose creatively them into your story and make them incarnate. Bruce can help, but it is for you to give them voice. Or *voices*—there is no law of narrative that says there can be only one version. But there it is: the road is open for you to take.

Oh Thunder Road!

11

Everything Dies: Facing Fatalism in "Atlantic City"

JOHN JACOB KAAG

Springsteen's "Atlantic City" is about passing and about passing away uncontrollably. It's about a type of fatalism, the type that keeps one up at night—out of despair or out of sheer defiance of the dark. When Springsteen points us into the *Darkness on the Edge of Town*, he is pointing us toward "Atlantic City," a song he would release six years later. Dave Marsh, in his 1978 *Rolling Stone* review of *Darkness*, says that the album could take as its text two lines from Jackson Browne: "Nothing survives— / But the way we live our lives."[1]

For Springsteen, however, this is not some stoic fact, but an invitation to explore the ways that "nothing survives," the way we might live our lives in the face of this nothingness. "Atlantic City" beckons. Thirty million people, undoubtedly many more, continue to return to this not-so-imaginary place, attracted to its fatal freedoms, intimate possibilities, and carefully disturbing atmosphere. It is here, in the darkness, that hopes and beliefs are lost and found.

This song is sung by and about a loser, one who comes to experience the loss that quietly underpins human finitude. At one point, Springsteen wails—"there are winners and losers / and don't get caught on the wrong side of that line." He, however, remains caught as if by fate on the "losing end." Winners, on the other hand, do occasionally win in Atlantic City. That is

---

[1] *Bruce Springsteen: The Rolling Stone Files* (San Francisco: Rolling Stone Press, 1996), p. 75.

to say, they are free to leave. They take off before night sets in. They end up in the suburbs or in enormous libraries with marble floors that remain peaceful and bright even in the darkness. They may even become philosophers of a sort—but not good ones. Springsteen, however, suggests that something has been lost in this sort of suburban and intellectual victory—the capacity to feel deeply, the sense of being crushed, the power to create in a fatefully fragile world.

A similar suggestion emanates from a corner of contemporary philosophy, from the writings of John J. McDermott (born in 1933). He writes that "some of us all the time and most of us most of the time are dead to the possible rhythm of our experiences . . . We look alive, but we are dead, dead to our things and dead to ourselves."[2] If McDermott has us pegged it is because he has come to know us from firsthand experience. He is not Thales, peering up at the sky, Descartes, staring out his philosopher-window, or Kant, never venturing beyond the gates of his familiar Königsberg. McDermott, a committed teacher, avid baseball fan, and city-dweller, is *not* a detached and isolated onlooker, which is to say that he is *not* your average philosopher.

Born Irish, McDermott grew up in New York, not too far— geographically, dispositionally, or spiritually—from the place that Springsteen would call home. I don't know him well, but he seems to be the personification of the country that he describes in his writing: "America / One of a kind, but special / Nonetheless / Pockmarked, heroic, bewildered / arrogant, sensitive, never / plodding." Yes, this is Springsteen's America also. I guess this is why McDermott's philosophy can accompany this sort of music. I once had the chance to take a look at his library that wraps around his house in College Station, Texas (Yes, he now lives in Texas). What I found did not surprise me. *On the Road, Being and Nothingness, Don Quixote, Emerson's Essays, The Twelve Steps and Twelve Traditions*—all of which seem at home with McDermott.

The only real conversation that we ever had was the one that motivated me to write this chapter. In truth, the conversation

---

[2] John McDermott, "The Aesthetic Drama of the Ordinary," in *Streams of Experience* (Amherst: University of Massachusetts Press, 1986), p. 139.

was more like a Springsteen show. McDermott talked, I listened, and afterward I couldn't remember most of it. But I did remember this. One of his students had missed class the week before and McDermott, like any good teacher, had remembered to give the student a hard time face-to-face. The student—a good student—responded by saying that her father had passed away and that she was at the funeral. McDermott does not take death—or life—lightly. It is deadly serious—this business of life. Sympathetic and fiercely sincere, McDermott tried to comfort the freshman. The freshman didn't need comforting. "That's okay," the student said with a shrug, "no big deal." McDermott was stunned: "No BIG DEAL!?" For McDermott, nothing is bigger. The mildness of the student's response betrayed a type of ignorance, or even worse, a blatant refusal to examine the questions that fatalism inevitably begs. Under his breath and with a shake of his head, he muttered, "If death doesn't matter, what about life? Are we even awake?"

Drawing heavily from European existentialism, American philosophy, and his experiences in the urban centers of America, McDermott encourages his readers to remain alive to their experiences and to return to the dark issues of tragedy, finitude, and death not as abstract subjects, but as meaningful ways of thinking about, and participating in, human existence. This way of thinking is highlighted in his most recent work, the *Drama of Possibility*, but the way was first trail-blazed in earlier works compiled in McDermott's *Streams of Experience*. It is by way of this stream of thought that we arrive at the meaning of "Atlantic City." In his early writing and in Springsteen's music, night creeps in and even winners can be drawn back to the flickering lights of the coastline city. I want to negotiate the fatalism that emerges in their cityscapes and explore the dim and intermittent glow that hope casts in the darkness.

Living in "Atlantic City"—Permanently Afflicted

In McDermott's words, "No reader of this chapter has died" (p. 157). But it is equally true that every reader of this chapter is dying, passing away as this word passes into the next. The inevitability of one's own death resides as the irreducible kernel of our human situation. To the extent that philosophy seeks to enrich and deepen our situation, McDermott insists that its job is to gnaw at this kernel. We will, for better and for worse, never fully digest the meaning of our terminality. Think about it. See how it sits in your gut: You are going to die next Wednesday and every moment is a moment closer to humpday. Perhaps it puts a new spin on the meaning of the "daily grind." Perhaps, in darkness of this grim situation, you ask the question that philosophy seeks to negotiate: "What should I *do?*" Perhaps you cry out with the question to which *all* philosophers *should* respond: "Can you help me?" Death remains, for all of us, in the words of Martin Heidegger, our "ownmost possibility." If death remains our "ownmost" so too must the questions that accompany it. They are always ours to ask and always ours to answer.

In this age of whitewashed hospitals and quietly secluded nursing homes, it is difficult to understand McDermott's claim that *all* human beings, *at every moment*, are "permanently afflicted." Our lives, for the most part, are so pleasant and so healthy. Death happens at the end of a full life—and not before. It happens quietly, in a geriatric playground of wires and ventilators and sodium-free meals. By means of technology and modern medicine we desperately pretend to hold death at bay. Death happens, but we would like to think that it always happens elsewhere. Death happens, but it happens to someone else. Death happens, but not right now: "How strange, how singular, how unusual is our understanding of death," McDermott says. "Each of us claims to know of death, yet our experience is necessarily indirect, vicarious, at a distance."

Poets and musicians have the uncanny ability to close the distance between life and death, or more to the point, to understand life as the personal process of dying. In the words of the seventeenth-century satirist, Bishop Hall, "Death borders upon our birth, and the cradle stands in the grave." After the *Darkness* tour in 1981, Springsteen seems to have confronted this dark fact; he gets the message and successfully relays it to us. We see that human finitude emerged as a central theme at the end of Darkness, in "Wreck on the Highway." In this case, Springsteen is still the onlooker, the innocent bystander who witnesses, or imagines, the death of another human being. The theme of death, and life as a process of dying, becomes more pronounced after 1981. The songs on *Nebraska* would be more personal, more suicidal. Is it any surprise that *Nebraska* did not sell well? As McDermott explains, Americans don't like to talk about death, especially when it is framed as *sui*-cide, described so vividly as "my own." I guess they don't like to hear about it either.

The title track is the story of Charlie Starkweather, the serial killer whose personality Springsteen assumes in a frightfully calm, almost pastoral, voice: "I am not sorry for what I have done / at least for a little while, sir, she and I had some fun." This is a life literally shot through with death—the death of others and the death of oneself. When Starkweather is sent to the electric chair, his response remains indifferent, as if this fate is just another part of life. Like Camus's *Stranger*, Starkweather reflects an unyielding candor concerning the terminality of our condition and the way in which our finitude may cut us off from others, may make us aliens in our familiar world. Like Franz Kafka's *Trial*, "Nebraska" invites us to sing along in a fatefully disturbing song: "They declared me unfit to live / Said into that great void my soul'd be hurled." We might not want to sing along, but Springsteen and McDermott suggest that we have no choice in the matter. At some point, all of us are declared unfit to live. This most lonely, but most common, of situations begs the question that McDermott's writing occasionally seeks to answer: "Can we experience ourselves as terminal yet live creative, probing, building lives which nonetheless, ask for no guarantees and for no ultimate significance to be attributed to this endeavor" (p. 84). This is the question that plays out in Springsteen's "Atlantic City."

The violence and terminality of "Nebraska" bleeds into "Atlantic City" and stains the song from the very beginning. On March 15th, 1981, a nail bomb went off under the porch of a row home in South Philadelphia. The explosion destroyed the house and killed Phillip Testa, the owner of a local poultry business and the head of the American Mafia in Philadelphia. Springsteen opens "Atlantic City" by recounting this story: "They blew up the Chicken Man in Philly last night / they blew up his house too." According to Testa's neighbors, his body parts were strewn for blocks—messy reminder of human brutality and vulnerability. The hit was supposedly initiated by a rival family from Atlantic City.

Why does Springsteen open with such an explosive tale? Let's look further into Springsteen's angle of vision. The early 1980s saw the sedimenting of suburban life in America, a kind

of human existence that had been, for various reasons, torn free
of its existential moorings. By then, we had not only actively
fled from but had lost sight of the dangerous prospect of our
vulnerability. Our mechanized lifestyles and technological habits
evidenced the deadening consequences of this cultural development. Our flight in the face of human fragility lay at the heart
of "white flight," the dispersal of our city centers in the two
decades before. It was safe outside the city. In the suburbs, life
became happily boring, forgetful. Springsteen, however, was not
happy and insisted that we ought not to be. Along with the
punk movement and the later works of the modern painter
Willem de Kooning (1904–1997), Springsteen's songs anticipated
McDermott's observation that "Boredom and ennui are signs of
a living death. In that the only time we have is the time we have,
they are inexcusable faults." To counteract these faults and to
remind us of the precariousness of our human condition,
Springsteen attempts to rouse us from our suburban compla-
cency. "Coming to consciousness," the point and purpose of
good philosophy and good music, stood in marked and violent
contrast to everyday suburban modes of living in the 1980s.
"Coming to consciousness," according to McDermott, "has nothing to do with the traditional pursuit of happiness, an attempt
illusory and self deceptive for a human organism whose
denouement is the inevitability of death without redemption."
Indeed, "Atlantic City" continues to be jarring to the traditional
pursuits of Springsteen's average listener.

The murder of the Chicken Man initiated a cascade of death
that swept across the crime families of the Northeast for the next
fifteen years, ending in 1995. It's in this sense that "trouble is
busting in from out of state" and why the "boys on the boardwalk are getting ready for a fight." This is precisely when my
own mother would have whisked *her* two boys back to the suburbs—more about that a little later. Springsteen, however,
encourages us to linger in the possibility of loss. Indeed, it is
precisely in the face of this "trouble," simultaneously existential
and criminal, that Springsteen cashes "out of the Central Trust /
and buys two tickets on that Coast City bus." He goes to Atlantic
City, to the city of loss, not in spite of the danger, but because
of it. This is not, however, a romanticized journey and this character, like Starkweather, is by no means your garden-variety
hero. This character is less a journeyman than a transient, for the

former "connotes a definite goal, an end in view, or at least a return home. A transient, however, is one who is passing through," and passing away. On his passing through "Atlantic City," Springsteen's only triumph, if one could call it that, is his coming to consciousness as shown in the refrain: "Everything dies, baby, and that's a fact..." Death is not something that happens elsewhere. It is not even something that "happens" per se, like some onetime event. Death *is* here and now—in everything. In describing the passing of time and human finitude, McDermott writes that "Time passing is a death knell. With the license of a paraphrase, I ask, For whom does the bell toll? It tolls for me and thee and for ours" (p. 132).

Celebrating Transience

The "fact" that is repeated in Atlantic City's refrain is also a question: can I deal with the fact of human finitude—can I live with this knowledge? McDermott directs us to Albert Camus's rendering of the question. Camus writes, 'I want to know if I can live with what I know and with that alone." The answer always cuts in one of two directions. Sylvia Plath, Virginia Woolf, Ernest Hemingway, Hart Crane, and Woody Guthrie traveled the path of suicide, whether slow or fast, or both; this is an alternative that may be reasonable if followed, not as a route of escapism, but as an existential choice that attempts to reject a dehumanizing fatalism in our lives. Springsteen flirts with the plausibility of suicide throughout Nebraska, but also seems to suggest another option.

This second option is defined, in McDermott's words, "by the imaginative and ameliorative strategies for coping with the stark reality" that "everything dies." It is only through these strategies that we might understand the second line of Springsteen's assertion: "Everything dies, baby, that's a fact / *but maybe someday everything comes back.*" Terminality and possibility are held together in the refrain of the human condition. There are, however, no promises here. As McDermott indicates, our hopes for amelioration and salvation are *possibilities*, tentative "maybes," rather than actualities. Like the "suicide machines" Springsteen describes in "Born to Run," McDermott places the volatile mix of finality and possibility under extreme pressure. The result is the combustion of human action—the "life of the live creature."

McDermott is taking this phrase from John Dewey (1859–1952), the American pragmatist, but recasts it in a tragic way that Dewey never quite pulled off. This creature, like Springsteen's character, is a homeless one. As soon as we come to face our homelessness, however, McDermott writes that we "can proceed . . . under the assumption that we do not belong." Along with Springsteen, he suggests that our existential situation is an invitation to explore the darkness of our lives. Remember that fatalism has the power to keep us up at night. That's why Springsteen's refrain of "Everything dies" gives way to entreaty: "*So* put your makeup on, fix your hair up pretty, and meet me tonight in Atlantic City." This is the way that we proceed in the face of finitude. This is a rendezvous with possibility in a city of unavoidable loss and risk.

This ongoing and active encounter in Atlantic City serves as the conclusion of experiential observation and belief. Here, Springsteen echoes McDermott and the pragmatist, William James (1842–1910): a resolute evaluation of our human situation should drive us out of the realm of thought and onto the road of action. The chauvinism and unstable power of Springsteen's character indicates that our response to human finitude will always, or less cynically, usually, be sub-optimal. This being said, if our fundamental situation, as Springsteen and McDermott suggest, is one of transience, we are to realize that the "meaning of the transient's journey is . . . the journey itself." Meaning-making is always on the way, embodied in precious and fleeting moments of transaction with the world.

Earlier I mentioned the way that de Kooning's late paintings—big, frightful pieces of abstract expressionism—might jar us from the inertia and "bad faith" of suburban life.[3] At the very least, they can shake us up. De Kooning, like McDermott, like Springsteen, seems to suggest that ennui and boredom are not proper responses to the tragedy of our human situation. Instead, in the face of our finitude, we are called by an aging

---

[3] Bad faith refers to the concept developed by the French existentialist Jean-Paul Sartre. It's often described as the counterpart to "authenticity," the willingness and ability to act freely in a fragile world that is outlined by the "nothingness" of human finitude. One acting out "bad faith" refuses to face the terminality of their situation in a personal and resolute matter. See Sartre, *Being and Nothingness* (New York: Simon and Schuster, 1992), pp. 86–112.

de Kooning to "paint (and act) like this stroke may be your last." McDermott agrees and reflects on the aesthetic character of ordinary experience; we may not have the artistic genius of de Kooning, but it is possible and suitable to "to make our (life) journey ever alert to our surroundings and to every perceivable sensorial nuance" (p. 165). We are to be alert, even in the fading twilight, noticing the specks of sand that might still reflect the sun's last efforts—and our own. This alertness, however, does not guarantee sunny days and smooth rides. Indeed, it often makes us prone to experience, with bone-jarring sincerity, the unavoidable potholes of life. Sensitivity can be a real pain sometimes. But everything, including a pothole, dies; this too shall pass.

McDermott says that "Transience as the 'form of life' can be celebrated . . . for us, novelty is crucial and even failure and mishap is to be integrated into the pedagogy of history." As "Atlantic City" plays out, Springsteen states that, "Luck may have died and our love may be cold / but with you forever I'll stay." The relations that we create in life are by no means permanent and immutable, but his character insists that he will, despite this fact, remain faithful to life's journey: "Were goin' out where the sands turnin' to gold / Put on your stockins baby, 'cause the night's getting cold." This journey is defined by hopes that are both intense and fleeting, like the sun on a shrinking patch of Atlantic City sand. Echoing Dewey, McDermott repeatedly claims that meaning is not realized in the duration or sustainability of an experience, but in its *quality*. The journey is defined by human *pathos*, imperfect in its expression, but meaningful in its emotional and qualitative resonance.

It is defined by its pathos, but also by its terminality: Just as we think that Springsteen is going to arrive at golden sands, at a lasting and terminal consummation, the song turns dark again: "Now, I been lookin' for a job, but its hard to find." And "down here it's just winners and losers and don't get caught on the wrong side of that line." The man has debts that no honest guy can pay and is "tired of comin' out on the losin' end." In light of this situation, Springsteen explains to his lover that a not-so-honest solution can be reached: "So, honey, last night I met this guy and I'm gonna do a little favor for him." Ironically, his attempt to become a winner draws him ever closer to the ultimate loss of being human. Echoing a sentiment expressed in

"The River," Springsteen searches for the cross-current of personal salvation, but those waters have ceased to flow. The Atlantic City sand won't be turning to gold. Or maybe this summary moment has simply passed away. Other inevitable waves crash on the shores—dangerous, self-destructive, tragic, violent. What is this "favor" to which the singer commits himself? The "trouble" that "busted in from out of state" seems to have found a home in the inner sanctum of his character, and he seems to have been caught up in the violent and fatalistic movement of the city, described in the opening of the song.

Citing Karl Jaspers (1883–1969), McDermott describes this movement as a "flux (which) sweeps us into the whirlpool of ceasing conquest and creation, of loss and gain, in which we painfully circle, subject in the main to the power of the current, but able, now and then, to exert ourselves within a restricted sphere of influence." Asserting oneself in, and against, this inevitable movement takes courage, commitment, and a certain amount of defiance. This is the fundamental challenge of our lives: "To convert the personal weaknesses into strengths and to drive our strengths into the teeth of a personally neutral, but relative pregnant world" (p. 151). It's not surprising that the challenge of life is, at once, a fight to the death. At least it is in "Atlantic City"

My grandfather still tells me about Atlantic City, the flourishing middle class Mecca of the early 1940s. When thirty million vacationers made their pilgrimage each summer he says that it was "a real city," and a beautiful one at that. I have never quite been there. Urban decay, white flight, "race problems"—things just died I guess. I am not nostalgic. I don't know what I am missing. As kids, my mother would take us on a few of the safer rides and let us run around the boardwalk and this was called "going to Atlantic City." *We would always leave before dark*. Her attempts to shield us from what the city had become were—at least temporarily—successful. My only real exposure to the town was through my father, an oddly fanatic Springsteen fan. He, like the city, parted company before establishing any real acquaintance—appropriate, since the song is about absence and loss. I guess my mother could not shield me from Atlantic City altogether. And, undoubtedly, I am better for the exposure. Now I return to "Atlantic City" almost willingly. Absence and loss have lessons to teach.

Lesson One: In passing into *Darkness*, one's eyes must work harder. Indeed, we are called to use all of our senses to negotiate the streets of "Atlantic City." Lesson Two: The darker it gets, the more sensitive we must become. If, in Thoreau's words, we are to be awake to the dawn, we are also to be wide-eyed in the night. It is in this way that death—imminent, present, ownmost—places demands on our lives. Lesson Three: Each of us has "Deadlines" that we can neither shirk, nor fully meet. We ought not bemoan this fact, but rather realize that we are to work away, fully awake, on this deadline. In doing so, we might have the chance to realize that this deadline is also a type of lifeline. I leave you to work away on McDermott's "Deadline" in your little corner of "Atlantic City:"

A festering presence
takes
on the inappropriate
Label
of
Dead
As in no life
no play, no more
How does a line
Die
only to live
forever
as a sign of
failure
if one goes over
the line
But if we meet
the dead
line
Then the line
dies
Living only when
not
met.

12

Living on the Edge: A Reason to Believe

ERIN MCKENNA and SCOTT PRATT

Springsteen closes his 1980 album *Nebraska* with the image of a vague figure standing over a dead dog along a highway. The man may have hit the dog with his car; it may be his own pet, lost and killed along a highway. But the man is not sad or angry or guilty, rather he is puzzled and expectant "Like if he stood there long enough that dog'd get up and run." The chorus demands attention: "It struck me kinda funny, seemed kinda funny sir to me / Still at the end of every hard earned day people find some reason to believe."

Nebraska is one of Springsteen's darkest albums featuring songs about mass murder, broken families, poverty, and death and seeming to claim that life is empty and filled with despair. The final song of the collection, however, almost makes a contrary claim: despite it all, people find a reason to believe. The reason they find is never identified.

We'll try to propose what that reason might be by considering several of Springsteen's songs, getting some help from the contemporary American philosopher John McDermott. McDermott, like Springsteen, grounds his art and reflection in the ordinary experience of those most at risk in American society, those least likely to have opportunities to change their lives, those who work hard but fail to make ends meet, who lack health care and education—but at once those who still find a reason to believe.

Edging toward the Darkness

Springsteen's art in much of his early work (stretching from 1975's *Born to Run* to 1984's *Born in the USA*) seems intent upon recounting a certain range of human experiences—urban and working class—in a way that will transform them from unreflective drudgery, empty of meaning, into rich events where life becomes characterized by pain and despair, but also the possibility of something more. His approach to this work is to present songs that, in effect, *are* the experience to be transformed, set out for listeners to take up and live themselves. Early songs like "Born to Run" and "Jungleland" emphasize a kind of meaning characterized by speed and risk. Driven by the E-Street Band, many of these songs call for young men to break free of the confinement of life in working class towns—to live or die in the escape. The songs seem to suppose that if the escape is successful, these young men will find themselves in some new place where they will find happiness.

"Born to Run," for example, describes the end this way: "Someday girl I don't know when / we're gonna get to that place / Where we really want to go / and we'll walk in the sun." "Thunder Road" ends in a similar way, contrasting the place of the singer's ordinary life with a place where he will find success: "It's a town full of losers / And I'm pulling out of here to win." "Badlands" (1978) seems to set aside the "place in the sun" for a place that, if it provides anything, seems to reject the experience of the song *itself*, and the need to sing it: "I wanna find one face," he says, "that ain't looking through me / I wanna find one place, / I wanna spit in the face of these badlands." Put another way, if the place beyond the present experience is a new place in "Born to Run," in "Badlands," it becomes a "beyond" close at hand— within spitting distance. Significantly, "Badlands" also asserts a connection between belief, salvation, and the place of one's ordinary life: "I believe in the love that you gave me / I believe in the faith that could save me / . . . It may raise me above these Badlands." But above is not beyond and salvation will not be some new place, but a place continuous with the old. The last song on the 1978 collection is "Darkness on the Edge of Town" and here we find Springsteen offering a new conception of experience and the first chance to imagine what, in the face of the despair, will constitute a reason to believe.

"Darkness" continues the established themes of Springsteen's early songs: cars and racing, women and love. This time, however, with "Badlands" as the opening song, Springsteen seeks no longer the escape from despair but rather a place at the edge of town. In contrast to "Born to Run," there is no escape for the driver in "Darkness." Instead, salvation is "a spot 'neath Abram's Bridge," a particular place, no longer outside his world but at its fringes. It is the place where dreams are lost and found, but also a place where there is a price to be paid. The experience of the driver is here reinforced by the musical arrangement that emphasizes a kind of argument structure. The escape he seeks is tracked by raising the melody from the tonic to the third and then to the fifth in each verse, and screaming the octave by the end. Let's follow his progress.

In the first verse, the settled life of a former lover is set in contrast to a declaration that the singer has escaped to Abram's Bridge. In the second verse, the constraints of keeping secrets are "cut loose," and in the third verse the loss of his job and wife demand that he break free to the edge. In each verse, the listener is drawn into an experience that should pass for stability, only to find the stability broken and the singer seeking something more by risking everything at the fringes of settled experience. The listener is brought out of the center (where folks live the good life or strive for it) through loss (love, secrets, money, and wife) to the edge where death and life are both present realities. The meaning found is found in the darkness at the edge.

Feeling Edgy

While Springsteen sets out this notion of experience and the possibility for its development as an experience within *music*, John McDermott presents a *conception* of experience—a way of thinking about being in the world—that he calls the "Promethean self." Following the American philosopher William James (1842–1910), McDermott proposes that human selves are "to build a personal world . . . in response to the 'push and press of the cosmos'" (*The Drama of Possibility*, p. 380). As McDermott sees it, human beings emerge into a universe of chaotic activity. The things that we recognize, that we desire and reject, that hurt and help us, are relations that emerge at the intersections of action, and those relations make us or break us. Our struggle is to sort among these relations, depicted by Springsteen as lovers, work, unwanted children, failed aspirations, Hurst shifters, fuel injectors, refinery towers, radio stations.

The problem with this overloaded world is that "if we were to follow each thing and event to its full perceptual implication, we would explode" (p. 382). Springsteen's songs, in a sense, present this complexity of relations and in most songs the singer tries to gain control, to cut things off and leave things behind. As he says, again in "Badlands," "I want control right now." As McDermott puts it: "Cutting off relations is therefore necessary for personal survival. But how do we cut?" (p. 382). It's not enough simply to cut oneself off and end the relationships that make us who we are, nor is it enough simply to pursue relations without a sense of our selves and our roots. Liberation depends on the dual activity of cutting and connecting so that, even in the most desperate circumstances, "the world we build is exactly akin to the way we cut relations, indulge relations, and celebrate relations" (p. 382). The process of building a world, while liberating ourselves, is nevertheless constrained: "our world takes off as novel and as distinctively ours precisely in response to how we make new relations of the relations already at work in the environ in which we find ourselves" (pp. 382–83). The singer of "Darkness" builds his world in relation to the desolation and confinement of his life by risking his life racing cars at the edge of town. The effort is dangerous, but it is transformative; as McDermott concludes, "Being in the world is not a cakewalk."

In "Darkness" we find the idea that, in facing death, life takes on its fullest meaning. Here Springsteen discusses the things people work for—"got a house up in Fairview"; the secrets people try to keep from others—even themselves; and the things lost along the way—money and wife. But none of this is where the richness of life is found. Instead we are told "I'll pay the cost / For wanting things that can only be found / In the darkness on the edge of town." The presence of death throws things into relief. It is in the wanting that we become alive.

The Cutting Edge

In the first verse of the song the woman who has the house in Fairview is trying to maintain a certain lifestyle (she's presumably the lost wife referred to in the third verse). She is seen as lacking something important—something necessary to truly appreciate life—her blood never burned. She needs to be told that there is "darkness on the edge of town." She is missing out on something important and the consequence is a boring life that meets the expectations of society at its center, not its edge. She buys into the values she has been given rather than exploring the darkness and making meaning herself. Speaking of such conformity McDermott says:

> To the extent that they do not learn to make their own relations, children are doomed to living second-hand lives. They become creatures of habituation who merely follow out the already programmed versions of their experience as inherited from parents, older siblings, and self-appointed definers of reality, such as teachers. Ironically, a child who knows how to make relations can convert even authoritarian and repressive treatment into paths of personal liberation, whereas a child who does not make relations converts invitation to free inquiry into derivative and bland repetition. This irony is made vivid for us when we realize that most often the lives of those whom we regard as "great" are characterized by affliction, suffering, and frequent rejection. In the hands of those who can make and remake relations, even negative events become the nutrition for a creative life. (*Drama of Possibility*, p. 463)

For both Springsteen and McDermott we must avoid living second-hand lives. In "Darkness on the Edge of Town," Springsteen points to the importance of the call to live a creative life, but also points to the accompanying loss and risk involved in such a life.

If death doesn't function as a fringe that helps give meaning and interest to life and our choices, it can be seen as something we must accept and move on. We must find ways to want and to go on even when things don't seem hopeful. In "Reason to Believe" we are faced with the death of a dog, desertion by a husband, the death of an old man, and a groom left at the altar. These are the kinds of losses that enter most of our lives. We will be left by others and we will leave this life ourselves; this is assured. And yet in spite of it all, "people find some reason to believe." Some will seek escape in various addictions or denial mechanisms, but most keep going. McDermott expresses a similar sentiment when he refers to life as a trudge.

As I have written elsewhere, "being in the world is not a cake-walk," although gratefully, it can have its celebratory perturbations and interpolations. If not a cakewalk, neither is it, for most of us, a walk on the wild side. Rather, the walk in the world turns out to be mostly a trudge, with occasional interstitial eruptions and an all-too-habitual tendency to live vicariously through the mediated ersatz reportage of person and events "in the news," as we are fond of saying. (p. 244)

So, we find ways to trudge through life. Even more, though, Springsteen calls on us to live actively and to dream. McDermott calls on us to do the same: "I still take as a personal and philo-sophical obligation to seek ways of coping, ameliorating, and understanding in the short run" (p. 243).

Between the Edges

The philosophical obligation is to cope, to ameliorate, and to understand. Ironically, it is rooted in the fact that we die *and* that we are aware we die. McDermott writes of a "metaphysics of transiency," in which "human life is seen as a wandering, a traveling, a bemusement which rocks from side to side, comedy and tragedy, break through and setback—yet, in all, a purpo-sive, even progressive, trip, in which the human endeavor makes its mark, sets its goals, and occasionally scores."

Meliorism—or looking for improvement without expecting perfection—emerges in life as an attitude and practice that bridges differences by their edges. It is neither pessimism nor optimism because it does not concede to the forces that would undo us nor does it expect that success is inevitable. The oblig-ation leads to "the deepest sentiment of human life, too often unsung and too often derided: that the nectar is in the journey, that ultimate goals may be illusory, nay most likely are but a gossamer wing. Day by day, however, human life triumphs in its ineluctable capacity to hang in and make things better: not perfect, simply better" (pp. 157–58). We might be tempted to take McDermott's meliorism for an acceptable state of affairs, at worst, neutral in its implications for us offering hope and worry in equal measure. But McDermott will not let his readers rest so easily. We are not destined for neutrality; we are destined to die.

The fundamental question is whether there is a median way between the self-deception of personal immortality, on the one hand, and the radical commitment to the moment, on the other. If we live within the bowels of the temporal process, can we not have also a sense of the future, a sense which does not delude us into thinking that we have transcended time? Put directly, can we experience ourselves as terminal and yet live creative, probing, building lives, which, nonetheless, ask for no guarantees and for no ultimate significance to be attributed to our endeavor? I, for one believe that we can live this way; nay, I believe that it is *only* in this way that we live a distinctively human life. (p. 285)

Creating, probing, building balanced against inevitable failure and collapse—this is what it is to be human. When we fail to live that kind of life we fail to give this life its due. We fail to pay proper attention to the growth of experience.

Springsteen appears to agree with this. Our recognition of the darkness also brings recognition of the edge which marks the presence of something beyond and the fact that this "beyond" will always exceed our grasp. Without the attendant hope for something more, we can slip into a hedonistic live-for-the-moment approach to life. We find examples of such lives in the case of addicts, for example. In "Darkness on the Edge of Town" the last verse speaks of the loss of money, wife, and meaning. One can read this as loss leading to resignation. With nothing left to lose why not risk whatever remains? But in "Reason to Believe" we find the activity of baptism and a plea for understanding, asking the Lord "what does it mean?" This song, which notes how people find ways to trudge on, seems to rely on the idea of something beyond. From this perspective one could argue that these two songs, together, send the message that facing loss without faith in a greater purpose results in reckless death seeking behavior—darkness. Hope and the ability to trudge on relies on faith in a greater purpose and meaning.

Over the Edge?

In light of our inability to know what makes the edge an edge, McDermott acknowledges the challenge. We don't know if there is anything beyond so that the same thing that underwrites hope underwrites despair at the same moment. Discussing the belief in salvation or immortality McDermott says:

> Certainly such hope is a legitimate and understandable human aspiration. But to convert this hope into a commitment, a knowledge, a settled conviction, is to participate in an illegitimate move from possibility to actuality. It's understandable that we wish to escape from peril, but it is unacceptable to translate that desire into an assured belief that we have so escaped. . . . Obviously, I have no final knowledge of these claims nor do I know of anyone who has. Evidence on their behalf is scanty, scattered, tentative, highly personal, and empirically dubious. (p. 283)

But this doesn't mean we must enter the darkness recklessly. Discussing the writings of the American philosopher John Dewey (1859–1952), McDermott notes the "absence of closure, of ultimate certitude, and of transcendent meaning. In short, there is no immortality. Yet, equivalently, make no mistake, we do *not* have nihilism" (p. 415). Instead we are called to come to the edge and find meaning, that is, to create, probe, and build. Nothing removes the bite from "the fact that we are born to live and destined to die. I contend that the utter frustration of this contradiction in our personal situation cannot be resolved. . . . Most likely, we have no ultimate future. This should not keep us from participating in the explosive possibilities of our present, no matter what the situation. Setback enriches as well as breakthrough. Our impending death is not the major obstacle to our becoming truly human. The obstacle is found in our running for cover on behalf of our escape from death" (pp. 289–290).

In the end nothing can "totally obviate our being ill-at-ease, for our disconnectedness is ontological and incurable." I can do something, though. "Make relations! Build, relate, and then reflect. Reflect, relate, and then build. Seek novelty, leave no stone unturned. . . . Above all, never close down . . . . The only acceptable denouement is death. Until then, all signs are go— that is, make relations until the maker is unmade" (p. 384).

Blurring the Edges

The result is a relation model of the world in which human beings—the voices of Springsteen's songs, his listeners and the lives they live—are regions marked by indeterminate boundaries where growth and transformation depend upon risking the boundaries in order to expand, cut, and connect. The result is life between two deaths: one by stasis, marked by drudgery and confinement, in which there is little novelty and little hope, and the other of death from risk or exhaustion when the boundary has finally been crossed. McDermott captures these deaths in his posit of five risks: relation starvation, amputation, saturation, seduction, and repression.

With relation starvation we find novelty unsettling and retreat into the familiar. Our world shrinks and becomes static. We are unable to make relations. Similarly we may participate in relation repression—hiding traumas even from ourselves. This can cause us to relate to the world in unhealthy ways. One way we try to protect ourselves is by relation amputation. Relation amputation refers to the risk of cutting off relations out of fear or habit—of being afraid to experiment. We must learn to cut, but not by being afraid to take chances. At another extreme is relation saturation. Here one overindulges in the making of relations, but then relations have little significance. Such a person is one "who eats without tasting" (p. 386). We must make relations, but we must also cut. We may also escape stasis in relation seduction—this can take the form of fanaticism—extreme, unthinking commitment to a cause or a chemically caused enhanced experiences, intense in its moment, but having no feet. The problem here is the return from the trip to everyday life only to find it baffling and disabling. "The trouble with relation seduction, be it local fanaticism on behalf of a visionary goal or pharmacologically induced, is that it is addictive, and therefore more a manacle than liberation" (p. 387). McDermott, like Springsteen, recognizes the need to build relations in order to foster meaningful lives. They both also recognize the difficulty and pain in the process, and point to dangerous side roads many of us take.

Death, from this angle, only marks the extreme edges and by itself provides little insight into the processes of cutting and connecting that mark life. This insight is not found in the worry over the extremes, but rather in life at the edge which is captured and made meaningful through the process of telling the story of the process. For McDermott this is a process of overcoming ontological disconnection through a narrative reconstruction of experience—of sharing the experience of disconnection as a never-fully-successful process of overcoming it. This process is expressed by Springsteen in the series of songs developed for the albums *The River* and *Nebraska*.

Living on the Edge

The song, "The River," by Springsteen's own report, represented a transitional moment in his work in which he recognized the value of narrative detail in making sense of the experience expressed in the more or less disconnected images of "Born to Run" and "Darkness on the Edge of Town." "The River" is the story of young man and his girlfriend who get pregnant and married and whose lives fall into a kind of numb desperation. The narrative character of the song allows Springsteen to set the aspirations and love of the young man in tension and, in the hearing, lets the listener experience tension and loss, hope and despair. In the end, the singer asks: "Is a dream a lie if it don't come true / Or is it something worse / that sends me down to the river / though I know the river is dry?" Significantly, the idea that edges remain central to this narrative construction of experience is captured in a song that did not make the final cut of *The River*. The song, "Living on the Edge of the World," was not released until 1998, but initially became a pair of songs on *Nebraska*: "State Trooper" and "Open All Night."

The first song, "State Trooper," is a plea by a late night driver on the New Jersey Turnpike that a trooper alongside the road leave him alone. The rhythm is regular but slow, the harmonies minor and the lyrics are sung as though the driver is strung out on exhaustion and amphetamines. He confesses that he has no license or registration but that his conscience is clear—though he does not say what he has done. His plea seems to be as much for the state trooper as for himself, as though, if he were stopped, the trooper's life would be at risk. Maybe the trooper has a family, but the driver sings, "the only thing that I got's been botherin' me my whole life." As he drives on past the trooper, the driver's attention shifts to the radio. The relay towers at the side of the road now point him to his distant lover while the same towers fill the air with talk stations: "it's talk talk talk till you lose your patience." His patience gone, the driver cries out for deliverance, "Hey, somebody out there, listen to my last prayer." But we don't expect that anyone will. The driver is at once leaving something behind and seeking some end beyond the turnpike, but his experience is there, on the highway, never escaping the talk and never reaching its end. The feeling of being between, strung out on a highway late at night, is shared by the listener caught up in the droning rhythmic chords and the strained voice of the driver. The meaning is found in the hearing, sharing an experience that becomes transformative by growing experience at its edges.

The second song drawn from the "Living on the Edge of the World," called "Open All Night," doubles the tempo of "State Trooper," but preserves the same rhythmic chords and melody. The result is a song that presses forward, conveying the singer's confidence in his journey and his ability to reach his lover at journey's end. The first verse offers assurance that his car is ready for the challenge, "hummin' like a turbojet." The second verse captures the landscape of his drive: a bleak terrain that recalls the drag-racing hill of "Darkness at the Edge of Town" and separates him from his home—the spooky turnpike at night, and New Jersey "in the mornin' like a lunar landscape."

The third verse recalls the radio towers of "State Trooper" and he asks them "won't you lead me to my baby?" The trooper still waits beneath the overpass, but for this driver he "hits his party light switch" and, we suppose, begins a chase. The driver seems ready for it and takes off. He is going to see his lover, Wanda, the reason for the all-night run. His confidence rises as he plans a phone call, but the last verse, shows again that the meaning of the experience is a product of the boundary between the hope inspired by Wanda and the impossibility of finally reaching her.

It is in this twilight region that the driver notices that the radio stations are no longer talk shows but gospel shows filled by "lost souls calling long distance salvation." And in the last line, the driver realizes that he is one of the lost souls. The two edgy drivers merge, both lost between where they are from and where they are going, desperate or hopeful. Taken together they seem to say that the locus of meaning is in a region between, seeking salvation and failing to find it.

Back from the Edge

Following McDermott, the reason to believe is found in the transitions where relations can be built and success and failure are near at hand. Our quest for meaning pushes us to the edges and, in this movement, reasons to believe keep emerging.

In his essay "Ill-at-Ease," John McDermott describes his own choice against suicide in order to see what happens next—life, he says, is a retrospect, like the place in "Badlands" that gives us perspective, but it is not achievable. Like the singer, we seek a place to spit in the face of the Badlands, but it is the seeking (being on the edge) that gives us a reason.

The last verses of "Reason to Believe" picture scenes of religious practice. In the third, there is a baptism and then a funeral that together pose a question: "Lord won't you tell us, tell us what does it mean?" The fourth and final verse, a wedding, seems to provide an answer. The congregation gathers; the groom waits, and the bride doesn't come. Then the congregation is gone and the sun is setting. The groom stands alone wondering what has happened and still finds a reason to believe. The answer is not in the comfort or the conformity of the congregation (which has left him) or in a return to town. It is not in some final arrival or permanent rest in the arms of a lover. The meaning is on the margin between hope and despair, lived fully in the darkness at the edge of town.

13

Living in "My Hometown": Local Philosophies for Troubled Times

HEATHER E. KEITH

Most Americans have a love-hate relationship with their hometowns. For better or worse, our towns and cities educate us, cultivate our values, nurture our characters, stock our imaginations, and create who we will become.

Then, for many of us, one day we decide that "Baby, we were born to run." We become Garrison Keillor's "exiles," dragging our families back for holidays but then counting the days until we can leave home again. We fancy that we have outgrown our hometowns and are too smart or cosmopolitan for the people who brought us up. At times, we may be right. Perhaps there is something stimulating and sexy about being a citizen of the world, and not a citizen of Hometown, U.S.A. However, many cosmopolitan and smart people are now suggesting that our cavalier attitudes toward the local, whether small town or big city, have gotten us in trouble. They say that our very environment and sense of community—our physical and social landscape—depends on recommitting ourselves to our hometowns.

In his bittersweet love song to a place, "My Hometown," Bruce Springsteen laments the troubled times of his hometown via depressing lyrics and gloomy, repetitive rhythms. The listener can feel the monotony of small town existence, punctuated only by tragic race issues and a deteriorating downtown. In the end, we are left to decide whether the best view of our hometowns is in the rear-view mirror. After all, why shouldn't Bruce and his family get the hell out of such a desolate and dreary place?

However, what if they find that other cities and towns are in the same kind of trouble? An alternative to selling out and moving for Bruce and Kate is to ask how they might help renew their hometown—not exactly by bringing it back to what it was when Bruce was eight and running through the streets on his father's errands (after all, in earlier days it was subject to racial tension and violence). Otherwise, they might as well view their town from the cemetery, like Thornton Wilder's Emily in *Our Town*, wishing they had done more to appreciate the people and places of their community. Rather, Bruce and Kate might help to cultivate a new community that is healthy, growing, and has at its core care and concern for its individual members and the social and physical landscape that gives us all life.

Troubled Times

One of the problems of hometown life, whether it's Manhattan, New York, or Manhattan, Kansas, is that people just don't seem to be joiners anymore, and communities are suffering. Robert Putnam, in his book *Bowling Alone*,[1] studies the decline of civic engagement and American community in recent times. In such important realms of engagement as the P.T.A., clubs, games and sports, informal socializing and neighboring, union membership, and political and community participation, America has seen a downward trend. Bowling leagues are replaced by video games and watching sports on T.V. It seems no one has time for the P.T.A. and for running for office or working on a campaign. Perhaps "Internet Monday" (the Monday after Thanksgiving) has replaced shopping in local stores, assisted by real people. Perhaps it's even replacing malls and outlet stores. For Putnam, this means that we're losing "social capital," the "connections among individuals" that make community work. We may be networking globally on our computers, while our towns and cities fall down around us due to a lack of face-to-face connection with our neighbors. The poet Gary Snyder notes that "For most Americans, to reflect on 'home place' would be an unfamiliar exercise. Few today can announce themselves as someone *from* somewhere."[2]

---

[1] Robert Putman, *Bowling Alone* (New York: Touchstone, 2000).
[2] Gary Snyder, "The Place, the Region, and the Commons," in *At Home on the Earth*, edited by David Landis Barnhill (Berkeley: University California Press, 1999), p. 94.

Bill McKibben, author of another sad-sounding book, *The End of Nature*, worries that the deterioration of community also has effects on our physical environment. By buying our food out of season, trucked in from far away places, we are doing more than our part in unnecessarily using up the world's resources. For example, McKibben notes that a head of iceberg lettuce (grown for most of us in California's Central Valley) offers just fifty calories of energy. Yet, it takes (resource-wise) four hundred calories of energy to produce, and 1,800 calories to ship it east.[3] That's a lot of wasted energy and resources. Think of the savings, in time, money, and resources that could be had by sourcing our food more locally.

The deterioration, or salvation, of our ecologies and economies go hand in hand. Both words come from the Greek *oikos*, household or home, and care for our natural and social households are both essential to strong community. Wendell Berry writes that "a healthy community is like an ecosystem, and it includes—or makes itself harmoniously a part of—its local ecosystem. It is also like a household; it is the household of its place, and it includes the households of many families, human and nonhuman."[4] Though Bruce may not be aware of it, his troubles are not just with a shuttered Main Street—the very air he breathes, the water he drinks, and the integrity of the environment around him are at stake.

On the other hand, the troubled times Bruce and Kate face entail more than the decline of bowling leagues or the pollution of local rivers. Their hometown, like many small towns and cities across the country, is subject to social capital that is exclusive, rather than inclusive. This results in racial tension, intolerance of outsiders (or, where I live, "flatlanders"[5]), disagreement about religious practices, and general closed-mindedness. Sometimes having things in common with our neighbors leads to "in" groups and "out" groups, perhaps an inescapable artifact

---

[3] Bill McKibben, "A Special Moment in History: The Challenge of Overpopulation and Overconsumption," in *Environmental Ethics*, edited by Louis Pojman (Stamford: Wadsworth, 2001), p. 305.

[4] Wendell Berry, *Sex, Economy, Freedom, and Community* (New York: Pantheon, 1992), p. 155.

[5] Here in Vermont, "flatlander" basically means "from somewhere outside of the state." Even Colorado or other non-flat places. Quaint, isn't it?

of human society. We bond with those who are most like us by
standing against those who aren't. Then, Putnam suggests, our
communities are vulnerable to gangs, NIMBY ("not in my back-
yard") movements, and groups such as the Ku Klux Klan. This
causes many politicians and scholars to celebrate globalization,
and to call on schools and colleges to turn out graduates who
are cosmopolitan, rather than parochial, and to prioritize world
citizenship over hometown values.

Many films from the past few decades showcase cosmopolitanism, where highly educated (or at least "citified") heroes infil-
trate urban neighborhoods and rural towns and enlighten the
masses. Think of "To Sir With Love," "To Wong Foo, Thanks for
Everything! Julie Newmar," or even the animated "Cars" in which
the racecar Lightening McQueen brings prosperity to the dying
town of Radiator Springs. Other films painfully detail the
parochial-cosmopolitan clash with more unfortunate consequences, such as "Boys Don't Cry," and "Deliverance." Certainly
when it comes to racism, sexism, homophobia, and intolerance
and violence of any kind, cosmopolitanism wins the day in any
ethics discussion, and it should.

We also need to recognize that something is lost if we all
become citizens of the world at the expense of our local values,
community feeling, and knowledge of the land. In his discussion of "Rootless Professors," Eric Zencey worries that by only
hiring professors who aren't "from around here," we're turning
out students who "are woefully ignorant of the value to be
found in being connected to place."[6] Zencey would likely use
my career as an example: I've taught the ideas of "Rootless
Professors" to many students, but never anywhere near my
Nebraska hometown.

But perhaps cosmopolitanism versus localism is a false
dilemma. For this professor's sake, I certainly hope that being
educated, tolerant, and worldly doesn't necessarily mean being
rootless. What we need to develop is an open-minded, pluralis-
tic, robust, and enlightened localism; a window on the world
that lets us see how they do things in Paris, France, and Kabul,
Afghanistan, but with our hometown in the foreground.

---

[6] Eric Zencey, *Virgin Forest* (Athens, Georgia: University of Georgia Press,
1998), p. 62.

Pluralism, after all, doesn't have to mean that one is disconnected from all values. "Make new friends, but keep the old." That's what our hometown Girl Scouts teach us.

So, Bruce and Kate might have a good reason to leave their closed-minded, closed-up and ecologically damaged hometown, but to where? Is anyone else's hometown going to be any better? Might they be better served with a fresh vision of the potential of their own community and a reinvigoration of social and ecological life? Perhaps they need an enlightened local perspective more than they need a moving van.

Local Philosophies

Philosophical rootlessness has long plagued American culture. In fact, many American students in introductory philosophy classes would surely be surprised to know that our country has grown its own philosophers, from Native American cosmology to neopragmatism. Maybe we're Anglophiles, or maybe we lack cultural-esteem, but the fact is that many American professors teach imported philosophy at the expense of homegrown. This is unfortunate because some of the best philosophies of community, social ethics, politics, and equality are American-made.

For example, the early twentieth-century American pragmatists George Herbert Mead and John Dewey offer unparalleled attention to the concept of the self as inherently social and the community as key to individual well-being. In his lectures and articles, Mead posited a self situated within an evolving social and physical environment, the very existence of which is utterly dependent on relationships with others:

> The self is something which has a development; it is not initially there, at birth, but arises in the process of social experience and activity, that is, develops in the given individual as a result of his relations to that process as a whole and to other individuals within that process.[7]

Mead and other pragmatists disagree with many contemporary ideas of the self which assume that we are all isolated individuals

---

[7] George Herbert Mead, *Mind, Self, and Society: From the Standpoint of a Social Behaviorist* (Chicago: University of Chicago Press, 1934), p. 135.

("atomic"—like little separate atoms, we philosophers say) who may bump into each other, but are otherwise separate and unique with our own little souls looking out from our own little windows. On the contrary, Mead thought that our very sense of ourselves, our character, is wholly a result of social interactions with others. We become unique and individualized only through a lifetime of experiencing ourselves through others. Mead famously said we "take on the attitude of the other" as we come to have a concept of ourselves as others see us. Maybe that's why so many of us have a love-hate relationship with our hometowns. When we look around, we see ourselves.

Dewey's philosophy slants the social self idea in a moral and political direction. If our very character and self-concept is cultivated through our interactions with others, then our moral commitments and political values, as well as the structure of our communities, is also dependent on our families and neighbors. Democracy itself, Dewey's favored political system, is more than just the ideals of a government, it is the form of community which actualizes the potential of its members. In *The Public and Its Problems*, Dewey writes, "There is no sense in asking how individuals come to be associated. They exist and operate in association. If there is any mystery about the matter, it is the mystery that the universe is the kind of universe it is."[8]

Thus, for better or for worse, humans live in an ecology of interaction—one that must be cared for in the same way that we are learning to care more and more about the physical environment. In this light, the social context from which we grow takes on great significance. It is clear that the health of our physical ecology is irreducibly connected to the health and growth of individuals. Likewise, the health of our community is undeniably bound up with the health of the individual characters which inhabit it.

There's increasing evidence in the sciences and social sciences, as well as philosophy, to support the pragmatist claim that even our basic conceptions of self and others always emerge from the context of a cultural or social ecology. Even biologists are looking at the relationship between individual organisms and culture as organic, making the health of the social ecology as

---

[8] John Dewey, *The Public and Its Problems*, in *The Later Works of John Dewey*, Volume 2 (Carbondale: Southern Illinois University Press, 1981), p. 250.

important as the health of the physical ecology.

We might seriously consider whether the great American ecologist Aldo Leopold's worry that "There are two spiritual dangers in not owning a farm" is transferable to a hometown philosophy. "One," Leopold writes, "is the danger of supposing that breakfast comes from the grocery, and the other that heat comes from the furnace."[9] Were he alive today, Leopold would probably think that most of us have become disconnected from our farms and our local economies. It's not just that this disconnection is ruining our hometowns; it is ruining us. It is a *spiritual* danger.

Avoiding this spiritual danger, Bill McKibben capitalizes on the shared household (*oikos*) of our natural and social communities in *Deep Economy*, in which he relates his family's attempt to live through a Vermont winter on locally sourced and preserved food. For McKibben, food consumption is exemplary of many of our consumption habits as we habituate ourselves to larger scale agriculture, marketing, and distribution, at the expense of local farms and economies. We're creating, with Bruce, Main Streets with "white-washed windows and vacant stores," preferring the (perceived) convenience and thriftiness of strip malls and the Internet for goods that have been shipped across the country or across the sea. At the same time, we're eroding the physical and social environment in which our children, including Bruce's son, are educated and their characters cultivated.

Though we may feel more cosmopolitan (in buying box store lead-painted toys made in sweatshops in China?), we're losing our own hometown heritage to thoughtless and valueless globalism. To combat this, McKibben works toward a revitalization of the local, in food choices and other consumptive habits. As Greg Brown, another great songwriter, warns the next generation, "Ah, the small and local must survive somehow, if it's gonna be your town now."

Hometown Security

Bruce's song to his hometown is a lament—a love song to a place he and Kate have already all but left. But, there's hope. As

---

[9] Aldo Leopold, *A Sand County Almanac* (New York: Ballantine, 1966).

Bruce asks his own child to take a good look around his hometown, we can imagine future generations doing the same, if only we can save the place. The good news, from people like Putnam, Dewey, Berry, and others, is that saving our local landscapes doesn't mean a lot of personal sacrifice. Rather, they argue, we'll find that we live better when we live locally and work toward the health of our communities—it just means slowly and systematically changing our ideas and habits. If Bruce, clearly an enlightened person with big ideas, can realize this, he can recommit to his hometown and get the boards off the windows for a thriving Main Street and a safe environment for his son and his son's children.

Novelist Barbara Kingsolver has a pretty good handle on the pleasures and benefits of living locally. In *Animal, Vegetable, Miracle*, co-authored with her daughter and husband, she writes about her family's adventures in gardening and local sourcing of food. Here, she notes the aesthetic pleasures of living locally and supporting the family farms and businesses in her Virginia county. Food suddenly tasted better to Kingsolver's family, and not just because they felt morally righteous in eating it. Food really does taste better when it hasn't traveled around the world in a freight container. Kingsolver writes that her family was surprised to learn that they wanted to be conscious of their food choices, and not just for moral reasons: "Our fretful minds had started us on a project of abstinence from industrial food, but we finished it with our hearts. We were not counting down the days until the end, because we didn't want to go back."[10]

Saving local farms and communities doesn't have to be lonely or parochial, or merely the projects of isolated families. Bruce and Kate might like to note that movements abound in consuming locally, even on a global scale. The international Slow Food "summit," Terra Madre, happens every couple of years in Italy. At this event (nicknamed the "food Olympics" by many participants), farmers, chefs, academics, and consumers from around the world come together to network, hear lectures, and enjoy foods, all in preserving the world's great food traditions. What could be more cosmopolitan than enjoying local

---

[10] Barbara Kingsolver, *Animal, Vegetable, Miracle* (New York: Harper Collins, 2007), p. 338. You might also try Michael Pollen's book *The Omnivore's Dilemma* (New York: Penguin, 2007).

cheeses, for example, while talking with farmers and academics about how to save the world? Slow Food groups on the local scale are growing in membership and number. Many folks are going "localvore" in their gastronomical habits, and food is just one example of enlightened localism.

I am fortunate to have become an active resident of a town that has a vibrant Main Street, a rebirth in family farming, genuine democracy in the form of town meetings, solid schools, and friendly neighbors. My town even has a small college that works hard to balance cosmopolitan ideas with environmentally and socially responsible habits. Plato's *Republic*, to take just one sophisticated set of great ideas, was, after all, focused entirely on what makes the best community. Education here means that students learn a sense of the importance of place and the human and nonhuman relationships that constitute ecological systems. We don't necessarily expect students to stay in their college hometown, but we do expect that they'll take this sense of place with them, whether it's to their childhood homes or to new communities. This, for Dewey, is responsible membership in a democracy.

And there's more good news for Bruce and Kate, should they choose to stay in their hometown. Contemporary psychologists argue that building community means better living for individuals. Jane Allyn Piliavin's research on "doing well by doing good" considers the emotional benefits of community participation from the perspective of the moral actor herself. Piliavin's studies show that good deeds, such as volunteering or donating blood can lead to rewarding and enriching feelings that can even bring about longer life and a buffer against depression and disease. Volunteering among the elderly results in better social integration (and less alienation) and volunteering among school kids results in their own greater retention and academic success.[11] So, if Bruce and Kate want to leave their sad songs behind and feel better about their times, they might consider pitching in at the schools and senior centers of their hometown. Not only will this strengthen their community and keep them from bowling alone, but it will be instantly gratifying.

---

[11] J.A. Piliavin, "Doing Well by Doing Good: Benefits for the Benefactor," in Keyes and Haidt, *Flourishing: Positive Psychology and the Life Well-Lived*, (Washington, D.C.: American Psychological Association, 2003).

Likewise, Jonathan Haidt studies "moral beauty" among college students in which he asks participants to report emotional and physical effects of witnessing good deeds, both in person and on video. Students report "warm, pleasant, or 'tingling" feelings'," and, perhaps most importantly, a desire to "help others, become better people themselves, and to affiliate with others." Recalling a situation when she witnessed a friend in her carpool asking to be dropped off to help when he saw an elderly woman struggling to shovel snow from her driveway, one student responded thus:

> I felt like jumping out of the car and hugging this guy. I felt like singing and running, or skipping and laughing. Just being active. I felt like saying nice things about people. Writing a beautiful poem or love song. Playing in the snow like a child. Telling everybody about his deed.[12]

As Haidt suggests, "A common theme in most of the narratives is a social focus—a desire to be with, love, and help other people."

I think Bruce and Kate feel this love. That's why they're so sad about what's happened to their hometown. But, instead of spending their energy loading up their moving van and getting that last glimpse of their town in the rear-view mirror, they might consider acting on the love they clearly feel for their community. As educated people, perhaps they can work to infuse their town with information on how community initiatives have been successful elsewhere, and *then do* those things locally. Information is good, even global information. So is saving the world through saving our social and natural households. A little enlightened localism might allow Bruce's son to look forward to a day when he can share a hometown Main Street, filled with neighbors and goodwill, with his child. Quit singing your sad song, Bruce, and get to work.

14
Bruce Springsteen *or* Philosophy

MICHAEL VENTIMIGLIA

What is the spirit of philosophy? What is the spirit of Springsteen? Can you find the spirit of philosophy and spirit of Springsteen's music in the same soul? I say "you" but, of course by "you" I mean "me"—it's hard to speak of Springsteen without telling the stories of our own lives. I'll put aside any pretension to omniscience about either of our topics, and I'll talk about what these two things mean for me.

The spirit of Springsteen is a stubborn hope or faith in the future despite an honest accounting of the harshness of the present. It is the space between despair and hope, between facticity and faith, that Bruce seems to understand deeply. I think the reason his work resonates so deeply with so many is that he draws on what might loosely be called the religious impulse. His story telling relates a basic human desire for transcendence from our everyday surroundings. At times Bruce hints at, or even offers, such transcendence, but he leaves open the question of whether or not this transcendence is really possible, at least in any permanent way. This, I think, is the essence of his appeal. Everyone really does have a hungry heart. This is true of the accountant and the mill worker. Without underestimating the importance of economic injustice in Bruce's writings, it's important to point out that Bruce's work is not merely about class struggle. Despite the political significance of much of his work—from stories of Mexican immigrants on *The Ghost of Tom Joad* to the anger of the often misunderstood protagonist of "Born in the U.S.A."—Bruce's work is not merely political. Despite his capacity for empathizing with criminals (without, by the way, glorifying them) his work is not merely about the social conditions that make the line between the right and wrong side of the law so thin. Bruce speaks to a yearning that itself transcends social or political place. He speaks to the dumb human sense that we are somehow trapped or limited by our everyday surroundings, that something better might exist, but it has somehow eluded us.

Is this spirit broadly consistent with the spirit of philosophy? Can one live in this space and seriously engage in philosophy? The easy thing to do here would be to talk about philosophy as a profession in order to reject its soulfulness. This would make philosophy a pretty easy target. But this is philosophy as an area of expertise, which is to say, most of the time, it is not really philosophy at all.

Although those of us who teach and write about philosophy for a living generally refer to ourselves as "philosophers," we do a lot more *explaining* than we do philosophizing. We explain other thinkers' philosophies to our students. We then go home, sit at our computers and explain other thinkers' philosophies to or our peers. We read Aristotle (or whomever) carefully. We read what other people have said about Aristotle. And then, for the most part, we try to make small little interpretive points about Aristotle and send them out there into the academic world hoping they will be read and liked. This isn't a bad thing. But it's not really philosophy. Sure, we have our own individual insights and add our spins to things now and again, but on a daily basis we are not really engaged in the quest for wisdom, we are not really, literally, lovers of wisdom. Rather than create a straw man out of professional philosophy, let's put professional philosophy, in the somewhat limited sense described here, aside. Writing and teaching about philosophy is not philosophy. So what is philosophy, really, and is it broadly consistent with the spirit of Springsteen's work?

A City of Winners and Losers

To begin to answer that question, I need to tell a story. Everyone's got a Bruce story. Even philosophers. Think of mine as a first case study in the distance between philosophy and Bruce.

I was approaching thirty. Unlike most of my friends—mostly first generation college students from Irish and Italian families in

New York and New Jersey—I decided to go into academia. Not a common move for people like me. It's not easy to come home from college for Thanksgiving and tell your dad that his tuition checks look like they'll be paying for a degree in philosophy. ("Oh, and by the way Dad, even if I get into grad school, I'll probably wind up driving a taxi when I get out.") Thinking back, one of my main motivations was that I wanted to make it as a musician, and I figured that a few years of grad school would give me more time to sharpen up my chops on the piano before I threw it out there. But graduate school turns out to be an insane amount of work and suddenly there I am, nearly ten years later, in the middle of Nowhere, Pennsylvania, working on a thesis without a whole lot of new piano riffs under my belt. I am a grown man with no real job, no marketable skill, no completed degree, and literally about two hundred dollars to get me through August until my next teaching gig.

So a buddy of mine and I decided it would be a good idea to take whatever money we had left until the next paycheck and bring it down to Atlantic city. Here's my memory of the subsequent events:

1. Fast food and cigarettes.
2. Singing the theme song to "Rocky" at the top of our lungs as we drive down the Atlantic City Expressway, the glow of the city on our horizon.
3. My friend—let's call him Bobby—drops his $200 at the Blackjack table immediately.
4. Bobby hits the ATM machine and gets a cash advance on his credit card.
5. My $200 is gone. Blackjack and craps.
6. Bobby's new money is gone.
7. ATM.
8. That's gone.
9. Repeat lines 7 and 8.
10. Repeat line 9.
11. Too late to drive home so we get an overpriced room.
12. Bobby hands me his wallet: "Do *not* give this back to me!"
13. Bobby asks for his wallet back.
14. Bobby steals his own wallet out of my pants while I am sleeping.

In the morning Bobby is down three thousand dollars. (Note: three thousand dollars in graduate student money is about a billion dollars in real person money.) I'm down about five hundred—my two hundred, and now I'm in the hole with Bobby for another three hundred, on *his* credit card. So. We are *still* thirty-year-olds, we still have no marketable skills, but now we're also broke. Worse than broke. Bobby is already paying twenty-seven percent on his cash advance. And we're out of cigarettes.

Silence in the car for miles. Depression. Gambling has a way casting a hue over your entire self-image, over every moment of your life which preceded your last win or loss. Your history seems entirely rewritten. You didn't just win or lose; you *are* a winner or a loser. And today I am a loser. The trip is now just one more bad decision in a line that seems to stretch back half my life.

Bobby turns on the radio. Some cheese-ball classic rock station that plays all the same hits over and over serves up "Thunder Road." And literally, from the first bar of the piano/harp intro, we are swept up in to that magical space between the real and the ideal that Bruce owns. "The screen door sa-lams . . ." We are singing again. "So you're scared and your thinking that maybe we ain't that young anymore . . . " We're singing loudly. We're smiling. "Roll down the window and let the wind blow back your hair . . . " We're screaming. We're laughing. We're driving faster. What the hell was I so worried about? "It's a town full of losers and I'm pulling out of here to win." Things are going to be fine.

Now, I don't want to suggest that the plight of the over-educated in America is anything like the plight of the people Bruce often sings about. I didn't have kids or a wife. I wasn't crossing over from Mexico to sell my labor or make drugs so my family would have money. I had choices. No one will mistake Bobby or me for working class heroes. But I think this is why everyone's got a Bruce story. Bruce talks about the space between the real and ideal like few can, but in a way most anyone can relate to. His stories are concrete, but his words and music capture the potentially universal experience of faith and optimism in the face of cold, harsh reality. Anyone can relate to this. Anyone can be uplifted by this.

This is a book about Bruce Springsteen and philosophy. For me, as we drove home from Atlantic City, it was clear that these two things just don't go together. You can't have your Bruce and your philosophy too. Philosophy was the over-thinking that I did for a barely sustainable living. Philosophy was the reason I needed to go to Atlantic City in the first place. Bruce was freedom from all that. Philosophy was pretension. Bruce was authenticity. Philosophy was unnecessary complexity. Bruce was sweet simplicity. The two were incommensurable.

I'd like to do another small case study to take us further into this question. Let's look not at professional philosophy, but at a philosopher—a philosopher with a profound sense of the transcendent who tackled one of the most universal, accessible, and ordinary of philosophical problems—in order to see how he and Bruce stack up.

This Tree of Evil

When I teach the problem of evil to my introductory students, I tell them that this is the one philosophical problem that even the least philosophical people find themselves asking. Few people bother themselves about the nature of true knowledge. Few people spend much time thinking about the essential characteristics of Being. But most people, at some point, ask themselves this central question of philosophy: "If God exists, and he is all powerful, and he is the good guy that we've been told he is, why is there evil in the world?" For many people this boils down to: "Why would God let evil things happen? Maybe he just doesn't exist."

Unlike many other philosophical questions, which only seem to become compelling when we have the leisure and comfort to address them, this is a question that kicks us when we are down. This is a question that arises not in comfort but in pain—when a friend's baby dies of a horrible disease, when people fly jets into tall buildings, when thousands of people slide into a crack in the earth as the ground beneath them gives way. It is the question many ask themselves when they have to deal with personal tragedy.

St. Augustine, a man from North Africa who lived from 354 to 430 C.E., is the most famous and influential Western philosopher to address this question. He is aware of what appears to be evil; he seems to share the sort of yearning for transcendence that animates much of Springsteen's work. His philosophy is complex, but he offers a solution to the problem of evil that can be sketched out in three interwoven strands.

As most students figure out pretty quickly, the idea of "free will" seems important for addressing our problem. When human beings slaughter, torture, and exploit each other, this isn't God's will; it's ours, Augustine says. God gave us free will so our choices would be meaningful. Sometimes we choose evil. This evil that humans commit against each other, "moral evil," can be blamed on us, not God.

Let's grant for a second that this gets us somewhere. Maybe it accounts for terrorism and genocide. But what about child-hood diseases? Earthquakes? What philosophers call "natural evil"? Well, we can try and pin this natural evil on free will too and blame it on Adam and Eve. This is part of Augustine's solu-tion—certainly more convincing for some than for others—but he also points out that what seems like evil to us may be part of something good from God's perspective.

Think of a little toddler being brought to the doctor for his shots. Out for the day with mommy. Maybe a lollypop. Life is good, until . . . some lady with what now appears to be a very deceptive smile whips out some very serious looking needles. Incomprehensibly, mom holds the kid down while this monster in a white coat gives him the pin cushion treatment. From the point of view of that kid what we have here is unquestionable, unadulterated, unmitigated evil, pure and simple. What the kid cannot see, of course, is that from a higher intelligence what seems like certain evil is, in fact, part of a larger good. Now, pre-sumably the gap between our intelligence and God's is far greater than that between a child and an adult. And so maybe what we think of as evil is in fact part of something bigger and better that we cannot begin to comprehend.

Finally, a third, complementary, solution of Augustine's is to deny that evil has any reality at all. Augustine wanted to save God the embarrassment of either having created evil or having to fight a cosmic battle against an evil being of equal power, so Augustine denied the reality of evil. Augustine argued that what we experience as evil has no separate existence, but is merely a "lack" of goodness, an "absence," a "privation." This solution helped make it intellectually possible for him to convert to Christianity—with its belief in one good creator God—away from the "Manicheanism" of his day which claimed that evil was a real power in the cosmos. This argument seems strange, far more speculative than the previous two points, but it was borrowed from Greek thought and, through Augustine, this view that evil has no reality has had tremendous influence on the history of philosophy and theology.

Nebraska

For Augustine, then, the problem of evil has solutions, and with God's grace, salvation or transcendence from this evil is assured. Let's compare this to Springsteen's implicit treatment of evil on *Nebraska*. Although *Nebraska* was not the commercial success Bruce's record company had hoped for, it is among the most philosophical and penetrating albums that Springsteen has ever created. It is likely the most haunting, bone-chilling album he has produced. *Rolling Stone* (October 28th, 1982) called it "the bravest of Springsteen's six records" at the time of its release, "his most startling, direct, and chilling . . . . as deep and unsettling as anything Springsteen has recorded." It is as close to having Bruce sing to you in your bedroom as you can get. This is because it was, famously, recorded in his. It is Bruce with his guitar and harmonica. He is recording on a piece of equipment any amateur could buy from a local music store. And it is the album, I think, that is most relevant to our case study on Bruce and philosophy.

Augustine's most important, though esoteric, solution to the problem of evil was that it did not exist. While Augustine did not mean to suggest that the perception of evil does not exist, he denies what philosophers call the metaphysical reality of evil. *Nebraska,* to the contrary, begins with a simple, concrete account of evil that seems to make all such distinctions melt into shallow chatter. The first song, the album's title track, was inspired by the story of mass murderer Charlie Starkweather. In 1957 Starkweather and his fourteen-year-old girlfriend Caril Ann Fugate killed eleven people from Lincoln, Nebraska to Douglas Wyoming, including Fugate's parents and her two-year old sister. In this first person narrative, Springsteen invites us to come to terms with evil in its simplest, most unapologetic terms. Evil with no accounting for itself. Evil with no remorse.

Bruce neither glorifies nor condemns. He just tells the story, as he understands it, on Starkweather's terms in a disquieting acoustic ballad. In response to our felt demand that the killer comprehend the pain and suffering he has wrought, the best we get is that for "for a little while, sir, me and her had us some fun." In response to our incapacity to process such heartlessness, we are told, "Well, sir, I guess there's just a meanness in this world." Bruce's lyric, ironically, is an unintended echo of the Manicheanism that Augustine tried to refute. Compared to this simple account of one man's unapologetic killing spree, Augustine's metaphysical gymnastics seem like pure sophistry.

Augustine speaks to the importance of free will for understanding moral evil. *Nebraska*, to the contrary, questions the meaning of free will when one is faced with few real choices. Twice on the album we learn about how people have "debts no honest man can pay." The first is the narrator of "Atlantic City" who can't find a job and realizes that in this simple gangland world of winners and losers the only way to climb out of his hole is to do "a little favor" for someone. The second is Ralph who, in "Johnny 99," loses his job, can't find another, and is losing his house. He gets drunk, gets a gun and shoots a night clerk. He doesn't claim that he is a victim or that he is innocent, but he points out that it was all these factors together which led to his drunken violence.[1] In "State Trooper," the narrator, who's got a clear conscience about whatever he's done, quietly chants "Mr. State Trooper, please don't stop me" as he drives the Jersey Turnpike with neither license nor registration. We don't know what would have to happen if he was pulled over, but the narrator's thoughts about the trooper's hypothetical wife and kids suggest that if the trooper flips the switch, his family is going to be devastated. While none of these men is cast as an innocent or a victim or a hero, Bruce seems to suggest that anyone in a similar position could do the same as they have done. Yes, free will accounts for some evil, but freedom, in practice, is often compromised.[2]

---

[1] Samuel Levine, "Portraits of Criminal on Bruce Springsteen's *Nebraska*: The Enigmatic Criminal, The Sympathetic Criminal, and the Criminal as Brother," *Widener Law Journal* XIV, p. 775.

[2] The basic idea of this paragraph, without the philosophical context, is Abbe Smith's. See Abbe Smith "The Dignity and Humanity of Bruce Springsteen's Criminals," *Widener Law Journal* XIV, pp. 787–835. My thanks to Justina Betro for her help with this and other resources.

Finally, in contrast to Augustine's suggestion that evil is part of the best possible world, we have *Nebraska* as a meditation on evil. The simplicity of the lyrics, the music, even the production make the ad hoc hypotheses Augustine is spinning out seem disingenuous. Despite what seems obviously true, Augustine seems to be arguing, things are as good as they can possibly be. *Nebraska,* on the other hand, is a straightforward and honest account of moral ambiguity and unapologetic evil. Bruce is wise to leave this ambiguity intact and unresolved where the philosophical urge might be to try to explain it away.

All the Redemption I Can Offer

Of course, both Bruce and Augustine offer redemption from evil, a faith in something better than that which hard experience teaches. Compared to Augustine's hard-won and reflective faith, it may seem easy to ridicule the religious tenor of Springsteen's offers of salvation through muscle cars and the open road. But Springsteen's work is about the need for deliverance, and the small ordinary ways in which we can temporarily find it, rather than any promise of final salvation. On *Nebraska* Bruce doesn't guarantee deliverance, but he speaks directly to the need to believe in it. In "Used Cars," a young child angered and embarrassed by his family's inability to afford a new car promises that he'll never ride in another used car as soon as he wins the lottery. And "Reason to Believe," the final cut on the album, contains three stories of persons whose need for faith blinds them to the obviousness of their circumstances.

Even though this is one of Springsteen's darker albums, it is worth mentioning that the transcendence or deliverance offered on other albums is also often explicitly temporary or even illusionary. "Born to Run," for all its gestures towards the eternal, ends with the acceptance that "till then" they were born to run. Someday, maybe, they will walk in the sun, but for the moment the narrator can offer something certain, a temporary transcendence in the most ordinary of situations. The hero of "Thunder Road" understands that he is no hero at all, but he can offer a moment's respite from the reality he and his girl will surely have to confront again when the gas runs out and the thrill is gone. What may seem on the surface like a facile synthesis of religious imagery and testosterone drenched adolescent angst may be, in its deep modesty and in its self-awareness, as profound as any promise of eternal salvation.

Without offering final judgment regarding which sketch of evil and redemption above is more compelling, it seems safe to say that Bruce's simple storytelling maintains an integrity that may be difficult to preserve in philosophy. This is because Springsteen offers no real solutions. Springsteen doesn't solve the problem of evil for us. He simply leaves it in the concrete as a problem. He doesn't guarantee eternal salvation, just small moments of deliverance which help sooth the desire for the eternal. Perhaps the best known and most explicitly philosophical lyric from *Nebraska* comes from "Atlantic City." After musing:

> Well now everything dies baby that's a fact.
> But maybe everything that dies someday comes back.

. . . the narrator refocuses on the here and now:

> Put your makeup on, fix your hair up pretty
> And meet me tonight in Atlantic City.

In this turn from eternal human questions to concrete moments of deliverance, in the here and now, we are offered a wisdom that may be incompatible with much of the philosophical tradition. And, yet, precisely because Springsteen appreciates the significance and depth of these eternal questions, we cannot fairly say that what is best in Springsteen cannot co-exist with what is best about philosophy.

Bruce and Philosophy

Philosophy is, again, the love of wisdom. Perhaps the most authentic and compelling image of the philosophical spirit is painted in Plato's *Symposium*. In the *Symposium*, philosophy is depicted as a passion, a desire, an *eros*. The lover of wisdom is, not surprisingly, on a quasi-religious quest; philosophy is itself an expression of the desire for transcendence. As a kind of "love" (*eros*) Socrates relays, it is neither good nor bad, neither beautiful nor ugly. It is between these extremes. Such love is the expression of a lack. It is a hunger of the whole person, an *eros*.

It is that which makes us aware of our poverty and points us towards something better. Socrates speaks of the condition of the god Eros, here translated as "Love":

> Love's circumstances are as follows: In the first place, he's always poor and far from being gentle and beautiful, as most people believe. On the contrary, he's tough, wrinkled, barefoot and homeless. He always lies on the ground, since he doesn't have a bed, and he sleeps in doorways and alongside the road in the open air. . . . he's a schemer after beautiful and good things. . . . He engages in the search for wisdom throughout his entire life . . . [3]

Love itself is not beautiful; it is the yearning or hunger for that which is beautiful. It is the desire to understand Beauty, to be in the presence of Beauty, to be "there with it," that draws one beyond his or her everyday surroundings.

Philosophy as a *passion*, a *desire*, a *want* to transcend time and place through wisdom or knowledge of eternal realities, is itself an expression of the sort of yearning that Springsteen seems to understand. Insofar as philosophy emphasizes the intellectual quest for transcendence, it is perhaps somewhat rarified and peculiar. Insofar as it thinks its quest is ever completed, the *eros* or the passion is destroyed and it self-destructs. But the philosophical *eros* itself, this pain, this need to transcend, is something that both Bruce and philosophers understand deeply. Philosophy is one, somewhat unusual, expression of this basic human need. In reply to Plato's question, "Do you think that this yearning, this love, is common to all human beings, and that everyone wants good things to be their own forever?" I think, we could say, with Bruce, that everyone does, in fact, have a hungry heart.

Moments of Redemption

As Bobby and I made our way back through the streets of State College, Pennsylvania, the magic of our Bruce moment had worn off. But my puzzlement about how Springsteen's music and professional philosophy could co-exist in my soul still has-

---

[3] Plato. *The Symposium* (203, c5–d7) in *Plato's Erotic Dialogues* (Albany: SUNY Press, 1993).

n't. For the moment, I have to find moments of redemption on the weekends and in the summers, when I get to watch how the music that comes from my fingers can occasionally travel up someone's body and make them sway or smile. I think the best, most honest thing I can say is that the closest I come to what I am looking for during the week is what I find on the weekend. I guess that will have to do.

IV

Tom Joad's Ghosts

15
Straight Time: Images of Oppression

LUKE DICK

The Boss seems to be obsessed with being free. Whether it's a crummy hometown, a crummy job, or a crummy family, Bruce punctuates his songs with some oppressive tension. Early on in his work, oppression is nothing an open window, a fast car, a willing female, or a tank of gas couldn't fix.

But it wasn't long before he was singing a different tune, in 1982's *Nebraska*, and later in 1994's *Ghost of Tom Joad*. Crowded with all sorts of destitute characters, these two records (more than any other in Springsteen's work) paint a different picture of freedom. In the title track of 1975's *Born to Run*, the chime of freedom is a glockenspiel climbing the scale like jangling keys hanging from the ignition of a glory-bound '69 Chevy. In *The Ghost of Tom Joad*'s "Straight Time," the chime is the sound of Charlie's hacked-off barrel of his robbery-bound shotgun hitting a cement floor.

These two different views of freedom and oppression offer insight into the Boss's songwriting, his views on life, and the difference between him and Charlie.

Got a Job at the Rendering Factory

Now, most every American knows who Bruce Springsteen is. Even the layman could associate a few things with the pop icon—America, working class, New Jersey, or fire departments might be some of the associations. Few, however, could name any songs from either *Nebraska* or *Ghost of Tom Joad*. Commercial success in the music business is a mysterious thing, and one could attribute commercial failure to any number of elements. I'm inclined to think that the "failure" of these recordings (as compared with *Born to Run* or *Born in the U.S.A.*) has a lot to do with the bleak, heady, and empathic demeanor of the stories and ideas that comprised the songs, as well as the un-climactic melodies. These recordings are commentaries on the plight of the human condition, of our economic system and the people in it—hardly workin' man's anthems. This is not to say that these collections of songs aren't good, as I believe they are some of his finest work, and so do many others—critics and democrats mostly. But, who are we to judge?

I don't know who you are, but I know you are reading a philosophy book about Bruce Springsteen, so I take it we have some basic things in common. Indulge me for a moment while I explain where *I'm* coming from, at least.

I'm probably the only dock worker in Nashville with a philosophy degree—and dock work is just one of the many attractive career paths open to those of us with such a degree. Knowing all of Kant's cognitive categories or that Socrates drank the hemlock has yet to come in handy while hoisting boxes and crates in a semi trailer on a hot day. I generally keep my book learning to myself, as it tends to put my fellow blue collars on the defensive. But I come from a working class family.

Off the top of my head, I can think of eight men in my family who can drive big rigs. For better or worse, none of them ever cared to crack a philosophy book. What's more, neither they nor any of my co-workers (even the music lovers) listen to *The Ghost of Tom Joad* or *Nebraska,* despite the fact that these records are wholly peopled with working-class folk. By contrast, according to my itunes play count, I've listened to both in their entirety at least a half dozen times in the past couple months, playing my favorite songs as many as twenty times. I think there's insight in this difference between the tastes of someone like me and my beloved fellow blue collars. And I think this difference says something about Springsteen, too.

Driving a forklift for twelve hours can make your back hurt. On that fact, me and my brothers—and Bruce—can all agree. It can earn you a decent wage, but day in and day out, it just plain sucks. In "Straight Time," the Boss creates Charlie, and Charlie works at the rendering factory—darkness before dinner comes. Charlie knows drudgery and long hours, too, but Charlie ain't like me and the Boss. He'd as soon tap his boots to Merle Haggard's "Workin' Man Blues" over a cold beer in a neighborhood dive than wade through the murky waters of Bruce's dark records. Charlie'd probably throw ASCAP a quarter to spin "Glory Days." Charlie might drive a semi; he would never, ever use a semi-colon.

Charlie just wants to escape his job, or so he thinks. Merle and a Pabst Blue Ribbon can alleviate that itch for a few hours. But Bruce wants to know why it itches in the first place. Sure it sucks, but by his own nature, Bruce internalizes its sucking differently than Charlie does. But there are Charlies everywhere, especially at freight docks and rendering factories, while Bruces are little less common.

This is not to say Bruce is more intelligent than any of them—he *is* more intelligent than some, but there are some very smart fellows running fork lifts, believe me, and if I were ever in a bar fight, I'd much rather have a Teamster in my corner than Bruce. It *is* to say that Bruce's way of thinking about the drudgery of a monotonous, hot, and dirty job is different than Charlie's. Where Charlie might see an incompetent, asshole of a foreman, whose orders he despises, Bruce sees another human cog, trying to find his way and make a life for himself the best he knows how. You see, Bruce dwells on others' possible perspectives. He's made a life of it and has a real gift in his empathy and how he expresses it. This is why his songs are so believable, even when they are about experiences that Bruce hasn't really had. The point is, Springsteen has developed the ability to both empathize and turn that empathy into a symbolic creation, a song. Such is the case in "Straight Time."

Got Out of Prison Back in '86

"Straight time" is when a prisoner is serving a sentence day for a day. If a straight-timer is serving a one-year sentence, he'll be there for 365 days. Through good conduct, the same prisoner can perhaps become promoted to double time, which would mean serving half a year. Similarly, when you're working on the dock, regular time is called "straight time." Thanks to Teamsters Local 480, if I work a twelve-hour day, four of those hours pay time-and-a-half, which is a nice consolation for sweating my ass off from dusk till dawn.

Charlie's job at the rendering factory wasn't his first tangle with oppression, and I'd venture to bet that if there were a chronicle of songs about Charlie, we would find that he never stops feeling oppressed. Right out of the gate, Charlie tells us that he "got out of prison back in '86." Come to find out, Charlie has another family member (probably several) who has known crime, too. His uncle "makes his living running hot cars." But Charlie wants to do right, so he gets married and goes to work.

In prison, Charlie was sick of doin' straight time. Out of the pen, probably a few years under his belt at the factory, Charlie says he's *still* "sick of doin' straight time." He doesn't differentiate between what he's doing now in his life at the rendering factory and what he was doing in prison. Wow. Within one short verse, the Boss has peered into a very real experience of a very real person and pointed out a very real anxiety by indicating the fact that the possibilities for folks like Charlie are often limited to doing straight time—whether in the pen or on the clock. Bruce believes the door to real freedom is always open (perhaps just barely), but he also thinks that Charlie's back is to the door, and Charlie is the type to whoop everyone's ass in the room out of pride rather than turn around and leave the darkness of the windowless bar.

Straight Time

Stepping back from this narrative, we find that "straight time" is not *just* a couple of words or a term referring to the technicalities of the penal system. Springsteen uses them intentionally to create an experience for us to try to help us see Charlie like he does. By virtue of the unique way Springsteen creates, "straight time" becomes an indication for us, a sign that points to a lack of freedom and to a cycle of drudgery. The phrase also means time spent walking the straight and narrow, staying on the accepted side of the long arm, bending his will to the requirements of the conventional path. And that's what good songwriters do. They bring us images from the void and make us see things that we haven't seen before, to associate words with new and unexpected meanings that can enrich our lives. How does he or they do it? The short answer is that they create aural and visual images through music and language through the medium of a song. Let me unpack that last sentence using a philosopher by the name of Jean-Paul Sartre (1905–1980).

Sartre belongs to a school of philosophy generally known as "French existentialism," having its historical roots in another school called "phenomenology." Phenomenology is distinguished by its unique methodological approach to understanding human experience. Phenomenology's method is to take subjective mental phenomena and extract general and essential features that make said experiences possible. That is, these people take a person's experience (oftentimes their own) of a certain conscious process and reflect upon that process in order to study and describe it, and make general claims about it. This requires reflection upon one's own experiences of certain phenomena. One could do a phenomenology of peripheral vision, for instance, and reflect upon one's own experience of peripheral vision and attempt to extract all of the features necessary to have such a capability and experience. This method has less to do with the physiological necessities of an experience (the material construction of an eyeball, retina, and iris) and deals primarily with the conditions and processes of the mind that are necessary to constitute a given experience (such as the factthat the mind and eye focus on one point yet take in perceptual data from areas around it, in the case of peripheral vision). Physiologically, it is possible to give facts about the brain, chemicals, and nerve impulses that serve as the organic means of its functioning. Phenomenologists believe that explaining how the brain physiologically works (for instance, that there are various interacting electro-chemicals) is quite different from explaining how one *experiences* the world, and they are essentially concerned with unpacking experiences and saying something definite about conscious experience.

Sartre believes that experience is centered on our processing of images. In his essay, "The Imaginary" (1940), Sartre makes it his task to explain the imagination. Now, before you go and start thinking about the "imagination" as something Walt Disney or Hunter S. Thompson (perhaps with the aid of serious drugs) has, it is important to know that what Sartre is talking about here is much more basic than an extraordinarily *creative* imagination. One needn't put together a Mickey Mouse cartoon or be an absurdly funny gonzo journalist in order to relate to Sartre's theory. Sartre is speaking generally of human consciousness, and we all have imaginations. He believes that all consciousness is a spontaneous imaginative act. If our minds are on, they are filled with images. Any image that the mind generates is called "intentional." For Sartre, *intention* does *not* have anything to do with our *willing* the image into existence, but rather it simply refers to the image that is the focal point of an act of perception or thinking. Although we often think of images as visual, they are often not. For instance, we can *imagine* the smell of a cake baking, the feel of your lover's lips, or the timbre of Bruce's voice. These are not *visual* images, but they *are* images in Sartre's sense of the term. Sartre's phenomenology is an explanation of how our consciousness alters and creates images in order to constitute our total experience of the world. For our purposes, I am going to focus mostly on Springsteen's lyrics and the visual images involved in them. Unfortunately, that allows only a cursory glance at how the aural images (such as Bruce's music alone) aid in presenting an overall image for the listener.

For most every Bruce song, there is a "concept."[1] In the songwriting world, people call these "song ideas," but we'll reserve that term for something else. Usually, these concepts are centered upon a chorus, and often these choruses hinge upon a hook line, which is often the title of the song. This "hinging" has to do with the title's being the conceptual focal point of the entire song. In our example, "Straight Time" is the title. Now, what is so special about the title of a good song? Well, a good song puts forth a concept that is a unique way of imagining the hook line, for instance, the way Bruce makes the correlation between straight time in prison, straight time at the rendering factory, and time spent on the conventional side of the law. These are three different uses of the phrase, but Bruce has united them in his song. This unification is special. He has made a rich association that moves beyond the ordinary use of the phrase, and this new metaphoric combination points us to Charlie's unending cycle of drudgery.

For Sartre, Springsteen has given us a "sign" with his title. If you think about a physical sign, for instance a stop sign, Sartre's

---

[1] I'm not using the word "concept" as philosophers normally use it. Philosophers mean something like "a reflective ordering function, a category subsuming particulars." I mean something earthier and more concrete, a vague image or idea drawn from past experience that brings other images together.

notion of sign and the notion of a song concept as a sign becomes clearer. Imagining a stop sign, the mind sees a red octagon with white letters spelling "STOP." By virtue of cultural habit, we've come to know the sign to indicate that we should bring our vehicle to a halt. I say "cultural habit" because stop signs need not be red or octagonal. That we recognize the sign as an indication of stopping our vehicles is all that matters. artre speaks of this:

> I approach these large black lines printed on a placard nailed above a door of the station. These black lines suddenly cease to have their own dimensions, color, place: they now constitute the words 'Assistant Manager's Office'. I read the words on the placard and I now know that I must go in here to make my claim.[2]

Sartre believes that when we see signs that we recognize, our mind recognizes letters, reads, and then goes on to the object or action that the signs indicate. Therefore, a sign directs the mind to constitute a certain image. The unique case of "Straight Time" (and most all good songs) is that upon listening and understanding the song, the song title or concept becomes a new sign that we must interpret and attach to an object, just like we would a stop sign. When we first hear a song, we don't have the luxury of habit tell us what it indicates, as we do with a stop sign. We must engage the song with our imaginations and let it affect us. "The essential role of signs," says Sartre, is that they "must enlighten and guide us" (p. 26).

Through the filter of Sartre, Bruce's "Straight Time" can be understood on various levels. First and most basically, we understand two English words that indicate something, namely "straight" as meaning something that is not crooked and "time" which refers to duration and change. Secondly, the cultural definitions of this phrase indicates a way in which a prisoner is serving his sentence, day-for-a-day, as well as getting paid hour-by-hour at a day job, and trying not to return to a life of crime. Third and most importantly for Springsteen, the phrase is a new and innovative sign that brings the cultural definitions together and posits them as a means to understanding perpetual drudgery.

----

[2] Jean-Paul Sartre, *The Imaginary* (New York: Routledge, 2007), p. 21.

Best Remember Who Your Friends Are

That's all fine and good, but Charlie don't give a shit about Sartre. Sartre's suspicious and French and looks to have hygiene problems.[3] What Charlie *does* give a shit about is that he's out of jail now, but he's still in prison, working his crummy job at the crummy rendering factory.

Despite the fact that he had a great song idea when he came up with "Straight Time," Springsteen had to fill up the song with lyrics and a story to guide us to the understanding of his concept.[4] For a song to work (that is, for a song to guide others successfully to an understanding of the song concept) the lyrics must have the potential to make the song concept *present* for us. The verse and chorus lyrics should lead the listener to generate in his or her *own* consciousness the song's concept. Bruce does so precisely by giving a shit about Charlie, and Sartre can explain the way the Boss affects his listeners, so I guess Springsteen *should* care about him, too—except that Bruce doesn't seem to need any help in performing this particular bit of magic.

According to Sartre, the mind naturally manipulates images depending on the context in which those images are given. In the case of watching an impersonator, the mind will manipulate the perceptual images. When we watch Dana Carvey, given that we know Dana Carvey is a popular comedian who often does imitations, we are naturally going to assume that we will get an imitation at some point. We anticipate this. Perhaps the imitation will be of Mr. Rogers, perhaps it will be of Jimmy Stewart, or perhaps it will be of Jimmy Stewart doing Mr. Rogers. When we watch and listen to Carvey, the mind readies itself for this, and when Carvey slips us something different from his natural face (if he even *has* a natural face—for all I know he's impersonating Dana Carvey), we almost involuntarily begin processing the

---

[3] If you don't believe Charlie, go ahead, do a Google image search and see for yourself. The expressive nature of consciousness doesn't have to work very hard at all to smell snails and cigarettes on his breath.

[4] It's not necessary songwriters come up with the concept and *then* fill in the rest of the lyrics. The order in which the creative components of a song are generated can vary. Sometimes they just tinker with song ideas and wait to see if a concept will emerge. Sometimes they have just a hook to create the concept and then fish around for associated song ideas.

imitation he is doing. It actually *is* voluntary, but the habit is deeply set, so it kicks in without any perceived effort from us.

Now, Dana Carvey looks nothing like Jimmy Stewart. In order to "make us see" Jimmy Stewart, he radically caricatures Jimmy Stewarts face. During Carvey's imitation, we get his best impression of Stewart's bulging eyes during the climax of *Mr. Smith Goes to Washington*; we get the most yokel-ly representation, as when Stewart comes back to reality in *It's a Wonderful Life*. These radical manifestations do not really look like Jimmy Stewart. I would be surprised if someone recognized Carvey as Stewart with the sound off. However, coupled with very believable vocalizations, we're willing to overlook all of the discrepancies of likeness between Carvey and Stewart. Once consciousness has been guided to interpret the imitation and then to recognize Jimmy Stewart, we ignore the discrepancies and see and hear only those that remind us of Stewart. Once consciousness has recognized Stewart, it takes all of the facial and bodily manipulations that *do* resemble Stewart's actions and brings them together with all of Carvey's other representations during the skit. That is, once consciousness shifts and recognizes Stewart, it ignores all things not-Stewart and unifies all things Stewart in Carey's performance. Sartre calls this affectation of consciousness the "expressive nature" (p. 29). The main point is that by virtue of an expressive nature, consciousness can ignore discrepancies and posit connections in what it perceives in order to unify these images into a single image of Jimmy Stewart. The process is spread out in time. The mind also *retains* the past moments and *protends* (anticipates) those to come; all these perceptions and connections generate a unified image of Stewart.

Sartre's notion of "imitation consciousness," which I have just described, can be used to explain Springsteen's method of affecting us with his song "Straight Time." While listening to Bruce's work, consciousness also posits and ignores details in order to create a unified understanding of the song and its character. We all know "Charlie" in about the same way we know Jimmy Stewart, even if we have never actually met either. There are lots of Charlies, and we already know how to "recognize" one such. Creating the essential details is the way in which Springsteen leads us to his song concept. When we recognize Charlie, we are in a position to understand what "straight time" is to him. Stylistically, Bruce is singing in first person, as if he's Charlie. Now, we know Bruce Springsteen isn't Charlie any more than Dana is Jimmy. We knew it before we pressed play, and it doesn't take the mind long to get over this discrepancy. Once we have done this simple work, we can accept another discrepancy—that is, that Springsteen is singing in a vernacular that is not natural to him. I'm sure that Bruce has read enough books to realize that "ain't" ain't a *real* contraction, because it doesn't quite join two words together. But Charlie mightn't realize this. Further, he ain't one to give a shit either way. Springsteen's colloquialisms help us connect the dots between verse and concept.

So, in the first verse, Charlie is out of prison and doing his best to get by, but he hates his lot in life. He hated it before prison, during, and now after. In the second verse, Charlie's car-smuggling uncle is there, and good uncle "slips" Charlie a hundred dollar bill and says, "Charlie, you best remember who your friends are."

By virtue of consciousness's expressive nature, it reads between the lines, and we just know Charlie has the itch so bad that he'll end up helping his uncle chop a Seville or cop a Coup de Ville. Bruce didn't explicitly tell us this, but we know it. And we also can gather that thieving is a one way ticket out of the rendering factory, and probably a one way ticket back to prison. We now have a description of *how* Springsteen did it.[5] And, *voila*, the mind is guided to see that "Straight Time" is all about a never-ending battle of oppression.

Eight Years In, It Feels Like You're Gonna Die

The title of this section is from the "bridge" of our song—that is the part where the music changes—and, like the concept in "Straight Time," it, too, is beautifully ambiguous. "In" could refer to prison or work or marriage or sickness, or so many other

---

[5] We've discussed how Springsteen used images to lead us to his concept and how we were led. The most mysterious question (that I will not attempt to answer here) is how does Springsteen spontaneously come up with the images and lyrics that he does? Are there any rules to the spontaneity of the imagination that could explain how his concepts and lyrics strike him from the void? How does the Muse work?

ways of being "in." Not to get too dark here, but life bombards us with problems. Human beings must eat, drink, co-operate, shelter ourselves "in" order to live. We *must* do this day in and day out, or else we perish. We're "in" a hell of a mess. The figurative "dying" Charlie speaks of here is the soul tax of laborious boredom, and Charlie's mistake is that he ties this feeling to his job instead of realizing that life itself is the ultimate penal colony that he must address.

Albert Camus (1913–1960), who was Sartre's existentialist *nemesis de plume*, speaks of something similar in *The Myth of Sisyphus*. Camus's book is an interpretation and commentary on the Greek myth in which Sisyphus, as punishment for aggravating Zeus, is forced to serve eternally in the underworld by schlepping a rock up a hill. Upon every try, Sisyphus loses grip of the rock only to have it tumble down the hill. Hoist, climb, sweat, drop, watch miserably, repeat infinitely. Camus likens Sisyphus's plight to life in general and refers to it as the "absurd reality" of life. We make the bed to mess it up. We work to eat, we eat to live, we live to work. We have kids, then we work to provide life for others, and then they live to work. Throw the many forms of suffering in the mix, and things begin to look infinitely bleak, which is why Camus says, "There is but one truly serious philosophical problem, and that is suicide. Judging whether life is or is not worth living amounts to answering the fundamental question of philosophy."[6]

Everyone reading this chapter has, up to now, chosen that life is good enough to keep living, else you wouldn't be among us, but few really address the problem of life the way Camus believes it ought to be addressed. Why is it that you get up out of bed every morning? Just to eat? Just to work? Just to live? Camus says many people live out of the habit of living.

So we know of some rocks Charlie has attempted to carry: prison, the rendering factory, whatever landed him in prison in the first place, and whatever keeps him on the straight and narrow, for the moment. And now he's about to help his uncle and leave that rendering factory behind. But we know that Charlie is just dropping one rock to pick up another, but despite what he imagines, neither he (nor anyone else) can get rid of the hill. We

---

[6] Albert Camus, *The Myth of Sisyphus* (New York: Random House, 1983), p. 1.

seem to have our choice of rocks, but the hill is the hill. Best get used to it and do as Camus does by attempting to enumerate reasons that the hill is worth climbing.

Charlie has what a friend of mine refers to as "shit hooks." To really nail this colloquialism in everyday conversation, it's necessary to employ it in the following way: "Here comes ol' shit hooks," or even better, "Shit hooks is what he got." Wherever he goes, whatever town he moves to, whatever job he has, Charlie always seems to find and drag his shit with him and pick up more along the way. Just because he changes one rock for another, he approaches the hill with the same set of hooks, with last attempt's waste on them. I know plenty of troubled folk who move to another town to seek "a new life" only to find that after the new has worn off, it's still life and they're still tailed by all they drug with them. They rarely, if ever shed their hooks and approach the hill with open eyes and clean hands.

Driftin' Off to a Foreign Land

In regard to the trifles of living, no woman, no Chevy, no Thunder Road, no Atlantic City, no new job, and no heist can transport us to a place where sorrows and drudgery disappear. Pre-'82 Springsteen is partly good, and I'm a sucker for it, in all its teenage splendor. But in regard to Camus's question, it yields only a youthfully naive answer. The answer it offers seems to be the result of having only carried the rock once. Early Bruce tells us simply to pick up a shinier rock. In "Straight Time," all bets are off, and older Bruce recognizes (probably after several trips up the hill with various rocks he found along the way) that the hill is the problem we must spend our lives dealing with.

In the 1947 issue of *The Nation,* Sartre's essay, "Americans and Their Myths," describes the cultural landscape that details America's peculiar hill,

> There are the great myths, the myths of happiness, of progress, of liberty, of triumphant maternity, there is realism and optimism— and then there are the Americans, who . . . grow up among these colossal statues and find their way as best they can among them. . . . But there are also these people, who, though conventionally happy, suffer from an obscure malaise to which no name can be given, who are tragic through fear of being so, through that total

absence of the tragic in them and around them. . . . There are
the thousand taboos which proscribe love outside of marriage—
and there is the litter of used contraceptives in the back yards .
. . there are all those men and women who drink before making
love in order to transgress in drunkenness and not remember.
There are the neat, coquettish houses, the pure-white apartments
with radio, armchair, pipe, and stand—little paradises; and there
are the tenants of those apartments who, after dinner, leave their
chairs, radios, wives, pipes, and children, and go to the bar
across the street to get drunk alone. (*The Nation*, October 18th,
1947).

Early Springsteen simply grabs the keys to these "myths of happiness" and lays rubber down a stretch of road. That's where the
songs end. Later Springsteen has to deal with gas stations, flat
tires, and faulty water pumps. And, let's face it, we'll be buying
tires the rest of our lives. So, Bruce, how in the world do we get
free? I mean, I wanna conquer the hill and build one of them
mansions of glory, you know?

I've listened to Bruce and am old enough to know that no
pop star can get you off the hill. There simply is no "top of the
hill." If the oppression of your home town, of a shitty job, or of
financial strains were the actual problem, do you really think
Bruce would still be putting out records? This hill goes on forever, or at least until we die. And Bruce knows this. So then,
how do we deal with the hill, Bruce?

If we look at his music and his life, I think we can say something about how Bruce believes this is possible. Early Bruce was
filled with beat poetry about himself like "Blinded by the Light"
or of his early notions of escape as in "Thunder Road." It seems
that folks like Charlie are still under the impression that the
Thunder Road can lead us to freedom, and then, presumably,
eternal happiness. But by creating, knowing, and communicat-
ing the character of Charlie, Springsteen shows us that eternal
happiness (on earth, at least) by Charlie's standards is but a
dream we drift off to in our warm beds after we've jacked,
stripped, and sold the car.

It's difficult to say how he truly lives his domestic life, but in
his art, Bruce seems to answer Camus's question by embracing
the hill in the labor of brotherly love. He carries his rock right
next to Charlie and empathizes in the fact that they're both car-

rying rocks. He also sees that Charlie is carrying the same rock the Boss carried back in '72 (or whenever Bruce was still wet behind the ears). The Boss *engages* the hill and most everyone on it he comes across. He finds their rocks interesting, too, and he talks with them on their way up. If Charlie happens to drop his rock in the middle of the conversation, Bruce says a musical prayer for him and then keeps truckin' up the hill, focuses on Billy or Johnny, or Mary instead.

The Boss also asks us to listen to his music, and I'd be surprised if out of all his records, he's not most proud of either *Nebraska, Ghost of Tom Joad,* or *Devils and Dust,* all three of which demand to be engaged as stories about dragging rocks and dropping them. See, I like to engage these stories and these people that Springsteen puts out there. I see Charlie through Springsteen's eyes, or at least, Springsteen makes me see *my* Charlie. These collections of songs demand that we engage "in" them, or else we won't "get" the songs. It takes work and effort, and the melodies and tags don't just find their way into your brain, like "Glory Days." And I believe we can really see what Bruce is up to when we recognize that "Glory Days" only requires that we look at the shiniest parts of our own rock, and "Straight Time" requires that we look at the hill and everyone on it.

16

Whatever You Say, Boss: Or, What the Thunder Road Said

MICHAEL F. PATTON, JR.

> April is the cruelest month, breeding
> Lilacs out of the dead land, mixing
> Memory and desire, stirring
> Dull roots with spring rain.
>
> —T.S. ELIOT, *The Waste Land*

> And now in Zanzibar a shootin' star was ridin' in a side car
>   hummin' a lunar tune,
> Yes, and the avatar said blow the bar but first remove the cookie
>   jar
> we're gonna teach those boys to laugh too soon.
>
> —BRUCE, "Blinded by the Light"

Hang on! The chapter you're about to read is about the death of Socrates, rock 'n' roll music, meaning, and the future of Philosophy itself. We'll have some laughs, ask some really hard questions, re-live some of our favorite Boss songs and, in the words of Bill Cosby, I'm coming at you with music and fun, and if you're not careful, you might learn something before it's done. So let's get ready, eh?

What Eliot is saying in the immortal passage from *The Waste Land* above is that we face a choice in this life between being dogmatic and unquestioning or opening ourselves up to possibilities, argument and changing views or, in a word, uncertainty. At least that's how *I* read it. You may get something else out of it. Who's right? Well, I vote for me. Of course I know you probably vote for you, so I guess it is a stalemate. What to do?

I want to talk about our options in this matter, using some examples from both ancient Greek and contemporary US history—and of course, the songs of Bruce Springsteen, our hero for this little tome. I'll be using a few famous quotes from the Boss and others, and I will tell you what they mean. Maybe. So let us go then, you and I . . .

I Mean what I Say and I Say What I Mean

I think it's good if a song has more than one meaning. Maybe that kind of song can reach far more people. (Syd Barrett)

How strangely will the Tools of a Tyrant pervert the plain Meaning of Words! (Samuel Adams)

Bruce Springsteen's long career has produced a large body of work that has become iconic across more than one generational divide. His lyrics and guitar licks can set many different moods, and his concerts are legendary events that people return to again and again. Despite the amount of attention paid to the Boss in dozens of books and hundreds of reviews and newspaper reports, people seem to disagree about what his songs mean, and they sometimes do so in very dramatic terms. What should we or could we make of cases in which intelligent people disagree about the meaning of some song, work of visual art, passage of prose or poetry, or what have you? Let's survey some bullet points.

- Ronald Reagan (okay, okay, so I'm not limiting this just to intelligent people. Give me a break) thought "Born in the USA" was a patriotic enough song to choose it as a campaign anthem in 1984. Everywhere Reagan showed up wrapped in the flag, the strains of the Boss were in the background, which seems to suggest that Reagan thought the song was a pro-America or pro-government song. Or at least, that was his idea until Springsteen told him "no way," and after all, Springsteen is the Boss.

- In the film *Roger and Me*, the citizens of Flint, Michigan, play "My Home Town" during a protest of *Money* magazine's designation of their city as the worst place to live in the United States in 1986. The organizers and the citizens alike seemed to believe that this Bruce tune was as an expression of pride in his home town and, by extension, a source of support for their pride in Flint.

- John Kerry chose "No Surrender" for his 2004 presidential campaign, suggesting that he thought it has some connection with the political campaign he was mounting at the time.

- There are perennial attempts by its citizenry to get "Born to Run" legally declared the state song of New Jersey. Apparently, they think the song expresses something good about their state.

All of these interpretations are pretty strange. While the folks who are too stupid to move out of New Jersey might also mistake a song which calls their locale "a suicide trap" for an anthem of state pride, the other mistakes are just as egregious and need explaining. Here is what the lyrics of those cited songs *really* say, at least in part:

> Born down in a dead man's town
> The first kick I took was when I hit the ground
> You end up like a dog that's been beat too much
> Till you spend half your life just covering up.

Suffice it to say that these are not the words of a Reagan revolution Republican. The thousands of people who share Bruce's view of things as expressed in this song are, at the very least, not patriotic about these sorts of things.

Likewise, in "My Home Town," far from lauding his own Flint-like home town, Springsteen actually describes both the economic conditions of Flint accurately and predicts the inevitable reaction of its citizenry:

> Now Main Street's whitewashed windows and vacant stores
> Seems like there ain't nobody wants to come down here no more
> They're closing down the textile mill across the railroad tracks
> Foreman says these jobs are going boys and they ain't coming back.

So much for a rosy memory of the northeast in the era of over-seas manufacturing.

And, finally, for a candidate who infamously urged the young to get good educations so they wouldn't end up in the Army and shipped off to Iraq, this seems like an odd verse to lead off your signature song:

> Well, we busted out of class
> Had to get away from those fools
> We learned more from a three-minute record, baby
> Than we ever learned in school.

Does Kerry actually think that the people who cut class to listen to 45s (or ended up settling for gentlemen's Cs in the Ivy League) end up in Iraq, one way or another, while their more bookish colleagues have nicer fates?

So how do we decide what to say about the yawning gap between what *I* think these songs mean and what these *other people* think about them? And bear in mind that I am going out on a limb here when I say that there is an obvious meaning to a Springsteen song. Besides my friends who swear "Backstreets" is a story of forbidden gay love and that "Thunder Road" is really some sort of Bible lesson, this is the guy who wrote these words in one of his first hits: "Some brimstone baritone anticyclone rolling stone preacher from the east; He says: dethrone the Dictaphone, hit it in its funny bone, that's where they expect it least." Okay, I have no idea what this means. I will be big enough to say I am willing to accept it.

Bruce's own views on this (as little as he has said anything about it) seem to be all over the map. In the past he has pointed out that Manfred Mann got the lyrics to "Blinded by the Light" wrong in some significant ways (those deucebags!), and he has explicitly told the public that "Born in the USA" is not a patriotic song in the sense that Reagan thought it was. But, in his most recent album's lyrics, Bruce seems to be untouched by actual occurrences, instead favoring his own lit-tle inner world: "Don't worry Darlin', now baby don't you fret, We're livin' in the future and none of this has happened yet." If he can go from settling the issue about some songs defini-tively while also penning a piece of such ostrich-like subjectivism, the Boss may need our help in deciding what to say about these issues. After all he's done for me, I for one am happy to lend a hand.

So on to the task: answering the question of what a song means. To do this even halfway adequately, we'll need to cover some far-flung ground, starting with the guy who started it all—Socrates.

The Sounds of Silence

Silence is a statement that is open to gross misinterpretation. (Craig Bruce)

And the poets down here
Don't write nothing at all
They just stand back and let it all be. (Bruce, "Jungleland")

Legend has it that John Cage composed his scoreless master-piece 4' 33" after a visit to an anechoic chamber. The chamber was alleged to provide a completely silent environment, but, of course, Cage could still hear his heartbeat, breathing, and the like. This led him to his examination of the entire concept of silence and left us with a song all accordion players should learn early and play often. Besides providing us with some interesting argument-fodder, the lesson of 4' 33" is that sometimes what is left out leaves room for disagreement about meaning. Like neg-ative space in the realm of the visual arts, often what you *don't* say is more central to the message than what you *do* say. And, short of just reciting a political manifesto (that would itself inevitably have omissions) set to music, any song, including Bruce's songs, will leave out enough to engender disagreement. So how do we decide what to think? How do we keep from falling somewhere on the continuum that lies between the Bruce Fundamentalists and the Bruce Unitarians?

Truth versus Opinion

The basic tool for the manipulation of reality is the manipulation of words. If you can control the meaning of words, you can control the people who must use the words. (Philip K. Dick)

Poor man wanna be rich,
Rich man wanna be king,
And a king ain't satisfied 'til he owns everything.
(Bruce, *Badlands*)

Long before the birth of Christ, Socrates was put to death by
the Athenian senate for a variety of crimes, but in my humble
opinion he was snuffed because he embarrassed the pompous
folks who were in charge of Athens by asking them questions
they couldn't answer. Socrates's typical *modus operandi* was to
find self-declared experts and then show them up by tying
them in knots with his questioning. Now nobody likes a know-
it-all, but they liked Socrates even less, because he was saying
that nobody knows anything, which is slightly worse.
Elsewhere in Plato's writings about Socrates, he claims that
uncertainty is the most unpleasant mental state for human
beings, and I tend to agree. Whenever I teach or talk about philosophy, I can see people getting unhappy as I try to undermine accepted truths. Or maybe I just have bad breath. Either
way, I know from experience that it is far more comforting to
be sure than to be in doubt, so it seems almost predictable that
the ultimate sower of the seeds of doubt, Socrates, would
annoy people enough to drive them to homicide. Anyone who
engages in philosophy at all is heir to this intellectual heritage
from Socrates—we are all worried about the question of truth
and certainty.

So one of the big questions of philosophy is this: is there
truth, or were the Athenians right to make Socrates (1) drink the
hemlock, and (2) shut the hell up (in that order, since the other
strategy didn't work)? This may seem surprising, but the issue
boils down to whether there is a difference between philosophy
and rhetoric. Philosophy is supposed to be the quest for wisdom, which a lot of people think takes the Thunder Road
through the truth. The fans of rhetoric, on the other hand, think
that all that matters is telling the most convincing story. It's more
like Rosalita deciding whether the Boss's plea to move to
California is good enough to defy her parents. This is not a discussion, it's a sales pitch. You would think that such a song
would woo the shoes off any girl, but since Bruce keeps singing
the song, I assume Rosie still hasn't made up her mind—or
keeps changing it (a woman's prerogative, after all).

The person who is "right," in the arena of rhetoric, is the person who gets the most votes. It was one of the charges at Socrates's trial that he engaged in rhetoric by making the weaker argument appear to be the stronger. The famous sophist Gorgias wrote his *Encomium of Helen* to convince those who heard it that Helen of Troy, contrary to all accepted wisdom and myth, was not blameworthy in her actions, even though they caused the devastating Trojan War. It is masterfully written and serves as an example of how powerful rhetoric in the hands (or mouth) of a master can be. Whether Gorgias believes his conclusion is beside the point—he can convince the audience to accept it. And the implication is that, if he wanted to, he could make the same audience come to reject that very conclusion.

The difference between Socratic questioning (called dialectic) and rhetoric can be elusive to the casual listener, but the difference is all-important. Rhetoric aims to convince the audience of a pre-established conclusion while dialectic urges the participant to convince others that her opinion is justified and worthy of acceptance. Philosophers like me take a pretty dim view of rhetoric as described here—I think the whole issue of being rational is to be engaged in the activity of giving and asking for *reasons*, while rhetoric is the activity of leading people to a belief you want them to have for *whatever* reason, whether it be political, personal or, in the case of advertising, economic.

So now we get to literary theory and the problem of Springsteen interpretation. Is literary theory rhetoric or dialectic? Are all interpretations equally good, or can we have a principled reason to prefer one to another? Let's go forward in history a few centuries and get some help from another source.

Multiple Meanings the Easy Way

Be sure that you go to the author to get at his meaning, not to find yours. (Salman Rushdie)

A man should look for what is, and not for what he thinks should be. (Albert Einstein)

God have mercy on the man
Who doubts what he's sure of. (Bruce, *Brilliant Disguise*)

St. Augustine (354–430 c.e.) famously discussed his idea that the Bible was "polysemous." Polysemy is demonstrated by any text that has more than one level of meaning. Augustine thought it was obvious that the God who framed the entire universe could write (or, more accurately, inspire) a text that had a symbolic or moral meaning, for example, a meaning that was different from the literal meaning of the text involved. The parables are a prime example—there are some messages about how we ought to behave in the story of the prodigal son that are beneath the surface of the actual accounting of occurrences. Surely if Aesop's fables can have a moral that is never explicitly stated in the story, then God could be giving us a history lesson and a moral lesson in the same passage. "But surely, Patton," you may be saying, "if God Almighty can co-author a book so rich in levels of meaning, the Boss can write some songs that have more than one 'correct' interpretation. You're being too literal." Well, maybe so. After all, I don't believe the obvious "literal translation of the following song snippet works, but I think it means something nonetheless: "I got a bad desire, I'm on fire." And the Boss is clearly aware that other people are capable of polysemy, since the target of his affections in "For You" has the coveted ability to "laugh and cry in a single sound." But there is still more work to do.

Now one vital thing must be kept clear here: in the polysemous works we are discussing, there is an actual intended meaning at each level. It not right to say that anything goes— after all, you don't get to be a saint in the Catholic church by being permissive about things like this. The surface meaning is clear to most anyone who can read competently and the more complex lessons encoded in the story are to be figured out by people who have studied theology. Augustine opens the door for fights between fundamentalists and more permissive readers such as Unitarians, but he doesn't throw open the floodgates of meaning altogether. That takes someone like Friedrich Nietzsche (1844–1900).

In *The Twilight of the Idols,* Nietzsche said that the text disappears beneath the interpretation. Later in the same work he says that no one gets anything out of any book that they do not bring to the reading with them. While I won't go any further into the mad German's ideas here, I think you can see that this shifts the focus away from whatever meaning the author of a text *wants* to convey and on to the pre-existing beliefs of the reader in this case. This is like the move from philosophy to rhetoric. Nietzsche writes these provocative words at the end of the nineteenth century and thereby plays a role in ushering in the postmodern era. (Note: the Modern era, when philosophers use the term, goes from around 1600 to around 1900—academics can make anything hard to figure out. We are in the "contemporary" or post-modern era, as far as I know.)

Maybe Nietzsche is right. In a somewhat paradoxical nutshell, he basically said that there was no capital "T" truth to be had. On his view, which later extended by Michel Foucault (1926–1984), truth was merely another instrument one could use to force one's views on others. I could, I suppose, get you to do what I wanted you to do by following you around with a baseball bat and threatening you with grievous injury. I might not be big enough to scare you, and even if I were, eventually I'd need sleep or a potty break and you could get away or get the bat. Thus, it would be a better plan for me to convince you that there was such a thing as the Truth, and that since it is not "up to us" what the Truth is, you'd better get hopping. (Of course, a better plan still would be to convince you that in addition to there being Truth, I *know* what it is and a powerful god would mess you up if you didn't abide by it. There—now you don't need to read Nietzsche. You can thank me later.)

Multiple Meanings the Post-Modern Way

What do you want meaning for? Life is desire, not meaning! (Charlie Chaplin)

The meaning of things lies not in the things themselves, but in our attitude towards them. (Antoine de Saint-Exupery)

Well you may think the world's black and white
And you're dirty or you're clean
You better watch out you don't slip
Through them spaces in between. (Bruce, "Cross My Heart")

The post-modern era takes this idea and runs with it. Thinkers like Jacques Derrida (1930–2004) and Foucault are among the postmodern philosophers who downplay the importance (or existence) of authorial intent as they start to treat everything as a text of some sort. Even the Boss expresses some doubts about absolute interpretive authority when he laments that the cops "busted Madame Marie for tellin' fortunes better than they do." Almost everything we do involves some sort of interpretation, and this interpretive act is essentially subjective. For the post-modernists, or at least for their followers, there is no longer any fixed meaning to any text—just whatever the current reader of the text takes it to mean at the time, through whatever crack in the binding she might happen to step through. I'm no expert here, but I can offer a few illuminating remarks, I think. Even though Bruce warns of the dangers of telling nothing but boring stories of glory days, I seem to have drunk my fill, so here goes.

Post-modern literary theory is tricky. In the hands of an amateur, it can lead to some pretty silly stuff. I often encounter colleagues and students who balk at the whole idea of literary theory. They react especially violently to a thing called "Deconstructionism." We snide philosophy grad students used to revel in going to the local pub and springing upon unwitting English and religious studies grad students who proclaimed themselves decontructionists. The first year students would always fall for our requests to explain deconstruction with some version of "Nothing is literally true," to which the obvious reply is "Is *that* true?" The hilarity was palpable. The more sophisticated budding deconstructionists would say something a bit more accurate, such as "There are no determinate meanings." This level of understanding of deconstruction required a better retort, which we neophyte philosophers gladly supplied. Typically, the silverback philosopher would say some variant of "I couldn't agree with you more wholeheartedly—All statements have completely fixed and unambiguous meanings." Almost no one got this right away, so it would go on for one or two more rounds, but eventually all but the dullest saw the difficulty involved in stating the thesis clearly. More hilarity ensued.

But let's try. Every time you read a text (or watch TV or talk to a friend or anything else), you get a theoretical reading of it. Snooty experts call this "seeing through a lens," and I think it has to happen all the time. While you might resist a Freudian reading of something, your reading of it has, at the very least, the theory "this means what it seems to me to mean when I read it." The problem is, this is about the worst interpretive theory you could have. For one reason, what a text means to you will change with multiple readings and with further experience, so this "null-theory" gets too many different answers. Second, this interpretive theory doesn't leave much room for fruitful discussion between many people. If it means what it seems to mean to you, and it also means what it seems to mean to me, and those meanings are different, then there isn't much for Reagan and Kerry to debate about. They are both right according to the theory each holds, even if they are completely contradicting each other. It's hard to get an intelligent discussion going here, even if it's not entirely due to a bad theory of meaning. Since texts, songs, shows and conversations are essentially social transactions, this is a big drawback of the null-theory. Now I don't claim to know whether we should use a Marxist lens or a Christian one, a Freudian one or a Structuralist one, or any other in our conceptual camera bag. It might just up being a case of 57 channels and nothing on, but I do think we should have slightly more sophisticated ways of talking about things than we might first be inclined to do.

While there are many interpretive strategies we could employ, it has always seemed to me that some of them are just flat-out wrong. No amount of dancing will make *War and Peace* into an allegory for the US Space Program, just as we might look all day long for the Paris Hilton references in *Romeo and Juliet*. More restrained authors might just say that there are just not very many good arguments for these interpretations, but I'm more inclined to reject them as non-starters. And there are some things that Bruce Springsteen just *doesn't* mean in the songs we listed at the beginning, even if we cannot say with certainty just what he *does* mean. But even if it isn't up to Bruce, even if we agree that the "author's intentions" do not determine the meaning of the text, there are plenty of things the lyrics themselves don't mean on *any* sane account. "Born in the U.S.A." does not mean that I need you to buy me a hybrid car. Even if I do . . . or a Camaro, if you'll also cover the gas.

The Final Word: That's Right, I Said Preliminary Thoughts

If I were doing something that the Bible condemns, I have two choices. I can straighten up my act, or I can somehow distort and twist and change the meaning of the Bible. (Jerry Falwell)

Somewhere along the line I got off track—One step up and two steps back. (Bruce, *One Step Up*)

So why argue about this? Isn't it just a game of mental give-and-take where neither side gains any lasting ground? Isn't the only message we can take away from the post-modern condition that things mean what we think they mean? Maybe so, but we need to watch out here. If there is no fixed meaning, truth, or what have you, we get plunged into a world where it is rhetoric all the way down. In other words, you may have to buy me that Camaro, if there's not truth. In such a case, it is the sophists (or their latter-day counterparts, the lawyers) who end up winning. This means I sue you for the Chevy, and you'd better have a good lawyer, because mine went to the University of Alabama, which means he's armed and dangerous, even if he talks slow. After all, whoever tells the most convincing story will get the most people to accept his account of what the Boss means, and if that turns out to be Reagan's campaign managers, then Bruce really was being pro-Republican, Flint is a good place to live, and "No Surrender" has something to do with adults. Me, I'm not ready to go there just yet.

Frankly, I'm of at least two minds about all of this. Or else I'm not. I really can't even tell you what my chapter means anymore—maybe I am not the one to ask. I can't give you any better advice than the lad from Scotland Yard, and he pointed out that after a while each of us is on our own. This discussion could go on all day—the choices are between dogmatic fundamentalism and openness to argument and the possibility of revising our opinions. Besides a personal belief that we should keep looking into this because philosophy (and Springsteen) is where the fun is, all I can do is leave you with the last verse Bruce himself chose to sing in his version of the traditional "Froggie Went A Courtin'":

Little piece of cornbread laying on the shelf, uh-huh
Little piece of cornbread laying on the shelf, uh-huh
Little piece of cornbread laying on the shelf,
If you want any more you can sing it yourself, uh-huh,
    uh-huh, uh-huh . . .

17

A Little of that Human Touch: Knowledge and Empathy in the Music of Bruce Springsteen

SCOTT CALEF

When I was younger I didn't care much for song stories, especially when they involved specifically named people. Narrative lyrics about Bad Scooter searching for his groove, the Magic Rat crossing the Jersey state line, Crazy Janey in the back alley tradin' hands, or little Early-Pearly in her curly-wurly (whatever that is!) seemed irrelevant and remote.

These moments, people, and events may have some autobiographical significance for Bruce, I thought, and be meaningful to him, but I don't know these people. I don't have a relationship with them. I don't even know if they exist. So why should I care? Ironically, because the characterizations were so well-drawn, so concrete, they seemed effective as stories but ineffective as *art*, if art is in part—as Tolstoy argued—about the communication of feeling.[1]

When bands like the Beatles sang about love, I could usually "own" the song because I felt love too, in all of its giddy and tumultuous ecstasy and heartbreak. Those sorts of songs had universal appeal because of their generality. When the Beatles sang about John eating chocolate cake with Yoko, on the other hand, or about Desmond and Molly Jones, well, the rhythm and guitars might still be fun, but something about the lyrics I found annoying. I'm sad to say it was somewhat similar

---

[1] Leo Tolstoy, *What Is Art?* (Oxford University Press, 1938; originally published in 1898).

with Bruce. It wasn't that I didn't appreciate songs like "Jungleland," "Tenth Avenue Freeze-Out," or "Johnny 99." I loved them, and still do. But because they seemed to be about somebody else's life, they didn't seem to be about mine. Lyrically, they didn't move me.

I have no idea whether the experiences I've just described are shared by very many other people, and my former attitudes now strike me as absurdly limited. But as a philosopher, I'm still interested in broad, universal, general questions and truths. I also think Bruce Springsteen is one of the most thoughtful, profound, and articulate artists in popular music. His music not only has the power to entertain, but to teach, to show us things we didn't see or notice before. It also prompts us to internalize truths we may already have known somewhat vaguely at a deeper level. But these facts about the Boss's work raise a couple of interesting philosophical questions.

How, for example, is it possible to "learn" from Bruce's lyrics if they tell stories about people or incidents that are imagined and not real?[2] After all, if the songs' narratives are "fictional"—that is, if they aren't "true"—how can we derive truth from them? How can an artistic *invention*—something false by definition—show us so much about the real world? Why should we assume that Springsteen's song sermons are valid, not only within the fictional world they create, but also to us inhabitants of the real world? And assuming we *can* learn from Bruce's story-song compositions, what exactly can we learn?

In sum, the following three statements all seem true, yet mutually inconsistent:

1. We can learn from Springsteen's narratively-structured songs.

2. Springsteen's narratively-structured songs are works of musical fiction.

3. We can't learn from fiction (and therefore, musical fiction) because *as fiction* its purpose isn't to convey the truth,

---

[2] I know Bruce often does research for his albums, and some of his songs invoke actual people, places and happenings. But I don't think most fans would say we can only learn from those songs. The puzzle that interests me is, how (and what) we can learn from the rest of his repertoire.

and accuracy can't be presumed one of the author's intents.

I'll basically assume that statements 1 and 2 are true. I believe that 3 is false, and that the Boss can help us see why it's false. Once we see why 3 is false and in what sense Springsteen's art can not only entertain but educate, we'll also be in a position to determine precisely what he can teach us.

I Got My Facts Learned Real Good

Some philosophers have thought that if music like Bruce's can teach us, it must be able to convey new truths. If Springsteen were merely repeating common sense or the folksy sort of wisdom our grandmothers love to dispense after the holiday meal or a few glasses of sherry, he'd only be telling us what we already know. We wouldn't be learning anything. So the question is: what kinds of new truths can his music communicate?

Well, where do new truths *usually* come from? One source is science, but Bruce doesn't seem to be offering us scientific truths. He isn't reporting the empirical results of carefully controlled physical experiments. And although his songs are rich in sociological, political, and psychological insight, he isn't really summarizing the findings of professional psychologists, sociologists, economists and the like either. Nor is he drawing conclusions from intuitively plausible or self-evident principles by means of rigorous logical analysis. That is, he isn't exactly doing what academics call philosophy either.

But now we're pretty much back where we started. On the one hand, I surmise, many of Springsteen's fans think they've learned something from his music.[3] But if this sense of realization that occurs from time to time while listening to Bruce's music is genuine, we have to ask what sort of truth is being communicated. And now we wonder, what sort of novel facts about the world can his music give us if it neither formulates empirically testable hypotheses nor makes inferences from

---

[3] They might be wrong, of course, but then we'd have to ask an equally difficult question: Why are so many Springsteen fans so deeply confused about what's happening to them when they think they're learning stuff and they aren't?

accepted facts to unforeseen, unanticipated conclusions? What can lyrical poetry teach us that science and philosophy can't?

Philosophers sometimes distinguish between two kinds of knowledge, knowing *how* and knowing *that*. The former concerns skills of various sorts. So, I might know how to make a C chord, case the promised land, walk like a man, dance in the dark, "prove it all night" or build "a '69 Chevy with a 396 . . . straight out of scratch" ("Racing in the Streets"). Unfortunately, however, this isn't the kind of knowledge I'm likely to get from listening to Bruce and the E-Street Band. No matter how many times I play *Lucky Town, The River*, or *Magic*, I still won't know how to win at Blackjack, re-plumb the kitchen or conjure a rabbit. Perhaps, though, there are some skills I might acquire or improve. Maybe, for example, I can become a more articulate critic of social injustice by listening to *The Ghost of Tom Joad* and *Born in the USA* again and again. Or, if I already know how to play the guitar, I might be able to figure out how to play some of Bruce's songs by strumming along while listening intently. I don't think, though, that our feelings that we've learned something while listening to albums like *The Rising* or songs like "American Skin" has anything to do with developing our talents.

"Knowing that"—the other commonly recognized form of knowledge—refers to factual knowledge. For example, "everything dies, baby, that's a fact" ("Atlantic City"). And if "I got my facts learned real good," I might know that "Poor man wanna be rich / Rich man wanna be king / And a king ain't satisfied / Till he rules everything" ("Badlands"). When I come to know *that* something is the case, I acquire information I previously lacked, and it's tempting to think that if we're learning from poetry and lyrics it must be this kind of learning that's taking place. After all, an awful lot of the factual knowledge we've accumulated we picked up by hearing or reading something, and lyrics are heard or read. And maybe we can learn from lyrics in this way, but it's doubtful.

Suppose, for example, that I didn't know rich men want to be king or that everything dies or that the Rangers had a homecoming in Harlem late last night. Or, to take an even more specific example, suppose that before listening to the first verse of "Youngstown" from *The Ghost of Tom Joad* I didn't know that in northeast Ohio in 1803 James and Dan Heaton found ore in Yellow Creek which was made into the cannonballs that helped the Union win the Civil War. Do I now know these things just because I've heard Bruce sing them? Probably not. Even if I assume Bruce is sincere and so believe him, and even if what he says is true, all I've now got that I didn't have before is a true belief. And true beliefs aren't the same thing as knowledge.

Plato makes this point in the *Theaetetus,* a dialogue on the nature of knowledge. Consider: Prior to my meeting across the river, I believe that making two grand is a dead certainty and that the money's practically sitting in my pocket. Eddie keeps his mouth shut and the deal goes down like it's supposed to. I go home and triumphantly throw the money on the bed, showing Cherry this time I wasn't just talking. I believed I'd get the money and my belief turned out to be true, but that doesn't mean I *knew* I wouldn't get burned and that tonight would turn out to be "everything that I said." A combination of wishful thinking, dumb luck and careful preparation might make for a Cinderella story, but that doesn't mean we knew the end from the beginning.

To constitute knowledge I'd also have to know *why* Bruce (or anyone else) believes these things, and determine that the reasons were adequate. That is, I'd need not just the Boss's charismatic authority, but something like sufficient evidence or independent justification.

A Little of that Human Touch

Since we're unlikely to acquire either "knowledge that" or "knowledge how" from an artist's lyrics, some conclude we can't learn from music after all. Fortunately, as it stands, this is too simple, for there's another sort of knowledge—often over-looked—which Springsteen imparts abundantly. This third way of knowing involves knowledge of *what something is like.* It's knowing how chocolate, oysters, or pineapples taste, or how Bruce's harmonica or Clarence Clemons's saxophone sounds.[4] It's the sort of experience we have when, in a field of blood and stone, the blood begins to dry and the smell begins to rise ("Devils and Dust"). But knowing what something is like isn't

---

[4] Although in these examples I talk about knowing *how* something smells or tastes, this "how" is different from the how-to knowledge exemplified in knowing how to ride a bike, play the harmonica, or speak Spanish.

necessarily limited to things we have experienced ourselves, and here's where a gifted artist like Bruce can really expand our horizons.

If I've never tasted a grape, I probably can't come to understand that flavor just by having someone else describe it to me using especially vivid metaphors or imagery. But we might be able to learn *what something comes to as a possible form of lived experience*, even if we haven't experienced it personally. In this sense, "Springsteen has always been the most cinematic—and literary—of rock composers."[5] When we listen to "The River" we come to know what it feels like to lie in the grass with a high school sweetheart and pass happy summer days driving and swimming. We understand the rude shock of discovering she's pregnant out of wedlock and the feeling of being forced into marriage and monotonous work at nineteen. We identify with the discouraged husband as he struggles to find work during an economic downturn, and drifts apart from the person he once loved so passionately, tormented by the memories of how things used to be and might have been.

But here's the key point. Fortunate circumstances or prudence (if you're a "Cautious Man" or woman) may have protected you from these sorts of disappointments. You might move in upper-middle class circles and have a stable, high-paying, white-collar vocation. Perhaps you're single, or married for the first time only later in life. You may never have been pregnant or had a child. Maybe you're fortunate enough to be in a long-term relationship where the passion burns more brightly now than it did at the beginning. In short, you may never have experienced the dashed hopes, desperation and heart-rending nostalgia of Mary's husband in "The River" and you may not be personally acquainted with anyone else who has, either. But when you listen to the song, you know what it would be like. You feel for *and identify with* this man, a fellow human being who returns to the river years later knowing all the while it's dry.

---

[5] June Skinner Sawyers, in her introduction to *Racing in the Streets: The Bruce Springsteen Reader* (London: Penguin, 2004), p.15. She elaborates that "In songs such as 'Meeting Across the River', 'Born to Run', 'Stolen Car', 'Johnny 99', 'State Trooper', 'Highway 29', and 'Straight Time', he creates strong characters and vividly rendered scenes in a matter of minutes."

Since most of us probably have experienced money worries or fading love, perhaps "The River" isn't the best example. So consider "Nebraska", a song about two serial murderers who went on a killing spree from Lincoln to Wyoming.[6] By the time they were apprehended, ten people lay dead. At trial, the male member of the couple denies feeling sorry for what they've done, remarking simply that it was fun while it lasted. All he can say by way of explanation for his brutal crimes is that "there's just a meanness in this world." The way the spare musical accompaniment complements the quiet, polite, resigned yet remorseless inmate is deeply affecting. Though bound for the chair, the killer is just as indifferent to his own death as to the deaths of his victims. All he wants is to be executed with his partner so they can take one last wild ride together. The stunned and outraged community spit that he's unfit to live and that his soul will enter the void, but the way Bruce represents Starkweather, we experience the numb void that *is* his soul.[7] Or rather, what it's like to have no soul.

When we learn what its like to be these people, we're engaged in what Springsteen has called "a collective event of imagination." In a recent interview Bruce emphasizes the importance of imagination to his work, which he describes as "an ongoing dialogue about what living means. . . . You create a space together. You are involved in an act of the imagination together, imagining the life you want to live, the kind of country you want to live in, the kind of place you want to leave to your children. What are the things that bring you ecstasy and bliss, what are the things that bring on the darkness, and what can we do together to combat those things?"[8] If, with Bruce's help and a little imagination, we can answer these questions we will have learned something important indeed.

---

[6] The song is based on actual events. It is Bruce's "retelling of the Charles Starkweather-Caril Fugate 1950s murder spree." He calls it "the record's center." Bruce Springsteen, *Songs* (New York: Avon, 1998), p.138.

[7] The cool, unemotional, detached way Springsteen characterizes Starkwell in "Nebraska" reminds me of Meursault in Albert Camus's 1942 novel *The Stranger*, where a convicted and emotionally lifeless killer also faces death. If *Nebraska* is one of your favorite Springsteen albums, as it is one of mine, I highly recommend *The Stranger* to those who've never read it.

[8] *Rolling Stone* 1038 (November 1st, 2007), p. 52.

Living Proof

Examples like those I've borrowed from "The River" and "Nebraska" could be multiplied indefinitely, but the point is, I no longer feel as I once did that songs structured around stories or narratives are, for all the scene setting and character development, oddly *impersonal.* For by entering the lives of these people through song, I have a momentary insight into what it's like to be them. On that level, I can relate and I can learn. By allowing us to empathize with and share the stories and emotions of others—even if those others are fictional and never existed—Springsteen lets us participate in a vast range of experiences that otherwise would elude us. As Bruce puts it in "No Surrender," we might learn more from a three-minute record than we ever learned in school. Springsteen's art gives us the opportunity to live more than one life. Perhaps in part because we're mortal, this is deeply satisfying.

This way of understanding Bruce's skill as a songwriter fits well with the painstaking effort he expends to get nuances and descriptions exactly right. He wants to show us something, and we won't have the experience he's trying to convey unless the details and moods are captured perfectly. In *Songs* he offers an explanation worth quoting at length:

> As with *Nebraska,* on "Tom Joad" and the songs that followed, the music was minimal; the melodies were uncomplicated, yet played an important role in the storytelling process. The simplicity and plainness, the austere rhythms defined who these characters were and how they expressed themselves.
>
> The precision of the storytelling in these types of songs is very important. The correct detail can speak volumes about who your character is, while the wrong one can shred the credibility of your story. When you get the music and lyrics right in these songs, your voice disappears into the voices of those you've chosen to write about. Basically, I find the characters and listen to them. . . .
>
> But all the telling detail in the world doesn't matter if the song lacks an emotional center. That's something you have to pull out of yourself from the commonality you feel with the man or woman you're writing about. By pulling these elements together as well as you can, you shed light on their lives and respect their experiences. (*Songs,* p. 274)

The Ties that Bind

Bruce emphasizes how important it is that he finds an authentic voice. When he sings, his vocalizations are really the voices and perspectives of the people in the songs. Otherwise, he says, the music doesn't ring true. In hearing their stories, however, we learn something of what it would be like to be those people suffering those hardships in those circumstances, even if we never have to go through those things ourselves. And if we *have* gone through them, the music enables us to relate to those experiences more universally. We no longer consider them purely personal tragedies, but human ones.

The ability of Springsteen's music to invest mundane circumstances with universal meaning also imbues them with philosophical significance. Jean-Paul Sartre (1905–1980) denies that there's any such thing as human nature, but he does believe in what he calls "the human condition." He writes:

> Although it is impossible to find in each and every man a universal essence that can be called human nature, there is nevertheless a human universality of *condition*. . . . And diverse though man's purposes may be, at least none of them is wholly foreign to me . . . . Consequently, every purpose, however individual it may be, is of universal value. Every purpose, even that of a Chinese, an Indian or a Negro, can be understood by a European. . . There is always some way of understanding an idiot, a child, a primitive man, or a foreigner if one has sufficient information. In this sense we may say that there is a human universality, but it is not something given. . . . I make this universality . . . by understanding the purpose of any other man, of whatever epoch.[9]

The ability to identify with others and so unite with them enlarges us and increases our humanity by joining us with the rest of humanity. Since we are humans, we become more of what we are. We feel more complete, and this is literally fulfilling.

---

[9] Sartre, "Existentialism is a Humanism", reprinted in Walter Kaufmann, ed. *Existentialism from Dostoevsky to Sartre* (Meridian, NY 1975) p.362

Ain't No Sin to Be Glad You're Alive

I've tried to argue that that Bruce's music can help us imagine lives and circumstances to which we're unaccustomed. And, I've suggested, he enables us to transcend our purely private worlds and exchange them for vaster realms in an intensely gratifying way. If I'm right about those things, they help to explain another phenomenon which is quite curious if you stop to think about it. Many of Bruce's songs—"Empty Sky," "You're Missing," "Reno," "The River," "Factory," "Born in the USA," "Reason to Believe," "Streets of Philadelphia," "Wreck on the Highway," "When You're Alone You're Alone," "Souls of the Departed," and innumerable others—are deeply sad. They come from, and dwell in, the darkness on the edge of town. Not only are many of his themes frankly depressing, but thanks to his artistic sincerity, we experience the futility, emptiness and loss of his characters to the full. Why then do we like listening to them? Who wants to feel sad or defeated? Ironically, Bruce is so good at what he does that no one should want to listen to him! So why do we?[10]

Aristotle gives an answer:

> Imitation is natural to man from childhood . . . and [he] learns at first by imitation. And it is natural for all to delight in works of imitation. The truth of this second point is shown by experience: though the objects themselves may be painful to see, we delight to view the most realistic representations of them in art. . . . The explanation [of our delight in art depicting unpleasant situations] is to be found in a further fact: to be learning something is the greatest of pleasures not only to the philosopher but also to the rest of mankind . . . the reason of the delight [in the unhappy episode represented] . . . is that one is at the same time learning—gathering the meaning of things.[11]

---

[10] I know many of Bruce's songs also bring a ray of light and hope—even romance—to the honestly acknowledged struggle of his working-class heroes. But not all his songs are like this. I don't see a lot of latent optimism in songs like "You're Missing," "Gypsy Biker," "My Best Was Never Good Enough," or "Devils and Dust."

[11] Aristotle, *Poetics*. Reprinted in *Art and Its Significance: An Anthology of Aesthetic Theory*, edited by Stephen David Ross (Albany: State University of New York Press, 1984), p. 71.

Aristotle is saying that people love to experience even tragic art because we love to learn, and we learn through imitation. Because we delight in learning, we can delight even in songs about unhappy people in miserable circumstances. When those lives are "imitated" artistically or poetically in song we learn "what it is like" to live those lives. We "gather the meaning of things."

Aristotle goes on remark that the poet's function is:

> . . . to describe, not the thing that has happened, but a kind of thing that might happen . . . what is possible . . . Hence poetry is something more philosophic and of graver import than history, since its statements are of the nature rather of universals, whereas those of history are singulars. By a universal statement I mean one as to what such or such a kind of man will probably or necessarily say or do—which is the aim of poetry, though it affixes proper names to the characters. . . .[12]

Bruce's more narrative lyrics "affix proper names to characters," but they are universal—and thus philosophical—nevertheless. Discovering "what is possible" and what a certain kind of person "will probably say and do" is akin to knowledge. Because art imitates life, though on a universal level, music like Springsteen's captivates us by broadening our life experience. By doing so, and quickening the imagination, it makes us more alive. The situations Springsteen sings about may be depressing, but the realization of what it would be like to live in those alternate realities appeals to us as rational beings who desire to know. In other words, the joy at learning from the Boss's songs compensates us for the sad facts that are learned. We love sad music, not just uplifting and hopeful music, because on some level it satisfies our natures as knowing, empathizing beings.

---

[12] *Poetics*, p. 77. According to Aristotle art can also be cathartic. It provides a release from the pressures of life by allowing us to live out our violent or sexual fantasies without actually injuring ourselves or others. Because music can help us know what it's like to live through imagined experiences, we don't actually need to abandon our wives and families. We can safely have the experience through vicarious identification with the subject of songs like "Hungary Heart" instead.

Lonesome Day

This may also clarify why so many people were so deeply affected by *The Rising*. For the rest of the country, far from New York and east coast values, the facts of what happened on 9/11 were clear enough. But many of us, confronting an event so unprecedented, so shockingly momentous and ruthlessly diabolical, were simply stunned to incomprehension. We couldn't process the total emotional overload. *The Rising* helped us collectively make sense of the numbingly unfathomable events of that day by reducing them to a personal scale. We could then relate to them in more familiar terms: "Shirts in the closet / shoes in the hall / . . . / TV's on in the den / Your house is waiting / For you to walk in / But you're missing." ("You're Missing"). "I woke up this morning, I could barely breathe / Just an empty impression / In the bed where you used to be" ("Empty Sky").

This isn't the whole truth about why *The Rising* was such a healing album, of course. While helping us to understand, it also gave us hope, hope that we as a people could again "rise up." Reminding us of our vast potential as a nation, it helped us to look forward and not just back. It showed us something important, not about the Magic Rat, Bad Scooter and Crazy Janey, but about ourselves and each other.

18
Socrates the Sculptor, Springsteen the Singer: Philosophy and Art Against the Tyrants

JASON M. BELL and JESSICA BELL

Socrates and Springsteen are the two most politically prominent philosophical artists who have ever lived. A first clue that you might be one of the most famous philosophical artists who has ever lived is that the powers-that-be abduct you for their entertainment, as happened to Springsteen in 1984, when Reagan and Mondale each falsely pretended to have received his endorsement.

Imagine that—one day you wake up and the television and newspapers tell you that both parties have claimed your endorsement, when in fact you don't like either of them because they are both bullies picking on helpless little states. What would you do? And what would Socrates do? Indeed we have the answer to the latter question, because in the *Republic*, Socrates was kidnapped in a similarly prominent way, although perhaps a bit more brutally, being forcefully brought, like Dorothy in Oz (and Springsteen circa 1984) "behind the curtains," to a gathering of the wealthy Masters of State who control the machinery of lying government propaganda, in service of its aims of endless consumption and Total War (from which they all profit most handsomely).

Bob Dylan in *Masters of War* prays for such direct critical access, but Socrates and Springsteen actually have it, not even having asked for it!

The Sculptor: Abducted!

Socrates was, according some, a stonemason, like his father. According to others he was a sculptor, responsible for the sculp-

235

ture of the the Graces that stood near the Acropolis. Whether Socrates was an artisan or an artist with stone, he was at the very least a sculptor of conversations, and artist with words. And it is for this that he was renowned and in demand.

There Socrates was, minding his own business, walking with his friend Glaucon back to the city of Athens after making a religious pilgrimage, when his garment was seized by a slave, on the order of his master Polemarchus, the son of a wealthy arms merchant named Cephalus. So there you are walking down the street, minding your own business, when suddenly you are seized from behind and ordered to wait, and told that you are being commanded to provide entertainment at a party. These people do not care that your wife Xanthippe and your two small children are at home expecting your return; and they don't take your "no" at all seriously.

What did Socrates do? He announced his intention to proceed back home, of course; after all, this is where Xanthippe and his children live. But Polemarchus, catching up with his slave, demands that Socrates provide conversational entertainment at a "party" at his house—really a gathering of his and his father's flatterers—and then Polemarchus appeals to the number of his mob to demand compliance: Socrates is brought to the party, occurring in a mansion of glory (327c),[1] filled with slaves and their masters. There are in fact good contextual clues, like the passionate threats of bully Thrasymachus, the lechery of Polemarchus, and the slurred arguments of the assembled group, that the only sober ones there are the permanent slaves and the "temporary" ones, Socrates and Glaucon.

It's a bitter pill that these abductors have stolen and swallowed. Socrates—with the aid of his own E-Street Band, Glaucon and his brother Adimantus—chastises their conspicuous consumption, their imperialism, and their attempts to con-

---

[1] We're following the translation of the *Republic* by Paul Shorey, in the widely used anthology *Plato: The Collected Dialogues*, edited by Edith Hamilton and Huntington Cairns (New York: Pantheon, 1961). But if the edition on your shelf is different (surely you have one somewhere), you will notice little numbers in the margins. We don't actually know what edition of Plato those margin numbers come from, but everyone uses them, so they must be important. We will use the little margin numbers too, because we don't want to offend the authorities, no matter how dead they surely are by now.

trol politics and manipulate the thinking of those around them. These elites exert control so as to maintain their privileged position. They live in a cave of pedagogical lies and make up "eternal forms" to supplement their paid armies. Socrates then warns that his captors' mercenary guardians will eventually see through the lies they have been told and turn against their oppressors; the end result of this civil war is to be a city enslaved, indebted, ruined, and under the yoke of tyrants.

Of course the very livelihood of this assembled group depends on the overconsumption and warmongering of others as well; if Athens stopped living in such splendor and fighting so many wars of imperialistic expansion, then Cephalus's arms-manufacturing business would go bankrupt, and his son Polemarchus would need to find a job and leave off his merrymaking and kidnapping. Thus the fiery Sophist Thrasymachus, a hired hand, is appointed to frighten and cajole Socrates so that he will stop his critique of the overconsumptive state. "Don't you understand," this august assembly says through its spokesperson, "that there is no justice beyond what we masters of the universe possess? We, dear fellow, control the levers of all power; we will make you rich, if we please, and we will destroy you, if we please. So please do stop using that concept of some other sort of justice to hurt our business interests. We here in this room, the arms merchants and their flatterers, *are* justice and the laws; while your boring 'just man' who is honest in his labor and fair in his dealings with his neighbors will be killed and forgotten, if we so order it. So, look man, just pull your chair up to this sweet table and receive the reward for your compliance. Or you will be killed and forgotten." Well, in Socrates's case, perhaps the threat was half true; he was killed.

The Singer: Abducted!

In 1948, George Orwell predicted that in 1984 a critic's opinion would be abducted and perverted into an endorsement by a ruling elite engaged in perpetual warfare and perpetual lying, supposedly for the good of the Republic. Precisely on schedule, Springsteen, engaged in a critique of imperialistic warfare and overconsumption, was abducted by the two major American presidential contenders, Reagan and Mondale, who supported invasions of weak states (like Lebanon and Grenada) that had offered no plausible threat, and who simultaneously pretended that Springsteen had endorsed them. This abduction was not a physical one, as in Socrates's case, but rather an abduction of his political endorsement. Perhaps you think that we oughn't to take such a kidnapping seriously compared to the ones that befell Socrates; but we must take political kidnapping at a quite literal level, since our political opinions may easily be so important to us—if we choose them to be—as our bodies. There is, after all, a connection between what we believe and what happens to our bodies—as tens of millions of deceased dissidents could easily attest, if they were still here.

Reagan and Mondale, like Polemarchus and Cephalus, are not so stupid as they might appear—they knew, of course, that Springsteen was a critic and not a flatterer at the time they pretended he would endorse them, and the point of the kidnapping was to cajole him to accept a prominent role—as offered by the latter-day Thrasymachus, George F. Will in a newspaper editorial entitled "A Yankee Doodle Springsteen,"—as the poet laureate of joyous overconsumption and the oppression of foreigners. Springsteen, of course, pointedly turned down all these offers. His critical voice has since been censored by some of the largest corporate-owned American radio stations who now refuse to play his music, perhaps because they well understand that his critique of overconsumption might mean reduced profits for them, if people heard it.

At any rate we may still be surprised that Orwell's bold prediction of the *year* 1984 came true, right on schedule. But I think that Orwell is here less a prophet than a good reader of history, as the same thing had happened on roughly the same schedule to the critic Socrates a couple of thousand years before—it was a few decades after the Greek defeat of Xerxes and his Persian army that Athens fell into the same sort of miasmic post-imperialist disrepair that undid Xerxes; likewise it was about so many years between Hitler et al., and Springsteen's critique of the decline of America. To the victors goes the spoilage, apparently. Several decades, that is, after defeating the tyrants Xerxes/Hitler, the once-just people, strong by virtue of minding their own business and leaving others to mind theirs, who nobly fought those who failed to mind their own business because they were in quest of lording over others' business, began to imitate the actions of their former oppressors: the children of the children of the "greatest generation" revel in luxury and think themselves better, in the words of Socrates, not merely to the unjust, but to everyone. The children of the children of the victors, enflamed with appetites and passions that far outstrip the ability of the land to provide for them, must, then, turn to despoiling the neighbor's land and censoring its domestic critics. Suddenly the wars have no purpose *but* to seize the excess of our rapidly proliferating desires. It's hard to understand, in a ghost city like Youngstown:

> These mills they built the tanks and bombs
> That won this country's wars
> We sent our sons to Korea and Vietnam
> Now we're wondering what they were dyin' for.

Elenchus and *Epoche*

The Socrates of *The Republic* and Springsteen are strangely, but almost universally, misread as succumbing to "Stockholm syndrome"—parroting the beliefs of their abductors, and endorsing a "patriotic" state that forcibly discourages dissent, censors art, encourages recitation of comforting lies, and seeks endless wars against foreign states, all for the one purpose of allowing consumption to grow exponentially. There are two main reasons for this misunderstanding. The first derives from the effects of censorship as earlier discussed; the second comes from Socrates's and Springsteen's shared critical method, wherein they do not obviously denounce overconsumption and imperialism "from the outside," so to speak, but they patiently consider those activities from within, first when people are apparently flourishing, and finally in their cataclysmic decline. To the unsensitive reader who hears Springsteen's repeated chorus: "Born in the U.S.A.," and odes to fast cars and street racing, and Socrates's encomiums in *The Republic* to the lying eternal forms, and to the self-serving "philosophical" ruling class of Athens, these critics seem instead to be paid celebrity endorsers. But if we read the songs and speeches in a broader context and listen for Socrates's and Springsteen's judgments as to the consequences of such beliefs and behaviors, we will easily see that Socrates and Springsteen are far from endorsing the debauched behaviors; this car-racing and these eternal universal forms lead to loneliness, death and suffering for those who believe in them and those with the misfortune of living near to them.

Both Socrates and Springsteen use the same method of *elenchus* to criticize those whose desires necessitate parasitic predation on the labors of domestic and foreign workers: both perform a sort of thought experiment that corresponds to actual conditions, beginning by humoring those whom they criticize by temporarily endorsing their message. After all, it's easier to catch a fly with honey than with vinegar. But then they run the experiment and show how, in the end, such beliefs and behaviors result only in unhappiness. Unfortunately, in both cases, readers and listeners often lose sight of this method of elenchus and ascribe to both Socrates and Springsteen those beliefs they are criticizing!

In Book One of the *Republic*, we learn that Cephalus—the wealthy arms merchant whose son abducted Socrates—is terrified of Hell, but he thinks that wealth alone (such as he possesses by an accident of birth) will enable him to make peace with the gods. He also asserts that the poor are almost certainly doomed to Hell since they must cheat their fellows and cannot pay off the gods. Let us pause here to remember that Socrates is an unashamed member of this working poor, and Cephalus knows this very well, so Socrates is being insulted quite directly. It's almost as if Springsteen were dragged to dinner at the Trump Palace in Atlantic City and then told by The Donald that all those working people back in Asbury Park were unworthy of heaven. It's not like he doesn't know where Bruce comes from. How would Bruce take that?

In Book Two Socrates praises the modest workers, in communion with the forms of particular expertise that enable their labor, and whose labors sustainably meet the needs of their people—meaningful work. It's this genuinely happy political condition that forms the "control" or *epoche* against which the experiment of the diseased overconsumptive state is tested, and found lacking. If you really want to know what ails Atlantic City, you need a healthy contrast—a happy, productive working class neighborhood. Later in the *Republic*, we are subjected to Socrates's restatement, now at greater and tragic length, of the conditions foreshadowed in the beginning, when the critics are kidnapped and horsemen risk death for the amusement of the wealthy—a horrible litany of abuses against the human person and collective intelligence that must be undertaken by the wealthy, overconsumptive, diseased state. There will be censorship of the artists, starvation, murder, infanticide, violation of the constitution and of taboo, and war without end; and finally, at the end, Socrates declares that the "smart but wicked men," the tyrants and the oligarchs who create them, shall be the sole inhabitants of Hell—and not the working poor, as Cephalus had assumed.

As with Springsteen in "Born in the USA," the doctrines that are widely attributed to Socrates—of eternal fixed forms, of the Cave as a good pedagogical model—are in fact descriptions of the hopeful beliefs of his kidnappers: that if they lie in just the right way, they can set things up so that they will be always able to overconsume and lord it over their fellows, just as they are now. Alas, the *Republic*, the most commonly read of Socrates' conversation, is very long. Scholars, tired by the many words, forget the elenchus, and begin to ascribe to Socrates the beliefs of his oligarchic kidnappers!

In the twentieth century, respected philosophers such as Karl Popper and Bertrand Russell, and indeed thousands of others, are shocked that Plato, writing in middle age, has stolen from us the humane Socrates he wrote about when he was younger. But such scholars forget that Socrates has been kidnapped, and that he is, by the critical method of elenchus, demonstrating what will happen to the censors, kidnappers and enslavers of critical domestic artists and unthreatening foreign peoples. Slightly more sophisticated readers like Leo Strauss (1899–1973) remember the *elenchus* but for some reason neglect the *epoche*, of Book Two, the healthy city or working people, and they fail to note the importance of the death sports that are the center of this culture—forgetting this, they implicate Socrates in other sorts of strange prescriptions, like the wholesale rejection of politics, when in fact he is merely rejecting the consumptive idealism of this group of wealthy abductors.

Likewise, with Springsteen, listeners are sometimes distracted by individual lyrics or refrains and miss the *elenchus*. The refrain of "Born in the USA!" is such an example; a casual listener hears uncritical patriotism and may assume that the proper response to invading weak nations like Grenada and Lebanon is to unfurl the flag and shout patriotically over the objections of the conscience of friendly cooperation. But if we listen more carefully, we hear the critique of a nation at pointless war abroad, with no respect for work or the natural environment at home. One does wonder why Springsteen chooses to deliver his lyrics in ways that make them hard to decipher on the first hearing. But Socrates is pretty hard to understand in his own somewhat different way. Perhaps Springsteen is inviting those who care to know to read the lyrics and let the fools who won't take the trouble think whatever they want.

Some slightly more sensitive critics of Springsteen's poems have understood the presence of the critique but hastily reduced it to an "anti-war" position that still celebrates other typical signs of American excess, notably its fetishistic love of automobiles. But these cars as ideal ends, too are tested by Bruce with the method of elenchus, and are found as tragically wanting as the diseased city of the *Republic*, as in "The Angel," where:

> The interstate's choked with nomadic hordes
> in Volkswagen vans with full running boards dragging great
>   anchors
> Followin' dead-end signs into the sores
> The angel rides by humpin' his hunk metal whore.

This isn't exactly the worship of the car on the road. Let's turn, then, to examine the *epoche* and *elenchus* in slow motion, so that we are not deceived into thinking the critics are endorsing what they in fact oppose. First we'll examine the "control," the good city; then the "experiment," the luxurious city. Then we'll compare consequences. We'll finish with a discussion of what Springsteen and Socrates's artistic criticism means for understanding philosophy itself.

The Good City

The first hurdle we face in understanding the philosophical criticism of the artists Socrates and Springsteen is fairly obvious—to realize that they are not finally endorsing the diseased cities in which overconsumption and censorship run rampant, but merely humoring the abductors. The second hurdle is more subtle, and it has tripped up many of the critics who have skillfully leapt over the first (by reading a little more closely). This subtler view regards Socrates's and Springsteen's criticism as so unrestrained as to negate *any* genuine patriotism. Thus Strauss mistakenly has it that Socrates asserts that the "good city," the ideal republic, inevitably must fall. The wise philosopher therefore turns entirely away from politics once he has dismissed it.[2] Likewise, for interpreters of Springsteen, the culmination of this period of his musical thinking is that he has become an "anti-war" musician. But for both Socrates and Springsteen the main point is not merely to criticize the bad city, but it is to examine it and the good city, and to compare them. Indeed by contrasting the horrible experiment of the *elenchus* with the control of the flourishing practical, working-class life (the *epoche*),— the overconsumptive, aggressive city of these captors is measured and found lacking by Socrates and Springsteen. But Strauss goes too far in taking Socrates to be rejecting any hope of a political good.

For Socrates and Springsteen, need, rather than pleasure, is placed at the center of the genuinely healthy city; and devoted work with our fellows is the only way to fulfill need with decency and dignity. This healthy city of workers is found in such places as Book Two in the *Republic*. Such a life turns out well, in love, as for Springsteen's "Cautious Man":

> Bill Horton was a cautious man of the road
> He walked lookin' over his shoulder and remained faithful to
>   its code
> When something caught his eye he'd measure his need
> And then very carefully he'd proceed.

And it is such a devoted worker who gamely faces troubles and pains, and doesn't seek to avoid them by forcing others, slaves and artists, to do his bidding. Only such as these, Springsteen argues, will taste the true pleasures that the Kingdom of Earth may provide, as in "All that Heaven Will Allow." The storms of life don't prevail:

> If you got a girl that loves you
> And who wants to wear your ring
> So c'mon mister trouble
> We'll make it through you somehow

---

[2] See Leo Strauss and Joseph Cropsey, *History of Political Philosophy*, third edition (Chicago: University of Chicago Press, 1987), pp. 43, 68.

We'll fill this house with all the love
All that heaven will allow.

In the healthy city, joy is constantly measured against need; loving co-operation in work with our fellows is the fundamental and necessary tool for this accomplishment. There is, for Socrates and Springsteen alike, a real and lasting satisfaction that accompanies such willing work, undertaken with our fellows. Such work is indeed a permanent comfort, even in times of dreadful social decline. As Springsteen has recently put it, "What others may want for free / I'll work for your love."

The double benefit of work, for the self and for others, and the dangers of avoiding it, are described in Springsteen's song "Galveston Bay," which discusses parallels between the working careers of two professional soldiers turned fishermen, one Vietnamese (Le) and one American (Billy), who fought for the same cause in Vietnam and who now labor in the same trade in America. In this poem, Springsteen requests a "do-over," so to speak, for our nation's "pre-emptive"—meaning unprovoked— strike against the Vietnamese who were minding their own business before the battle of Chu Lai, who were then attacked in their yards by invading American forces. In the song, racist Texans plan to burn the Vietnamese fishing boats, and Le shoots two of them one night as they attempt to carry out their plan. Billy, their friend, seeks vengeance, but at the last moment he "stuck his knife into his pocket / Took a breath and let him pass." Billy returns to his work and family, and lets his Vietnamese compatriot do the same.

It turns out, indeed, that the Vietnamese were able to figure out how to mind their own business, even without French or American oversight. Socrates in the *Republic* likewise requests a "do-over" of the Peloponnesian War, in which, rather than Athens choosing to treat those of these other neighboring cities as "barbarians" who are to be fought and controlled, they are instead to be treated as fellow Athenians.

The Luxurious City

Witness what passes for entertainment in the Athens on the day of Socrates's abduction. Not only is Socrates abducted to put on a free show at the house of Cephalus,[3] but on this same night, a new kind of death-sport will be invented!: a "torchlight race," wherein "they carry torches and pass them along to one another as they race with the horses," (328a). The allusion and danger are identical in Springsteen's "Racing in the Street": "Tonight tonight the highway's bright / Out of our way mister you best keep / 'Cause summer's here and the time is right / For goin' racin' in the street."

But all this is repaid by Socrates and his E Street band, Glaucon and Adimantus. After Cephalus's and Thrasymachus's insult of the working poor and the artists, Glaucon asks Socrates a crucial question, one that immediately follows Socrates's description of the healthy working city in Book Two: "If you are founding a city of pigs, Socrates, what other fodder than this would you provide? [You must provide] what is customary, they must recline on couches, I presume, if they are not to be uncomfortable, and dine from tables and have dishes and sweetmeats such as now are in use" (372d). This is at least an accurate description of hopes—Socrates's kidnappers are adorned in chaplets, and sit on cushions (328b–c), they eat fancy Athenian pastries, and drink fine wines. For them, salvation quite literally is to live amongst these pleasures, having escaped the need to work with others. It is like unto Springsteen's "Seaside Bar Song," where the tempter, the proud owner of a "a Chevy '40 coupe deluxe" becomes the seducer, the enemy of the work of the day, a denier of the consequences of the morning:

> Well don't let that daylight steal your soul
> Get in your wheels and roll, roll, roll, roll, roll, roll, roll . . .
> I wanna live a life of love while the night's still young.

---

[3] The legislature of South Carolina demanded, of all things, a free show of the Dixie Chicks for the soldiers stationed there, after that group of singers dared to criticize the president for fighting an unconstitutional war. http://www.scsenate.org/sess115_2003-2004/bills/3818.htm. Most curious! Should they sing "Not Ready to Make Nice"? Hopefully, in the spirit of Socrates's *Apology*, someday they will provide just such a free concert in South Carolina, but without the Hemlock afterwards, and not under coercion.

This is roughly the attitude of this assembled group of partiers at the house of Cephalus, who want to live for the night and not worry for the brutal hangover of the next day. For them, seeking profit for self-advantage is all there is to justice, and justice for its own sake is burdensome (359a–b), and it's interesting only insofar as it pays (364a–c). Indeed, profit is the only important thing, the work that produces it is a tremendous bore: business for them now is mere "huckstering." Even controlling most of the levers of power, this group still hopes for a "Ring of Gyges" (the fabled Ring that makes the wearer invisible—an idea famously copped from Plato's *Republic* by J.R.R. Tolkien) that would enable them entirely to escape the constraints of the law, so that they might be pure parasites; and even without such magic, they use the more modest means of their actual control of the government so as to make a "fillet of the state" (465d), and design ways around paying taxes for it (551e). Others shall pay, we shall enjoy.

In this luxurious city, the government of this assembled group's ideal state, rather than including workers, is for the richest who have bought the best education that money can afford—philosophy, they expect, is for the rich masters who can afford tutors to teach them, while the working poor shall ignore it (474c). Indeed, no one who does honest labor is to have a role in governing the state (551b). Here again, many readers have been lulled into believing that Socrates endorses such nonsense, and that his ideal of philosophy is a lazy one, a strictly *a priori* affair, conducted with clean hands in a life lived on the isle of the blest. But Socrates shows that children of "educated" oligarchs, like Cephalus's impetuous son Polemarchus, are not so smart after all, despite the seeming evidence of their wealth and the array of flattering tutors set before them: the general conditions of lying advantage that have been arranged for them mean that such a child is "defeated for the most part—and finds himself rich" (555a). No thanks, indeed, to his own intelligence; but thanks to the machinery of the state that holds his competitors down while it robs their wallets. How could Socrates endorse such an order any more than Springsteen could? For Socrates such a position would be a denial of his own origins, his situation, and the life of poverty he freely chose. For Springsteen it would be acting as though he were entitled to the gifts he has been given, which he has never done. The truth is that Springsteen believes in hard work.

A look at the successive drafts of the song "Prove It All Night," reproduced in Bruce Springsteen, *Songs*, second edition (New York: Harper, 2003), pp. 82–91, shows how hard he works to retrieve a song from an idea. His work ethics at his concerts is, of course, legendary. Never has a word of entitlement come from him, only gratitude. No doubt he earned the wealth he has, but he knows better than to confuse it with virtue and entitlement. This is what working class origins will impress upon a person who is at home with his or her own way of life.

The Bad City

What happens when these masters, these who live the highest lives of luxury in this most luxurious city, become rulers? As we have already seen, they abduct artists, for one; and they censor them when they do not obey. If any doubts remain whether Socrates and Springsteen endorse the corrupt and overconsumptive cities, the city that builds the cave, the eternal forms of lies, the one that puts on spectacles of car and horse races by torchlight at night, let us put them here finally to rest. Socrates and Springsteen need to practice their art freely in order to secure their livelihood, and so it would seem quite a bit silly for them to *endorse* the conditions and the practices of abduction and censorship. Alas many still believe that they do so endorse it, and that their ideal of patriotism is one that ignores the truth in a jingoistic desire to steal the neighbor's right to self determination.

The overconsumptive city must procure what it cannot produce, so it must go to war (373d–e). Eventually so many wars will need be fought that everyone must be called up, even the *Jugend* brigades; but these child warriors, as Socrates gamely said, shall only be sent to the safest battles against the weakest foes, and they shall be set upon the fastest horses should the fight turn bad. Nevertheless, these conditions may mean the slaughter of your offspring. The war profiteers, far from being frightened of this proposal, and unworried (since it is not *their* children who will be called up—indeed they think this prospect of Total War sounds mouth-wateringly delightful) just imagine the profits. Yes, let's arm women and children! (466e–67e).

Once again, many scholars read this nonsense while falsely thinking that Socrates really hopes that Athens becomes such a wicked state, but of course he doesn't. He is no more endorsing the condition of imperialism than Chaplin was endorsing Hitler in "The Great Dictator"—and with the same sense of humor: when Socrates attempts to explicate for his audience the innate worth of pursuing mathematical knowledge for the sake of cooperation, this audience can only understand the good of math by analogy to the profit of war, and Socrates laughs at them in response: "I am amused by your fear of knowledge in itself!"

Work, as we saw in the discussion of the Good City, is the necessary condition of sustainable pleasure; but there are few jobs in the overconsumptive city: why work at home when the excess can be seized abroad? Jobs are most notable in Springsteen songs and in the *Republic* as a departed ideal— these jobs are leavin' and they ain't comin' back—as Sprinsteen puts it; honest labor is demeaned in the city they criticize. The troops return from imperialist adventures abroad only to find that few opportunities for honest labor await them—this is the economic tragedy of "Born in the USA," "Lost in the Flood," "Brothers Under the Bridge," and "Youngstown," among many others.

But things get still more dire for this group. Let us recall that Cephalus is very pleased because his inherited business success means that he is able to keep his contracts with men and with gods; were he poor, he thinks, he would be doomed in his old age—he would be forced to cheat men and the gods. But now we learn that things are also quite doomed in this city that was created for his amusement, not despite but because of his predatory wealth—it is now a city divided against itself, a city of the desperately rich and of the desperately poor. In it, there is a huge criminal class (552c–e). This is a favorite topic of Sprinsteen's as well, as explored in the *Nebraska* album, in "Atlantic City," "Murder Incorporated," "Souls of the Departed," "Sinaloa Cowboys," and "Straight Time," among others. In "Souls of the Departed," the valleys witness the murder of poor-on-poor violence, while: "In the hills the self-made men just sighed and shook their heads." Indeed the law itself has often gone awry, even so far as to join the criminal classes in oppressing the criminal poor and the self-minding poor alike. In "The Line," the policeman succumbs to sexual temptation in clear violation of the law; in "Balboa Park," "Zero and Blind Terry," and "American Skin," the innocent are literally killed by both official and mercenary enforcers; and in "4th of July, Asbury Park," the oracle herself is censored: "Well the cops finally busted Madame Marie for tellin' fortunes better than they do," just as the Athenians killed Socrates because his Oracle at Delphi had told a fortune better than they did.

Benjamin Franklin and George Washington had more important matters to attend to than to censor and fine the public press for obscenity; whereas the massive fines levied by our contemporary government for the appearance of a female singer's partially clad breast on broadcast television ($500,000, if the singer in question is Janet Jackson) indicates plenty of time for meddling and a dearth of attention to real problems. This governmental censorship of artists is prominent among our contemporary perversions, as are the corporate censorship of artists, like Springsteen and the Dixie Chicks, who are rebuked for having dared to criticize the political powers that be. The reasons for such censorship are several. Artists, as Socrates and Springsteen show, call loud attention to the tragic consequences of mistakes; but these masters of war and wealth want their slaves to do their bidding courageously and without questioning the results or the reasons. Likewise these masters of taste are obsessed with pleasure and worship the pretty things, whereas much of the more honest art is ugly and displays tragic passions. The tyrannical leaders simply decree that there is to be nothing of the madness or Aphrodite in art.

Of course this overwrought government happily will allow your children to watch copious violence on TV (the FCC does not consider *that* obscenity), but this is not due to any deep moral inconsistency. It comes from absolute consistency with the necessary purposes of overconsumption at home that necessitates war abroad—if your children are fated to become soldiers in the next war, we had better teach them to suppress their natural squeamishness about blood and pain, and their desire for sex. After all, in their future experience they will be getting only blood and violence; sex is a disorderly distraction. There is no real *hatred* of eroticism here implied by the censorship, since indeed the rulers love debauchery for themselves, but they simply decree that whatever does not conduce to that end of producing warriors amongst the working classes is to be strictly forbidden (see 530e–531a). The decree is indeed simple, but there are a million tentacles: We are to be expunged of our human emotions (387b–e), we are to ban dirges and laughter (388c–e), we are to be rid of music, certainly Springsteen's sort (397a–d), except for simple cadences. There is to be music and plot fit only for preparing us for battle—as in the theme song for *24,* the television program that stringently equates torture of dark colored neighbors with the attainment of truth. Harmony is forbidden (399a–e), rhythm is unseemly, which would certainly include all the boogie and driving rhythms on E Street (400a–e). And poetry is to be against the law except for the boring sort. The overconsumptive state must also censor religion and literature and must *compel* the poets to do its bidding; it must even decree the shape and content of art and architecture.

Such a life without art wouldn't be very enjoyable, seemingly—but this group can still appeal to their ring of Gyges to secure their own enjoyment. They compel others to work, and must secure compliance by forbidding *them* most art. But surely, we think, we can enjoy these things in private for ourselves? For Socrates and Springsteen alike, punishment for violation of the compliant forms of labor meant quite direct consequences for the soul/psyche of the individual violator. Springsteen reports this phenomenon, as part of his own elenchus (and not endorsement), in "Souls of the Departed," "Out in the Street," "You Can Look," "The Price You Pay;"—indeed in such songs, like "The Long Goodbye" and "My Beautiful Reward," the animalistic consequences and even temporal terms of the recurrence of punishment are quite identical to Socrates's version as reported in Book Ten of the *Republic.*

It's on epistemological grounds that persecution abroad so strictly revenges itself on stupidity at the home front: the elite become the caricature of the underclasses, in which: "the mob of motley appetites and pleasures and pains one would find chiefly in children and women and slaves and in the base rabble of those who are free men in name" (431b). Even if you keep your ring of Gyges on all the time, the punishment for overconsumption will be strictly internal, as you become the thing the law mocks, because you are envious of what criminals can get away with. You have a debt no honest man can pay, when the ring is on your finger. Still your punishment is that your desires multiply fervently once they are first nourished by overconsumption, and the consequences are both internal and necessary: nothing will cure the overconsumer (426a–b).

The quest for pleasure is likewise adjudged by Springsteen in "My Beautiful Reward":

> Well I sought gold and diamond rings
> My own drug to ease the pain that living brings
> Walked from the mountain to the valley floor
> Searching for my beautiful reward . . .

Needless to say, the search doesn't end in reward. If fact, it doesn't end at all.

As for Socrates, when you respect the one practical eternal form, namely work in yourself and your fellows, you are saved; whereas, in your theoretical isolation, living in this isle of the blest at Polemarchus's house, with slaves to fetch glasses for you and Thrasymachus to write arguments for you, you are strictly doomed. Now you are truly lonely, persuasion is impossible, and you are left unable to co-operate with your fellows. Your slaves will surely hate you, and escaping from your cave, if they are able, they will have contempt for you, for the law, and for themselves. They become rebels. They'll enslave you if they can. In short, the city many depict as "ideal" in the *Republic* is a finely sculpted conversational elenchus, an artwork commissioned by and made for the presumptuous wealthy. But the joke's on them. Don't be surprised when an artist of conversation, when enslaved, creates a work that is hard for his abductors to recognize as a condemnation of all they hold to be true and valuable. The "good" city is the bad city, for those who can read, as surely as "Born in the USA" is a critique in song of like kind. Socrates would no more endorse this city than would Springsteen say that his protagonist is a happy man.

Springsteen's Martyrdom

We know how things end only for Socrates, and for Winston Smith in *Nineteen Eighty-Four*, not yet for Springsteen. But hazarding guesses of probability, I would suggest that Springsteen has a better chance of being made a martyr than you or me—if you speak of the oracle's judgment to the oppressive abductor classes, they will eventually forbid you:

> Well I learned my job I learned it well
> Fit myself with religion and a story to tell
> First they made me the king then they made me pope
> Then they brought the rope.

Springsteen hopes to avoid the fate of martyrdom, since he clearly loves this life as much as does Socrates of the *Apology*:

> Now some may wanna die young man
> Young and gloriously
> Get it straight now mister
> Hey buddy that ain't me . . .
> And I want all the time
> All that heaven will allow.

Both of these artists are able to love life so much precisely because they refuse to submit themselves to the selfish whims of the oligarchs. Socrates and Springsteen alike know the joy of the artisan who *makes* something; they know the joy of being abducted on its behalf. And apparently they have no desire to be like their abductors, even though they both had the easy opportunity to join in their oppressive splendor.

I am afraid we may all be long dead before some scholar of the distant future figures out how Springsteen did choose to "Apologize" to his abductors. Like Socrates the sculptor? Or like Winston Smith, the low-ranking bureaucrat? Or surely some other novel way. And what will Janet Jackson and the Dixie Chicks do? But even at the present moment we may safely say that Springsteen is criticizing the powers that be at a dangerous time. When wars against seemingly weaker neighbors are incessant; when our nation is in love with blood sports, in "Ultimate Fighting" and in the ritualized humiliation of the underclasses on much of the new so-called "Reality Television"; and when we are especially beginning to attend to the "need" for official and corporate censorship of artists.

Conditions are not yet so bad as Socrates experienced under the reign of the Thirty Tyrants, but as with the bodily disease that can quickly strike down the once-healthy, we may recall that we are living at a time when our president has suddenly self-decreed a theoretical and practical right to name anyone he so wishes an "enemy combatant," and thereby to order them exiled, tortured, killed; when he may haughtily ignore Constitutional provisions regarding the need for Congressional authorization of war, believing himself to be allowed to wage war against any state he wishes to invade (again, not merely as a theoretical right, but it is an actual affliction that has struck several groups of our neighbors). In conditions such as these, the best thing that you can hope for is that, like Paul, your Roman citizenship will mean a little something for a little while; or better, that the people of the state will begin, once again, to respect its constitution, namely by consuming less, working more, and engaging in more real processes of co-work with neighbors and ceasing in attempts to oppress and enslave them.

Socrates and Springsteen here may help us to understand the nature of the philosophical art. It does not always go looking for a fight, but sometimes it is surrounded by bullies. Here Socrates and Springsteen alike appear to be of the courageous stock, staying to fight those who would bully and kidnap justice and wisdom. They are nothing like such "philosophical" interpreters of Socrates as the Roman Emperor Marcus Aurelius or the defender of Nazism Martin Heidegger (1889–1977), who became bullies and sought to oppress weaker peoples; nor are they like Aristotle, Strauss, and Popper, who fled from tyrants and conducted their critiques from a safe distance. The first two are hardly comprehensible, the latter three are perhaps more so; but why would anyone take the path of those philosopher-artists-martyrs, such as Socrates, and perhaps Springsteen? And why do these two speak for slaves and women and the oppressed Greeks, or the Jews of the ghetto, or for the defeated general Santa Ana, or the "Black Cowboys," when it has been decreed that we are supposed to be in antipathy to our "enemies" and not in sympathy with them? For each philosophical artist alike, the conditions of knowledge, and the expertise in the art, quite literally needs others in order to exist. Meanwhile creation is an enjoyment that solves the problem of need, and artisanry of different sorts is also its own reward.

Contrarily, to attack and enslave these fellow people in quest of our amusement, or to justify our own sense of entitlement or superiority, is to condemn ourselves to the insoluble problem of need, but now in an inferior position compared to our pre-imperialistic condition, since now we have negated actual and possible fellow laborers who could have helped us to address need by means of joined labors. We have let our desires grow so immense that nature has neither interest nor ability to fulfill them.

Here Socrates's problem is not so much with the tyrant Xerxes, and Springsteen's not so much with Reagan, Mondale, or Bush; these oligarchs or tyrants are results, not causes, of the business of the luxurious overconsumption of a people. As Socrates puts it: "Do you not suppose that such a one will then establish on that throne the principle of appetite and avarice, and set it up as the great king in his soul, adorned with tiaras and collars of gold, and girt with the Persian sword?" (553c). The artist feels the consequences of the rise unto power of such a one, when the law is sent to greet him. And here Springsteen, in 1973, was as prescient in predicting his own kidnapping at the hand of the imperialistic powers of the state as Orwell was—less accurate about the year, but more accurate about the character:

> Oh, some hazard from Harvard was skunked on beer playin'
>   backyard bombardier
> Yes and Scotland Yard was trying hard, they sent a dude with
>   a calling card
> He said, do what you like, but don't do it here
> Well I jumped up, turned around, spit in the air, fell on the
>   ground
> Asked him which was the way back home
> He said take a right at the light, keep goin' straight until
>   night, and then boy, you're on your own.

I don't see how his current situation could have been more accurately foretold even by Madame Marie. Springsteen, like Socrates, seems to endeavor to uphold the decrees of the law, even some of the strange ones. But the critical voice of the artist accompanies every decree with its own rhyme of consequences, as Socrates and Springsteen, at the same time, uphold the genuine law of justice by comparing these edicts to the good city, in the light of critical examination of *epoche* and *elenchus*:

Well I unsnapped his skull cap and between his ears I saw
A gap but figured he'd be all right. He was just blinded by
   the light
Cut loose like a deuce another runner in the night . . .
Mama always told me not to look into the sights of the sun
Oh but mama that's where the fun is.

19
Elvis, 57 Channels, and a .44 Magnum: A Cross-Section of Springsteen's Imagination

RANDALL E. AUXIER

We've followed Springsteen from coast to coast, border to border, and across the seven seas (or at least around the Great Lakes). The essays in this volume really do run the gamut of the Springsteen experience. How to bring it all together and leave you with something you can really get your pearly whites into? I have something for your cerebral palate—it won't make you wise or virtuous, but it might sometimes cheer you up.

I want to teach you how to do "ontologies." First let's do just a bit of background on what this odd word means, and then on to the fun stuff—and it *will* be fun, I promise. When you've learned the trick, you can do ontologies with your friends, at parties, at home alone, or when you're camping, just any old place. If you doubt that it'll be fun (there *is* some boring stuff first), flip to the list of proper names in Springsteen songs that follows this essay. I'm going to play with that list, philosophically, and show *you* how to do it for fun and profit—well, at least *I'm* making a (thin) profit from this; if I can, so can you.[1]

Ontology is a powerful tool for thinking—in fact, while there is a difference between *thinking* and *imagining* (see Chapter 8 in this volume), they're closely related: what if your "thinker" has its *own* imagination? Well, it does. Immanuel Kant

---

[1] And my parents wanted me to study law, of all the boring practical things. I'll bet they're glad now, with all this money in philosophy, that I went my own way . . . and a note for the IRS: I am reporting all of this, I swear, or at least I promise to, at some point.

(1724–1804) went on and on about it, and he is the third best philosopher in Western history (the judges all place Plato and Aristotle ahead of him). But Kant didn't explain very clearly the point *I* am making. I think Abraham Joshua Heschel (1907–1972) said best what I am trying to say: "Thought is like touch, comprehending by being comprehended."[2] Heschel had a great economy with words. I don't. I need to explain this.

Neural Novacaine

Have you ever noticed what it feels like to touch a part of your body that has been anaesthetized with a part of your body that *hasn't* been? Like when you've been to the dentist, and you touch your jaw (while it's asleep) with your finger? Weird, right? On the other hand, if you just touch your cheek with your tongue, while they're *both* asleep, there is an odd sort of "nothing" that you feel, it's like a total *absence*, and you sit there wondering if you're hurting yourself, biting your tongue without knowing it. Better stop that. But when you touch your jaw with your finger when your jaw is asleep, it's sort of like touching another person, made weird by the fact that you *know* it's *you*. I'm getting paid to think about this, believe it or not.

It's a valuable experience (the jaw thing, not the money thing), apart from whatever dental benefits were bestowed during the process, because it shows you the difference between the feel of *reciprocal* touch, that is, what it feels like to touch your jaw when your finger and your jaw *both* feel it, and what it's like when that normal experience doesn't happen. Feeling yourself feeling you, when everything is normal, is like seeing yourself in a mirror holding a mirror in which you see yourself, *ad infinitum*. It's like instantaneous, total and infinite reciprocation—your finger feels your jaw, which feels your finger, which feels your jaw, and so on. Take away the first reciprocation and it's like looking in a mirror and seeing someone else looking back at you, but someone who moves when you move, and you know it is you, but you don't recognize the dude (or dudette). Weird.

---

[2] Abraham Joshua Heschel, *The Prophets* (New York: Harper and Row, 1962), p. xvii.

Now, what I think Heschel is saying above, oh so beautifully, is that *thought* is like that too—your finger and your jaw, when awake, comprehend each other, mutually, by touching, and thinking is comprehended the same way. And what *I* am saying is that your imagination, among the many things it can do, is like the finger that touches the jaw, and the jaw is like the idea you're thinking. That *idea* just sort of sits there, doing what it's doing (being thought), without a lot of self awareness, until the imagination reaches out and touches it. And then, in being comprehended by the finger of imagination, the thinking comprehends itself, says "well, I'll be damned, I'm an idea being thought about." But it is difficult to give an idea a shot of Novacaine, to make an act of thinking altogether numb, unfelt. But it's sort of like 2 + 2 = 4. You *know* it all the time, but aren't working with it all the time. And then somebody (such as me, your devoted author) mentions it, and whether you like it or not, you get an image of it, floating around in some sort of imagined space . So is the image the same as the idea? Not exactly, but the image seems to wake the idea up.

Unfortunately, it's hard to think about things without also imagining them. And for lack of contrast, you also don't notice that you are *feeling* what you *think* with your imagination. I know of some politicians, I don't need to name names, whose ideas come very close to that benumbed, unimagined condition, but even *they* must have *some* intellectual imagination, even if it doesn't extend so far as going to war with an exit strategy.

But you know that you *feel* what you *think* because sometimes just thinking about something or someone makes you happy or sad or anxious, and you can feel your body change as the idea comes up. The *image* that accompanies your thought is the medium by which you feel what you think. Change the image, and it'll change how you feel about what you're thinking. For instance, think of Bruce. That should be a pleasant thought. Now think of someone mistreating or hurting Bruce, someone like Bill O'Reilly. That should give you a different feeling. It does that to me, for sure. According to the neuroscientists, the way our brains generate images is by *initiating* an action in the back of the brain and then *inhibiting* the action in the front of the brain. We do that and up pops the image as a sort of substitute for a bodily movement. When the image appears, we feel and think simultaneously. It's hard to know what it would mean to "think" without images—it would be like a "pure idea" with no image at all, an utterly static thought, with no future, no past, and existing in an eternal present that had no consequences, no history, and no concrete meaning. Can we do that? I doubt it, but I can't say it's impossible.

Now, ontologies enable you to have *some* control over *how* this touching of thinking by imagining *occurs*. You're doing this all the time anyway, but there is a discipline and an art, a sort of Tai Chi of intellectual imagining, that you can learn, with practice. Welcome to my Dojo. You are Kwai Chang Caine, and let me be your Master Po, for a few pages, and when you can snatch the pebble from my brain, you'll know it's time to go wandering through the list that follows the essay.

"What It Is?!?"

I have always thought that this colloquial greeting pretty well says it all. Is it a question? Yes and no. It's an expression that rivals "Namaste" for acknowledging the divine in everyone you meet. And it is also a fair translation of the Ancient Greek *to ontos on*, from which we get the term "ontology." The (untranslatable) Greek phrase means "What it is that is," or something like that. Another interesting translation of the idea is the name God gave to Himself when Moses impertinently asked for His proper name from the burning bush. God said "I am that I am," except He apparently said it in Hebrew, and it is best not to write or speak that word in the sacred language. In Hebrew, the expression is first person, while the Greek is impersonal and infinitive—and there in a nutshell you have the difference between Greek and Hebrew ideas about God. In Hebrew you can say, "What it is, man!" to God, if you have the nerve, but it wouldn't make sense in Greek. In Greek God is like, on some serious Novacaine, thought thinking itself.

So ontology is about "what it *is*, dude." But as Aristotle pointed out, "*Being* is said in many senses," and he went on to enumerate ten properly distinct ways of saying "is," called "categories"—substance, relation, quality, quantity, action, position, and a few others I can't recall. Never mind. It isn't important for us right now. And then there are a few *bad* ways of saying "is," according to Aristotle, as Bill Clinton's attorneys once argued (I don't know if they cited Aristotle, but it would have helped their case). We'll avoid the bad ways of saying "is." But the word "ontology" is a more recent invention, based on the Greek root. It started appearing in European languages towards the end of the eighteenth century, and then really became popular at the end of the nineteenth. Now it's a cottage industry.[3] See, there *is* profit in this.

The Famous Ontologies

This would be a good name for a band. They could open for Springsteen, except that no one opens for Springsteen. Every philosopher has an ontology or two, or several, that is, ways of imaginatively arranging whatever exists so as to reveal some connections and relations that will be discussed. For example, in this volume, Gary Herstein works with an "events" ontology that he adapted from Alfred North Whitehead. James Couch is using an approach he adapted from Hans-Georg Gadamer called "regional ontology." Doug and Russell Anderson are entertaining (and rejecting) the ontology of dialectical materialism, in which reality is treated as a history of material human needs in competition with economic institutions and practices. All of these are ways of imagining reality, the "is" of things, in order to think about it. So, perhaps reality *is* temporal "events" in relation (Whitehead), or maybe reality *is* the way that horizons of "meaning" fuse at the edges of whole regions of lived experience (Gadamer). Or maybe reality *is* just the story of human beings trying to survive in the face of the impersonal juggernaut of history that is driven by alienation and economic practices (Marx).

But there are so many other ways to imagine reality. It is common for famous philosophers to *get* famous by coming up with a way to carve up The Real, and then to claim that their way of doing it is either the *best*, or the *only* way to do it—that somehow they've finally "touched bottom" on the issue of how reality *has* to be thought about, because that's how reality *is* (or at least how it *has to be* experienced by beings such as we). Among those who thought highly enough of their ideas to make

---

[3] Check the following websites: http://obofoundry.org/ and http://www.ifomis .org/ and http://www.loa-cnr.it/DOLCE.html and http://www.ontologyportal.org/.

so grandiose a claim, none was more full of himself than Martin Heidegger (1889–1977). He began his ontology with what is called "the Question."[4] "The Question" is a way of launching a sneak attack on what we already vaguely understand, namely "Being," but have failed to make explicit. When we have slunk quietly behind our quarry (our own vague awareness), we pop up, say "boo!" and then wait to see what we've flushed from hiding. But there are lots of ways to sneak and slink, lots of ways to say "boo!" and still more ways to list and count the things we may glimpse.

In the case of the splendid Dr. Heidegger, he did something he called "fundamental ontology," which outlines the bare essentials one must assume in approaching the Question of Being. He transforms that venerable question from "why is there something rather than nothing?" into the slightly less obvious "what sort of being asks such an impossible question?" It turns out, after much hand wringing, that the answer is, "well, the sort of being who asks that question is one that has a *problem* with its own being—and that would be *me*, and maybe also *you*, but definitely me." But according to Heidegger's zealous and numerous followers, none but the Master himself is deep enough or smart enough to carry out the weighty task of Fundamental Ontology (the capital letters are my own, but I think I can hear them in their tone of voice when I am in the presence of such self-importance). Let the snobs have their Fundamental Ontologies. I'm after something more suited to their estimation of *my* depth, or lack thereof. I want a slice of the Springsteen worldview, not the existential structure of all possible worldviews. I'm sure that would be too mundane for Heidegger.

Elvis and the .44 Magnum: The Poetic and Aesthetic Use of Proper Names

Among other things, ontologies help us sort out levels of generality and make us aware when we have hopped from what is

---

[4] Heidegger's book, *Sein und Zeit*, first appeared in 1927. The two-part introduction to this work sets out Heidegger's phenomenological method and raises the Question of Being. For a recent translation, see Martin Heidegger, *Being and Time*, translated by Joan Stambaugh (Albany: SUNY Press, 1996), Sections 1–8, 12–36.

more general (more abstract), to what is more concrete (less abstract). An ontology provides a kind of schema to remind us of *which* slice of reality we are considering, and which we are not. To give an example, let's look at some Springsteen lyrics.

Sometimes a character simply has a "gun," as in "Johnny 99." That "gun" could be anything from an AK-47, to a deer rifle, to a Saturday night special. The picture your imagination forms will depend on context. Since Johnny 99 (aka Ralph) uses it to shoot a store clerk, and later waves it around, most of us will picture a small gun, but that's up to us. The word "gun" is very general, covers a lot of possible things. One can wave a deer rifle around. But sometimes Springsteen is more specific, like when he describes that heart-breaker gal who walks down the street with her boot heels clicking like "the barrel of a pistol spinnin' 'round" in "Livin' in the Future." Now I don't actually know what sound the barrel of a pistol makes when it's spinning, but I do know that this isn't just a "gun," it's a *pistol*, and since it has a barrel, I'm not picturing a snub nose .32. I have a long barrel pistol in my imagination, spinning on the pavement where the boot heels should be. But I don't know if it's a Colt .45 or a Luger. "Pistol" is more specific than "gun," but it's still quite general.

But in "57 Channels and Nothin' On," Springsteen tells us that he got a .44 Magnum and shot his TV. He was doing what Elvis did one day (and what I want to do, and probably you too). Now, historically, the .44 Magnum was apparently Elvis's weapon of choice in the famous incident. But notice that our hero (or he's my hero at least) in "57 Channels" gets *a* .44 Magnum. A lot of those have been made. But in fact there is also *the* .44 Magnum Elvis actually used. Now we are approaching something that we might give a proper name—let's call Elvis's .44 "Betsy."

Now, a question. Isn't it interesting to consider whether *the* .44 Magnum, Betsy, is the gun to imagine in *all three* songs? It would connect them, in an odd sort of way—not only to imagine that it was the same *kind* of gun, but the same individual gun. I am not suggesting Springsteen intended this or anything of the kind; rather, I am pointing out a *way* of imagining a path through three songs. With such an ontology as this (and this *is* an ontology), you could actually write a movie script: three vignettes, the story of Elvis's gun that ends up, ironically, being used to shoot a second TV years later, bought by a frustrated viewer at a pawn shop, who had no idea he was courting Betsy. And how did Betsy get to the pawn shop? Well, there was a corrupt guy at the evidence room (apparently Betsy really did disappear), and then a fencer, and an accidental switch of two .44's he had, and a twist or two, and Johnny 99 buys Betsy at a pawn shop. Then a hold-up, and an incompetent police officer . . . and a hooker in boots with the same name as the pistol . . . you get the idea, finish the story any way you want, so long as the guy with the satellite dish and the Japanese car ends up shooting his own TV with Betsy—and the gun needs to find its way back to the evidence room in Las Vegas, because that's how stories work.

Now, how did I do that? Am I an imaginative genius? Hardly. I used a *very simple* ontology.[5] Recognizing four levels of generality, I imagined the same individual gun as fulfilling all four levels. It fit, basically. Then I took all three song stories, added them to the historical event with Elvis, took it all down to that very specific level of concrete thinking, and started telling the story. The *idea*, "this is Elvis's .44 Magnum," was filling itself out with an imagined possibility, bringing to life an otherwise inert thought with something I could have *feelings* about. I mean, why *not*?

You can look at the list of proper names after this essay and do the same thing. Some of those Johnnys and Billys and Marys could be the same person, couldn't they? In the case of Mary, I'm pretty sure it *is* the same person in a couple of songs. And who knows how many other names the actual Mary has had in Springsteen's lyrics? Is she also Wendy? And Rosalita? She might be. And it doesn't, in the end, matter all that much what Bruce intended, since this is your imagination (and mine) at work. Bruce gave us a template, a schema, a context, and that is his catalogue of songs. Of course, you don't have to use Bruce's songs; anything that offers a specific context will suffice. But Bruce's songs are so much *fun*.

You can go another direction with this simple ontology. You can look at a Springsteen song and find a general noun—like

---

[5] In my college dorm I lived across the hall from a guy who became a famous Hollywood director and screen writer. If he is reading this, and you know who you are, why don't we reconnect and discuss this movie about Elvis's gun? I already know what music we can use . . .

gun, and work your way down to something individual, by asking "what gun is this?"—or you can start with something that is very specific and search for general ideas that might describe it. I could have just as easily started with Betsy and imagined my way from "57 Channels" to the spinning pistol, to Johnny 99's "gun," as to move the other direction. But the list of proper names I compiled is *far* more interesting than a list of general nouns and verbs from the same songs. Why is that?

Shaniqua's Coffee and Theresa's Backbone

Even proper names display various levels of generality. For example, I know a bunch of people named Johnny, Bobby, Mary. The more common the name, the more people we know. When Springsteen calls such a name, we immediately try to form an image so as to follow and feel and think the story of that person, but *my* Johnny is different from *your* Johnny, as Springsteen knows very well. He's giving us imaginative space and something to do. Sometimes the image comes in clearer, sometimes it's as Hazy as Davy. But when Springsteen wants more control over what we picture, he can choose a less common name, or add a nickname.

For example, in "Girls in their Summer Clothes," some gal named "Shaniqua" serves the coffee. I have never known anyone with that name, but I know she is African American. Bruce made sure I would picture her that way, didn't he? Another more exotic instance is "Theresa" in "I'll Work for Your Love." Here, because of my own background, I have no choice but to picture two things: a bartender, whose name I never knew, in Oklahoma City, who was *definitely* the woman Bruce is singing to, and also Bernini's famous sculpture of "The Ecstasy of Saint Theresa." If you don't know this artwork, you need to Google it. Bruce spelled the name Theresa with an "h," leaving me no choice, although I *heard* the silent "h" in my imagination and I *knew* that was how he spelled it before I ever saw the lyrics. I just knew. I have met several Teresas in my life, maybe even a Theresa or two, but Bruce littered the song with a dozen allusions to Catholic mysticism, and perhaps even drew directly from the writings of Saint Theresa. He took more control of the imaginative space and left less to me. The bartender was mine, but St. Theresa is common property.

And that is how proper names function in poetry and stories. They tap into the past experience and context of the reader and generate images, and the images then become the animators of the ideas. In "I'll Work for Your Love," the *idea* is something like erotic and intimate reciprocation, whether in love-making or in building a life. Yes, yes, a very nice idea. But frankly, it's obvious and uninteresting until Theresa shows up, with her irresistible backbones, like stations of the cross –and I assure you that Bruce is counting them from the top down, not from the bottom up, because Theresa apparently has a nice ass, and redemption is *down there*, in this song at least. Bruce is so naughty.

We learn how much control Bruce *wants* over us by noticing the level of generality. The more concrete the image, the more control he has. But these proper names are also ways of engaging the listener's active imaginations and conveying ideas. At the same time they reveal a cross-section of Bruce's imagination –how he concretizes, how he specifies, and what is important to him. Recurring themes show up. For example, consider immigrants. They show up all over the place in Bruce's songs— Mexicans, Vietnamese, Europeans of all sorts. In the song "American Land," we get a list of family names of immigrants, and on the list is the Zerillis. The Zerillis? For heaven's sake, why not the Rosminis or the Corleones? Well, Zerilli is the name of Springsteen's mother's family. That's not just trivia, that's a message in this song. Springsteen *feels* his own immigrant roots, and they are crucial to his self-understanding. He sees his own family in the story of the Brothers Rosales in "Sinaloa Cowboys," and perhaps also the historical Brothers Heaton in "Youngstown." He builds it into the song and reveals something of his world.

Perrineville

Another example is "Perrineville" in "Highway Patrolman." There *is* a Perrineville, New Jersey, and I'm sure that's where Bruce got the name. But the song is set in Ohio, so that a car chase can cross the Michigan line, ending in an escape to Canada. Now, not even Springsteen can make us imagine an escape to Canada from New Jersey—or at least it would have to be an epic chase. Imagination has rules and limits. And

"Highway Patrolman" is a Rust Belt kind of song, so a town on the Mexican border isn't right. So, I know that Perrineville, Ohio, in Bruce's imagination is somewhere near Toledo, but of course, it doesn't exist—and neither do Joe Roberts and his no good brother Frank.

But this isn't pure *fiction* either. In this case, I think the narrative requirements of the song dictated the place. Bruce chose the escape to Canada as the outcome of the narrative tension in the song. He also decided he needed a *proper name* for the town, not just the phrase "rust belt town," or something similar. He wanted more control. He pictured Perrineville, NJ, placed it outside Toledo, and told the story. Would the song work if he didn't use a proper name? Maybe, but not in the same way. I mean, we *all* know Perrineville, we've *all* seen such a town, and we *know* what sorts of people live there. I have an in-law who just *is* Joe Roberts, a good guy, and he would have done exactly what Joe did—let his no good brother escape. But my people don't come from the "rust belt," and I don't identify with that name—I push it away from my imagination. But I'm neutral on Perrineville— where the hell is that? Well, I don't know because I'm not supposed to know. It needed to be some podunk town I've never heard of, and it doesn't matter whether it really exists, which is why it is better if it doesn't. Perrineville exists everywhere. And a podunk town by any other name stinks just as bad.

At the same time, these characters, places, and things (like Frank's Buick with Ohio plates), can just as easily be masks behind which Springsteen (or any writer) conceals himself. For example, is it true that Bad Scooter in "Tenth Avenue Freeze-Out" is a self-reference: BS = Bad Scooter, Bruce Springsteen? Is that you Bruce, or just a brilliant disguise? I don't know, but I do know that Bruce is the primary decider of what we do and don't know about him in his songs. Yet, the full slate of proper names, when turned over in our imaginations with the tools of ontology tells us a lot about him, a lot about ourselves, and a lot about our world.

And Try to Stay Awake

One reason, then, why songs are interesting and philosophy is usually boring is that songs and stories can move fluidly through levels of generality, whereas philosophy usually tries to deal with everything at a very general level, to make ideas stand still instead of setting them in motion, and moving from one level of generality to another with great deliberateness—there's just no responsible way to move fluidly in philosophy. In the hands of a philosopher, there's also a certain carelessness about individual, concrete existences. When a philosopher invents an example to help with thinking about something, it's usually as innocuous as possible—sure, they'll use proper names sometimes, even historical names or places, but the whole *point* is not to think about the individual, but about the type of *idea* it indicates. So, in philosophy "Paris" is not the vibrant place you can visit, it's "Paris or a city *like* Paris, or any relevantly similar city, in some specific sense." And "John" is not Spanish Johnny or Johnny 99, it's any one specific individual at all. And that is *boring*.

Now, what we have done here is a very simple ontology. You have finished the introductory course. I am afraid I will now have to blow your mind. Sorry.

A Brief Stab at Advanced Ontology

You can get college credit for this. Michel Foucault (1926–1984), a somewhat notoriously odd French philosopher, began his most famous book, *The Order of Things*, with a passage he copped from the Argentine writer Jorge Luis Borges (1899–1986), who cited a certain "Chinese dictionary" he had supposedly "found" (it is difficult to know when to *believe* what Borges says, and that is how he wanted it). This extract from the Chinese dictionary has become famous. It goes like this:

> Animals are divided into: (a) belonging to the Emperor, (b) embalmed, (c) tame, (d) sucking pigs, (e) sirens, (f) fabulous, (g) stray dogs, (h) included in the present classification, (i) frenzied, (j) innumerable, (k) drawn with a very fine camel hair brush, (l) et cetera, (m) having just broken the water pitcher, and (n) that from a long way off look like flies.[6]

Oh really? Are *those* the real classifications of types of animals? This is dizzying. Let's get a bit more specific, like, how many of

---

[6] Michel Foucault, *The Order of Things* (New York: Vintage, 1970), p. xv.

these categories would apply to, say, dogs. By my count, dogs could show up in every category except (d) and (e), and I am uncertain about whether there might be a way to get them into (e), if the howl is seductive enough to other dogs. Of course, the *same* dog may show up in several categories at once—for example, a tame dog belonging to the Emperor, viewed from a long way off. Or at different times, the *same* dog may belong to *contrary* categories—for example, a stray dog, later adopted by the Emperor, which then broke the water pitcher in a frenzy, and ended up embalmed. The lesson here is: don't decide too quickly what kinds of dogs there are—or anything else for that matter. You may miss some types, and it is best to remember that there are lots of ways of looking at "order."

Foucault built his book from noticing just how much we *assume* about how to "order" things in a given culture or historical period, and how much this may differ in other places and times. There *are* rules (or common "practices") in every period about how to imagine order, but there are no permanent rules that reach across all places and times, according to Foucault. What I did above is a highly conventional Western ontology of how to get from the general to the specific ideas and back again. But ontology is not limited by such conventions. It is a *highly* flexible philosophical tool, just as the human imagination is a highly flexible finger for touching the jaws of an idea. Now you're on your own.

Suicide Machines

My imagination was captured by the words "suicide machines" in "Born to Run." Let me explain. That's a motorcycle, right? A "cage" is a car, and we are sprung from them. I could follow the path I used earlier by asking what sort of motorcycle, and then looking for it in other Springsteen songs. But we are ready for more. Let's steal a lick from Heidegger, if we can risk offending his cheerleaders. Whenever you find a question that you sort of *know* the answer to, but you don't know *why* you are so sure of yourself, you have the makings of a kind of ontology. But there are so many questions and so little time. We should choose our questions carefully. This is a book on Bruce Springsteen. I have a question, and I know the answer, but I don't why I'm so sure of myself. I think most people will quickly see that this question has a lot of torque; it is indirect, but it might spring us from our cages.

My guiding question is: "Would Bruce Springsteen ride a Honda?"

First off, I don't mean "Has Bruce ever ridden a Honda?" Maybe he has, but ours is not a factual question about Springsteen's biography, it is about two cultural icons, Springsteen and Honda, icons that press upon us an immediate *contrast.* Our imaginations try to place Bruce on the Honda, and we have a sense of what Walt Disney called the "plausible impossible."[7] We feel we're imagining a fiction when we try to place Bruce on the Honda. We all know Bruce would not "ride a Honda" in the intended iconic sense, even if curiosity or circumstance might have led him actually to try one out at some point.

But how do we *know* the answer to this question with such confidence? I want you to think of the question itself as a vehicle, a motorcycle. Let's collect our insights like needed parts, and one by one install them. Eventually we will have a question that purrs, and later we may take it out for a ride.

The Passion of the Boss

Would Bruce ride a Honda? No. Consult the list. One reference to Honda, and it's a car, and it isn't an endorsement. But before we can get to the stuff that is so very boss about the answer, we need to spend some time tinkering with the question while we're still in the ontological living room (yes, we work on this bike in the living room, not in the garage; if you are worried about the mess, go read a different chapter). Put on some old clothes in case you get substances on yourself.

---

[7] Walt Disney explained the principle of "the plausible impossible" in Episode 55 of *The Wonderful World of Disney*, originally aired on ABC, 31st October 1956 (the series moved to NBC in 1961); it is part two of a trilogy called "The Art of Animation," and is currently available as part of the Walt Disney Treasures DVD set called *Behind the Scenes at the Walt Disney Studios* (directed by A.L. Werker and J. Handley, December 2002), ASIN B00006II6P. For the phenomenological basis of Disney's principle, see Edmund Husserl, *Ideas: General Introduction to Pure Phenomenology* (New York: Humanities, 1931), §23, pp. 90–92.

We learn much about the value of the question when we imagine variations. Ontologists always imagine variations.[8] I think the question needs to be formulated just as it is, and not, for example, "would Bruce ride a Harley?" to which the answer is "duh." That question leads us nowhere we have not already been, many times, although maybe we could have an interesting chat about what *model* Harley Bruce *should* ride, but that would be a pretty technical discussion; it's a spare part. The question also cannot be "would Woody Guthrie ride a Honda?" which is a jarring enough question, but I fear it is too great a project for any but Heidegger and his most profound followers . . . and maybe Bruce and Pete Seeger and Bob Dylan and Arlo. It's too much for us.

A much more predictable conversation could be had if we asked "Would Jesus ride a Honda or a Harley?" To this one, we can all agree he wouldn't ride a Honda (see below), but I fear we would be split over the Harley question, with a small minority insisting not only that Jesus *would* ride a Harley, but that he actually *did* enter Jerusalem on such a Hog (which may explain why things soon started looking like Glen Hanson's demise in *Easy Rider*—am I the only one who has noticed the similarity between that scene and Mel Gibson's *Passion of the Christ?*). This is my own view, in fact; not that Jesus *would* ride a Harley, but that he actually *did*. But let's keep it light. I think we can easily agree on the Bruce part of the question. Maybe Jesus on a Harley, definitely Bruce, no Honda for either one.

The "Honda" part of the question is equally crucial. It's an uncomfortable truth that there are two manufacturers of real motorcycles in the world today. One is Harley-Davidson, the other is Honda. The rest are wanna-be's. I am not saying Suzuki and Yamaha have made no real bikes. They made and make inferior Hondas. I'm not saying BSA, Triumph, Norton, and Indian never made real bikes. They made and make inferior Harleys. Here is another uncomfortable truth: Honda knows how to make a great motorcycle. Hondas are fast, they are effi-

---

[8] For an explanation of the method of imaginative variation, see Husserl, *Ideas*, §§68–70, 195–201. For an explanation of the explanation (trust me, you'll need it), see Erazim Kohák, *Idea and Experience: Edmund Husserl's Project of Phenomenology in Ideas I* (Chicago: University of Chicago Press, 1978), pp. 143–47.

cient, they last forever, they require very little maintenance, and yes, they even look good (to the middle-class, suburban eye). But they are McMortocycles. After some initial experiments, Harley-Davidson made the decision soon after Hondas appeared in the US market not even to compete, and Honda reciprocated (initially at least). Our first needed parts in this rebuild project: most battles are won or lost in the choosing, and there is no dishonor in letting someone else make a buck you never needed anyway. How different corporate America would be if it grasped this lesson! Bruce gets it.

Thus, I claim, we ask "would Springsteen ride a *Honda?*" precisely because it is the most informative contrast available to us. Honda makes an outstanding bike and they always did. The question is about a profound relation between, on one side, very defensible, conservative, thrifty middle-class values and on the other side, well, a somewhat impractical craving for freedom from those same values (not to reject them wholesale, but to take or leave them, as conscience and the sense of self may demand).

So what does Honda mean? Again, we seek contrast. By way of illustration, for instance, we intuitively recognize the ridiculousness of a Honda with extended forks. There are some things that just ought not be tricked out, like June Clever in a thong and pasties or a Honda 750 with extended forks (the 750 is still the "manliest" bike Honda ever made, but even *it* is something that could be respectably featured in an article for *Redbook*). The Honda as an icon helps us understand that this is a contrast not just of values, but of fundamental (even existential) relations. The truth is that Bruce could never *love* a Honda with all the madness in his soul, and the reason can be summed up in this phrase: Honda cannot make a suicide machine.

Honda cannot make a suicide machine because that would contradict every value they have poured into their bikes from the first. In fact, this is part of the reason we all know Jesus wouldn't have ridden a Honda. He had no use for middle-class values of this sort. What we may disagree on is whether he went into Jerusalem in a final act of defiance and there committed suicide willingly by the hands of others. But *if* he did that, he did it on a Harley, because a Harley is not first and foremost a bike or even a machine. A Harley is a *decision* about life and what makes it valuable, and how it needs to lived. When that decision comes to be embodied and epitomized in a machine, we *call* it a Harley. Here we have another needful part: Harley-Davidson, as cultural icon, represents not a machine first or foremost, but an existential decision and the life that follows upon it. We have seen, or so I claim, that "it's not just a bike, it's a choice," but have we understood it?

But I Digress

I will return to my question about Bruce in a moment, but we have a bolt stuck here and we need an impact wrench. Peter Fonda's bike "Captain America" seems to have clinched the iconic standing of the Harley, which had long been associated with a certain conception of freedom and individualism, but in the wake of *Easy Rider*, the popular imagination had crystallized around this idea. Part of the genius of Captain America was its symbolic insistence upon the association of patriotism with this very notion of freedom and individualism—this bike gave us permission to think for ourselves about *what* devotion and loyalty to the ideals of America really means, and the irony that this bike conveyed its rider towards making a drug deal (outside of the current laws) is also a source of creative tension. Brilliant. This reminds me of what happened with the song "Born in the U.S.A." I welcome you to picture the album cover in one half of your mind and Peter Fonda sitting astride Captain America in the other side.

It's worth pausing to consider how Dennis Hopper's film and its impact would have been different if Fonda had ridden *any* other bike (not just a non-Harley, but even any Harley other than Captain America—and you see our earlier method of ontology at work here, I hope). It's dangerous to make assertions about "might-have-beens," because no evidence can exist that fully demonstrates the falseness of such assertions. But with that disclaimer noted, I want to suggest that the film becomes close to meaningless, and numb, without the rolling American flag. That bike is the iconic key to the kingdom, not only of that one film, but to the America in which "Born in the U.S.A." can be received as a patriotic song by people who can't understand the words and never bother to read them (see the chapters in this volume by John Shook and Michael Patton).

Well, the song *is* patriotic, in a totally subversive way, just like Captain America. It is not an accident that our celluloid sacrificial

lamb, Glen Hanson, is a rogue lawyer incognito, and that, sym-
bolically, it is precisely the *law* that suffers a brutal death at the
hands of those who believe themselves to be defending it and
its ideals, because, after all, the letter kills the spirit, according
to Jesus, just as surely as the rednecks kill Glen Hanson. I think
both Jesus and Glen were only sons.

The Story of the Moral

Well, complicated ontologies can unfold as slow as Christmas
(another notion we wouldn't have without Jesus, not so much
Christmas, but the idea that it is slow—he sure took his sweet
time showing up, what with Babylonians and Assyrians running
amuck, and all those depressing lamentations, I mean, incarnate
already, would ya?).

Some people choose to serve appearances in making decisions about what products to buy, some chasing after what they
believe *others* will see as "cool," while others are attempting to
please the expectations of a conventional society. Such persons
will have more complicated journeys to self-understanding than
those who confront the decision for what it truly is. The ones
who choose their rides based on appearances have been consumed in what Heidegger calls the "they self," or in German
(since all ideas sound deeper in German, and this is a very ominous idea) *das Man*, which is the self that conceals its own fundamental modes of existing in order to live "inauthentically,"
caught up in the world of images and slogans and RVs. John
Kaag has discussed this in Chapter 11 of this volume. But bik-
ers have more straightforward terms for such people, such as
"assholes," but the nomenclature isn't crucial here. We will leave
such persons to the things they believe are important.

In the domain of those who confront existential issues more
directly, Robert Frost would have appreciated the depth of the
choice between a Harley and a Honda and would have been
able to summarize it better. I confess, that I have always chosen
Hondas, for reasons of my own. I am not much like Bruce,
which explains why I'm writing philosophy and he is playing
sold out concerts. Whether a person can actually *sell* his own
authenticity, is, of course, an intriguing question. Doug and
Russell Anderson have addressed that matter in their essay for
this volume. But that's another spare part.

My own confession about riding Hondas, however, seems to be the essential part we needed to get our question running. I might be too lazy to mix gas and oil in a two-stroke engine, but there is more than one kind of laziness. We haven't been lazy about our question. Let's check it over, see if this beast will start. We asked: would Bruce ride a Honda? We knew he would not. We considered variations on the question. We discovered that Bruce and Jesus have something in common, which can be summarized as: "live free or die," as they say in New Hampshire. Both Jesus and Bruce have a *passion*, meaning they are open to the world, a certain intense ontological longing, they "want to know if love is wild" and "want to know if love is real." That mode of existing, the "passion of the Boss," is compatible with mounting a suicide machine, whether it takes one to the "mansions of glory," or Highway 9, or Sturgis, or Golgotha. The cultural ontology of the suicide machine shows us something about identity and the moment of decision. It has shown us something about America and the ambiguous relationship between freedom and authenticity.[9] And it turns out that I am conventional and boring, not a risk-taker, and a stodgy middle-aged professor who wishes he was Springsteen, which is why I'm writing this. I'm not exactly living free or dying, here.

Yet, it was my choice, after all. The key to living free, if there really is one, is knowing who you are, and the path to learning who you are is your own responsibility. Respect the people who respect themselves, guard your own honor, and follow your own *daimon*, the voice that comes in through the back of your mind in the quiet moments, and you can probably learn what you need to know. Another important commonality among free spirits like Bruce is an intuitive awareness that happiness is fleeting, uncommon, not to be expected, and always to be celebrated wherever it alights for a time, as Kaag points out in his essay. You might call this pagan fatalism, but I don't see that naming it something so ominous gets you any closer to understanding it, especially since it is really all about freedom. Courage is also indispensable for a life that strives to be free,

---

[9] Since I know he won't cite himself, let me direct you to a very different take on almost exactly the same subjects, see the essay by my co-editor, Douglas R. Anderson, "Born to Run: Male Mysticism on the Road," in his excellent book *Philosophy Americana* (New York: Fordham University Press, 2006).

which involves a willingness to face and accept the consequences of your choices, even the consequences that are yours by bad luck.

Straight Time

With this much said, it might now be safe to say that our ontology of contrast rests on an uncommon willingness to put embodied practice and action ahead of reflection and hypothesizing. Springsteen's imagination doesn't proceed according to reflective hypotheses, it moves on the highway of existential possibilities, as several of our authors have said, in different ways. People like Bruce are really post-industrial, post-modern mystics, making of our world whatever remains to them to make of it. It is difficult to look upon what we have done to this world and not be moved to complete silence. And there is a very great silence that surrounds the culture of the post-modern mystics. This silence speaks volumes however, saying to the whole world of, well, the technical term is *assholes*: "if I fight your wars, I do it for my own honor, not for your gain; if I obey your laws, I do it because I choose them for myself; if I break your laws, I accept my punishment not at your hand but as the consequence of my own decision to live as I choose; and above all, do not ask me to believe your bullshit."

That's what I find when I survey the list of characters and their values, their places, and their things. I know Bruce would not ride a Honda, and now, surveying the whole cross-section of his imagination on the list, his masks and his revelations, I can see why I know the answer. Springsteen's imaginative world, and probably his actual world, is animated by a kind of philosophical practicalism that refuses to divorce body from spirit. The conventional life *does* divorce body and spirit. That seems like a shame, and it is at the root of our ingratitude about life. But there is an alternative, and we feel it and think it when we hear Bruce's songs. I recall another song about being "born" in John Kay's lines "Here and God are gonna make it happen, take the world in a love embrace, fire all of your guns at once and explode into space." Perhaps readers will recall the scene of Jesus's ascension. There is a certain sense of striving to *love the world* that informs this deep-seated quest for freedom and self-identity.

Plenty of suburbanites or conformists may be able to find this experience of being at home in the world without leaving the comfort of their living rooms, but as Bruce puts it, *his* love is bigger than a Honda, bigger than a Subaru. For people who have and need Big Love, the Harley recommends itself. So we see that Bruce wouldn't ride a Honda, not just because it isn't a suicide machine, but because there just isn't enough *love* in it. How can you really *love* a Honda? Does anyone want to *die* on a Honda? The Honda conserves itself, and those who ride them do not give themselves to the world in a reckless quest to love life and be loved in the midst of it. Hondas bespeak good sense, but Harleys are for people who can understand that he who would save his life must be willing to lose it. That is where the free love is, which is to say, this ride ain't free.

Epilogue

I am not certain I *believe* what I just wrote –it's a problem for philosophers. It sounds right, basically. But it really is just a way of following a road through a territory. The question suggested my ontology, and once I had the question defined, I knew what I had to say, or at least I knew the options that the question pointed to –and this is what Heidegger says about formulating questions. The answer is already *in* the question, and that's why we have to spend so much time with the questions. My question suggested that I needed to examine some relations among freedom, authenticity, and self-knowledge. I had to depict myself as conventional in order to praise Springsteen. But in plenty of ways, he's conventional and I'm a free spirit. So are you—both, I mean. Fortunately, the questions are infinite, and nobody forces you to ask ontological questions in just one way. I hope you can now have some fun with the list, and with this book in light of the list. I did.

V

Greetings from . . .

Proper Names in Springsteen Lyrics

The numbers after the proper names indicate the number of *songs* in which the name occurs, not the number of occurrences of the name. Names with no number occur in only one song. Due to the omission of "Terry's Song" from the official Springsteen website, searches of the proper names in that song will yield no results. Other songs from Springsteen's early work, before *Greetings from Asbury Park, New Jersey*, are also not listed here.

Persons

Fictional or Proto-fictional Characters

Bad Scooter
Big Bones Billie
Big Jim
Big Man (the)
Big Pretty
Billy (Bill) 8
Bill(y) Horton
Billy Devon
Billy Sutter
Bishop
Blind Terry
Bobbie
Bobby 6

Bobby Jean
Bobby Ramirez
Candy
Carol
Catherine LeFevre
Catlong
Charles
Charlie 2
Cherry
Cochise
Crazy Janey
Cynthia
Dan
Diamond Jackie
Dirty Annie
Doreen
Early Pearly
Eddie 2

Frank
Frankie 3
Franky
G-man
Gloria
Go-cart Mozart
Hazy Davy
Jack 4
Jack Knife
Jack the Rabbit
Janey 3
Jenny
Jim
Jimmy Lee
Jimmy the Saint
Joe 4
Joe Roberts
Joey 2

John 2
Johnny 6
"Johnny 99"
Johnson Lineir
Kate
Killer Joe
Kitty
Kyle William
Le Bing Son
Leah
Lena
Leroy
Lieutenant Jimmy Bly
Lieutenant Ray
Linda
Little Angel
Little Dynamite
Little Gun
Little Jack
Little Spider
Louis Rosales
Louisa
Lynette
Mac
Madame Marie
Magic Rat
Margarita
Maria 2
Mary 9
Mary Beth
Mary Dove
Mary Lou 3
Maximum Lawman
Mean John Brown
Miguel Rosales
Missy
Missy Bimbo
Mister Trouble
Monatuk
Ocanuk
Power Thirteen
Puerto Rican Jane
Raphael Rodriguez
Rainey Williams

Ralph
Rex
Ricky
Rosie (and Rosalita)
  2
Sally
Sam
Sampson
Sandy 2
Scott
Shaniqua
Sherry
Sonny 2
Spanish Johnny
Sue
Terry 3
Theresa
Tiny Tim
Tommy
Wanda
Wayne
Weak Knees Willie
Wendy
Wild Billy 2
X-man
Zero

Historical or Literary People (i.e., Bruce didn't make them up)

Abel 2
Adam 2
Allah
Bo Diddley
Brando (Marlon)
Broadway Mary
Bruce Lee
Buddha
Burt Reynolds
Cain 2
Casanova 2
Cheshire (Cat)

The Chicken Man
  (mob boss)
Columbo
Columbus
Daniel (prophet) 2
Danny Heaton
David (King)
Delilah
Devil (the) 13
Dinah
Elvis Presley 2
Eve
Ezekiel
Farouk (King)
God (includes
  "Lord" and
  "Heavenly Father")
  33
Hitler
Isabella (Queen of
  Spain)
Jack Thompson
  (boxer)
James Bond
James Dean
James Heaton
Jesus 6
Joan Fontaine
Joe (Joseph,
  stepfather of
  Jesus)
John McDowell (Big;
  politician?)
Juliet 3
Junior Johnson
Kid Cole
Kojak
Mars (god of war)
Mary or Maria
  (Mother of
  Jesus) 3
Moses
Rambo
Rembrandt

Rockefeller (John D.)
Romeo 4
Roy Orbison
Sam Houston
Samson
Santa An(n)a
(Antonio Lopez
de)
Sheena, Queen of
the Jungle
Tom Joad
Venus de Milo

Groups of People Bruce Apparently Made Up

Charlie Company
Duke Street Kings
Flying Zambinis
(the)
James Young and the
Immortal Ones
Little Melvin and the
Invaders
Little Willie and the
Soul Brooms
The Pythons (street
gang)
The Skulls (street
gang)

Historical or Literary Groups of People

Beatles
Blacks 3
California Border
Patrol
California Highway
Patrol (CHP)
Canadians
Catholics

Chinese
French
Germans
Gypsies 9
INS (Immigration
and Naturalization
Service, USA)
Irish
Italians
Japanese 2
Jews
Johnstown Company
(McClure)
Mohawks
Rolling Stones
Seminoles
Spanish 4
V.A. (Veterans
Administration)
Viet Cong
Vietnamese
Whites

Family Names of Fictional or Proto-fictional Characters

Bly
Brown
Devon
Horton
Le
LeFevre
Leneir
McNicholas
Posalaski
Ramirez
Rodriguez
Rosales
Smith
Sutter
Williams
Zerilli

Places in the USA
Individual Locations (both fictional and actual)

Abram's Bridge
Al's Barbecue
Appalacchia [sic]
Astrowash
Badlands (SD, per-
haps)
Balboa Park (San
Diego)
Bellevue (Hosiptal,
NYC)
Boardwalk, The 2
Bob's Big Boy
Breaker's Point
Bronx, the 2
Cadillac Ranch (TX)
Calvary Hill (Holy
Land)
Central Line (train)
Central Trust (Bank)
Charlotte County (FL)
Chelsea (NYC)
Club Tip Top
Darlington County
(SC)
East Compton (L.A.)
East of Eden
Easy Joe's
Eden
Ellis Island (NY)
Everglades (FL)
Exxon (station)
Fairview (NJ)
First Street Station
Frankie's Diner
Fresno County
Gethsemane (Holy
Land)

Greasy Lake
Guadalupe
  Mountains
Gulf of Mexico
Harlem (NYC)
Harvard
Holy Cross (church)
Howard Johnson
  (HoJo)
Innerlake
Jackson Cage
Jungleland
Kingsley
Liberty Hall
Little Eden
Madera County (CA)
Manhattan (NYC)
Mesabi Iron Range
  (MN)
Michigan County
Monongaleh Valley
  [sic] (probably OH)
Mott Haven (Bronx)
Ohio River
Our Lady of the
  Roses (church)
Palace, The (NJ)
Pinball Way
Pop's Grill
Rainbow Saloon
Rio Grande (Rio
  Bravo del Norte) 3
Riverside (hospital)
Sacramento Yard
  (train yard)
Sacred Heart
  (school)
Sal's Gracery
San Diego County
  (CA)
San Joaquin Valley
  (CA)
Seven-Eleven Store
Shawnee Lake

Sierra Madres
  (mountains)
Signal Hill
Sistine Chapel
Soldiers Field
Southern Trust
  (Bank)
St. James Parish (LA)
St. Mary's (church)
St. Mary's Gate
Stockton's Wing (NJ)
Telegraph Hill
Texaco (station) 2
Transcontinental
  (Railroad)
Trestles, The
Waynesboro County
  (UT)
Willow Bank
World Trade Center
  (NYC)
Wyomie County
Yellow Creek (OH)
Zona Norte (San
  Diego)

Streets and Roads (actual and fictional)

12th Street
53rd Street
57th Street
82nd Street (NYC)
95 (highway)
101 (highway)
A Street
Alvarado Street
Baker Street
Bleecker Street
  (NYC)
Blessing Avenue
Bluebird Street
Bond Street

Broadway (NYC)
Carson Street
Chelsea Road
Dixie Highway
Duke Street
E Street
Easy Street 2
Eighth Avenue
  (NYC)
Eldridge Avenue
First Street
Flamingo Lane
Highway One
Highway 9
Highway 29
Highway 31
Jane Street
Kokomo, the
  (a freeway) 2
Lover's Lane 2
Madison Avenue
  (NYC)
Main Street 5
Michigan Avenue
Route 9 (NJ) 2
Route 39 2
Route 60
Route 88
Shanty Lane
South Street
Sunset and Vine
Tenth Avenue
Thunder Road 2
Turnpike (NJ) 2
Twelfth Street (San
  Diego)
Union Street 2
Valentino Drag

Cities (actual and fictional)

Asbury Park, NJ
Angeline

Atlantic City, NJ
Baltimore, MD
Baton Rouge, LA
Brownsville, TX
Calverton
Darlington, SC 2
Detroit, MI
Englishtown, NJ
Firebaugh, CA
Fort Irwin, CA
Galveston (Bay),
    TX 2
Germantown, PA
Hollywood, CA
Houston, TX
Johnstown, PA 2
Kingstown, MD
Lafayette, LA
Lincoln, NE
Linden, NJ
Los Angeles, CA
    (L.A.)
Mahwah, NJ
Marysville, CA
Memphis, TN
Monroe
Needles, CA
New Orleans, LA
New York City,
    NY 3
Perrineville, OH
Philadelphia (Philly),
    PA 2
Pittsburgh, PA
Ponchatoula, LA
Red Hill, FL
Reno, NV
Rikers Island, NY
Sacramento, CA
San Diego, CA 3
Seabrook, TX
Stockton, CA
Stovell
Tampa, FL

Truth or
    Consequences, NM
Youngstown, OH

States

Arkansas
California 5
Carolina
Colorado
Florida 3
Indiana
Maryland 2
Michigan 2
Nebraska 2
New Jersey 6
New Mexico 2
Ohio 4
Oklahoma 2
Pennsylvania 2
Texas 5
Utah
Virginia
Wisconsin
Wyoming

Places outside the USA

Nations

Canada
Egypt
Italy
Korea
Mexico 3
Vatican
Viet Nam 3

Cities

Basra (Iraq)
Calgary (Alberta,
    Canada)
Chu Lai (Viet Nam)

Hong Kong
Khe San (Viet Nam)
Matamoros (Mexico)
Nazareth (Holy
    Land)
Quang Tri (Viet
    Nam)
Rome (Italy) 2
Saigon (Viet Nam) 4
Tijuana (Mexico)
Zanzibar (Tanzania)

Individual Locations

Amatitlan (Mexican
    river)
Guanajuato (state in
    Mexico)
Jordan (plains of)
Red Sea
Rio Bravo del Norte
    (Rio Grande) 3
Scotland Yard
Sinaloa (state in
    Mexico)
Valle de dos Rios
    (Mexico)

Things

007 (spy watch)
.32 (handgun)
.38 (handgun)
.44 Magnum (hand-
    gun)
.410 (shotgun)
350 (GM engine)
396 (Chevrolet
    engine)
455 (Oldsmobile
    engine)
B-52 (Boeing)
Bar-M (choppers)

Batmobile
Bible 4
Bronco (Ford)
Buick 3
Cadillac 5
Camaro
Cassiopeia
    (constellation)
Challenger (Dodge)
Channel 5
Chevy (includes
    Chevrolet) 3
Coast City Bus
Coke (Coca-cola)
David, the
    (Michelangelo)
Dodge
Eiffel Tower
Eldorado
    (Cadillac) 2
Elkhorn Special
    (train)
Exxon (station) 2
Ford 6
Goodyear (blimp
    and tires)
Greyhound Bus

Harley (Davidson) 2
Honda
Hurst (Shifters)
I-Spy Beeper
K-bar (knife)
Liberty (ship)
Mercedes 3
Mercury ('49)
Mission Impossible
Mona Lisa, the
Orion (constellation)
Psalms (of David)
Rembrandt paintings
Revelation (Book of)
Roadrunner
    (Plymouth hemi
    engine)
Southern Queen
    (riverboat)
Subaru
Taj Mahal
Tanqueray (gin)
Titanic
Trans Am (Pontiac)
VW (Volkswagen) 2
Vistavision
Woolworth's

Events

4th of July
    (Independence
    Day) 3
Christmas 2
Election Day
Great Depression
Indian Summer 2
Santa Ana Winds
    (CA)
Valentine's Day
Veterans Day

Days of the Week

Monday 2
Friday 9
Saturday 7
Sunday 6

Months of the Year

May
June
July 2
August

Hey, That's Me

DOUG ANDERSON teaches philosophy at Southern Illinois University, Carbondale. He first encountered Springsteen in the early 1970s while playing harmonica for two guys from New Jersey who had grown up with Springsteen and said he just had to be heard. He's been listening ever since.

RUSSELL ANDERSON is a medical writer, student filmmaker, and weekend philosopher living in Boston. Raised on classic Springsteen, Russ is living evidence of the cross-generational influence The Boss has had, and harbors nothing but respect for the man who makes us all feel like we grew up next to the Jersey boardwalk. Russ has a BA in Philosophy from Bates College in Lewiston, Maine.

RANDALL AUXIER teaches philosophy at Southern Illinois University, Carbondale. He writes fairly boring essays and books on classical American thought and the philosophy of religion. On the side he plays music in bars, hosts a radio show on the local community station, and is an activist in the teachers union. Springsteen's music was a prime inspiration for at least two of those activities. His favorite Springsteen song is "Born to Run," although he hopes he wasn't born to do anything of the sort.

JASON BELL writes philosophy and **JESSICA BELL** teaches science in the land of Woody Guthrie and Rainey Williams. They have taught at Vanderbilt University, Casady School, Middle Tennessee State University, and Harding Academy. Across the street from their alma mater, Oklahoma City University, they are building a little café on the once-Route 66. You can buy philosophy books there, too, like this book (which would go better with a cup of coffee, wouldn't it?) and

Plato. But no Heidegger. And it's a music venue: Bruce Springsteen, The Flaming Lips, Randy Auxier, and Doug Anderson will have played there by the time you read this.

Scott Calef got his facts learned real good, so they made him Professor and Chair of the Department of Philosophy at Ohio Wesleyan University. He's published in Ancient Philosophy, Applied Ethics, Political Philosophy, Metaphysics and the Philosophy of Religion. He's also contributed to volumes on The Beatles, Pink Floyd, and Metallica. Although Scott's been listening to Bruce since the release of *Born to Run*, he only saw him live for the first time at a John Kerry rally before the 2004 election (perhaps the only perk of living in a hotly-contested battleground state). He remembers it as one of the most heartfelt and honest musical events of his life. Scott's favorite Springsteen song is "Thunder Road," even though *he* spent *his* summer waiting in vain, not for a savior to rise from the streets, but for a decent tan to rise on his pasty white skin.

James Couch currently teaches philosophy at Keene State College in New Hampshire. He is interested in the question, what defines being human, as well as the social, artistic and existential elements that relate to this question. His work has explored thinkers and artists on both sides of the Atlantic. Though he does not play a musical instrument himself, he enjoys when others do. "The Ghost of Tom Joad" and "State Trooper" are two of his favorite songs by Bruce Springsteen.

Luke Dick is a professional songwriter and performer residing in Nashville, with his daughter, Emily. He will die happy knowing that he's talked people into giving him money for writing songs. While not writing or being a daddy, he drives a forklift for Yellow Transportation, strictly for pleasure and inspiration. Other than that, he is a man of love and leisure and enjoys loyal friends, good books, thoughtful sermons, cheap scotch, and long talks with all sorts. Luke wishes he had written "I'm On Fire."

Steve Gimbel teaches philosophy at Gettysburg College, but lives with his wife and kids a short drive from where he grew up in Baltimore, Jack. His professional interests range from the philosophical ramification of classic rock to the foundations of relativity theory, and he writes the daily weblog Philosophers' Playground.

Gary L. Herstein got his PhD in philosophy after spending some twenty-five years in the computer and high-tech industries, when he decided to abandon the Bill-Gates-Business-Model-of-Life for the fame and fortune of academics. Dr. Herstein has never been well informed about monetary matters. He is currently an assistant professor of philosophy at Muskingum College, New Concord, Ohio, but nothing he does can be rightfully blamed on them. Dr. Herstein's current areas of research include the logical bases of measurement, particularly as these connect with the work of Alfred North Whitehead. Other than the fact that he likes Springsteen's music, nobody is altogether sure why he has an essay in this volume (there are rumors that one of the editors owes him money). He presently keeps house with his three cats, all of whom despair of his ever learning anything interesting.

JOHN KAAG is visiting scholar at the American Academy of Arts and Sciences and a research associate at the Harvard Humanities Center. This means that he spends a good deal of time digging through dusty archives and around the roots of classical American thought—the writings of Ralph Waldo Emerson, Margaret Fuller, and William James. He does occasionally escape the library in order to satisfy his love of running, rowing, coaching, teaching . . . and his wife. His favorite Springsteen song is "The River."

When she's not snowshoeing, canoeing, or working in the garden, **HEATHER KEITH** teaches philosophy and directs a progressive education program at Green Mountain College in Vermont. She is a member of the college's CSA (community supported agriculture farm), a volunteer at SolarFest renewable energy festival, and enjoys small village life in Vermont, as well as her hometown roots in Nebraska. Her favorite Springsteen song is "Badlands," though she notes that the real Badlands are actually kind of pretty.

ERIN MCKENNA is Professor of Philosophy at Pacific Lutheran University in Tacoma. She shares her life with three dogs and two horses. Much of her philosophical work focuses on issues of human-nonhuman relations and ethics and social philosophy. This focus brings her in touch with issue of death and dying. Her essay here represents this interest in death and the task of making meaningful lives. Springsteen helps us all face this task head on.

STEVEN MICHELS is an assistant professor of political science at Sacred Heart University. In addition to a handful of articles on political theory that no one has read, he is the co-author (with Mike Ventimiglia) of "Can The Daily Show Save Democracy?" in *The Daily Show and Philosophy*. He also plays bass and "sings" in The Extra-Credit Project, the band of professors at Sacred Heart. His favorite Springsteen album is *The Ghost of Tom Joad*. He'd like to dedicate his chapter to his aunt Pat, a huge Springsteen fan who had a large role in his music education.

MICHAEL F. PATTON, JR. lives, loves, and teaches in the Philosophy Program at the University of Montevallo in Montevallo, Alabama. He thinks he is quite funny, and his friends and students either like or fear him enough to keep the illusion alive. In his free time, he and his wife Cheryl run a small coffee shop-bookstore-bar in Montevallo to the delight of hundreds. When he was younger, he had the best stereo in the world and played Springsteen and other music all the time. While he'd like to pick some cool Bruce song like "Born to Run" to list as his favorite, he's going to pick "Does This Bus Stop at 82nd Street?" as emblematic of his general state of confusion.

SCOTT L. PRATT teaches philosophy at the University of Oregon. He is the author of articles on race, Native American philosophy, the philosophy of pluralism and of the book, *Native Pragmatism: Rethinking the Roots of American Philosophy* (Indiana University Press). In the moments when he's not teaching or writing, he fly fishes in the Cascade Mountains, scuba dives at the Oregon coast, and listens to a lot of music. "Reason to Believe" is his favorite Springsteen song and, not coincidentally, a reason to believe.

JOHN SHOOK is Vice President for Research and Senior Research Fellow at the Center for Inquiry Transnational in Amherst, New York. He received his PhD in philosophy at the University at Buffalo, where he is Research Associate in Philosophy. His primary philosophical interests center on American philosophers, and the mutual influence of culture on the currents of American thought. His favorite Springsteen song is "Thunder Road," but he can be observed singing along to "Glory Days" at stoplights.

MICHAEL VENTIMIGLIA teaches philosophy at Sacred Heart University in Fairfield, Connecticut. He also plays piano for blues artist Roxy Perry. His favorite Bruce song is "Reason to Believe." He is waiting patiently for Mr. Springsteen to contact him and offer him a spot on his next album or tour.

Index

on music, mind and body in,
    xi–xii
"My Beautiful Reward," 250, 251
"My Best Was Never Good
    Enough," 25
"My Hometown," 4, 173, 212, 213
"Nebraska," 79, 153, 189–190, 228
Nebraska (album), xiii, 20–21, 41,
    152, 161, 170, 189–191,
    197–98, 210, 230, 248
need versus want in, 243–44
and negative freedom, 94–96, 100
"Night," 28
"No Surrender," 213, 230
"Open All Night," 21, 170–71
oppression in, 197, 200
"Out in the Street," 251
"Out of Work," 21, 28
and passion, 275
as Peter Pan, 104
and philosophy
    contrast between, 187, 192
    similarity between, 193
"Pink Cadillac," 36, 60, 65
as poet, 84
as populist, 65
as post-modern mystic, 276
"The Price You Pay," 131, 250
"The Promise," 26
proper names in, 223, 265–67
and prophets
    concept of, 3–4
    differences between, 12
    similarities between, 4–5, 6
"Prove It All Night," 247
"Racing in the Street," 93, 94, 96,
    98, 99–100, 244
"Radio Nowhere," 63, 65
"Reason to Believe," 165, 167,
    172, 191, 232
and reason to believe, 161, 162
redemption in, 191
and religion, 81, 81n9, 83, 183,
    191
"Reno," 79, 232
"The Rising," 6, 13, 14
    as lamentation, 14
The Rising, 26, 234

"The River," 158, 170, 228, 232
The River (album), 19, 170
    tour for, 143
    in *Rolling Stone* interviews, 28,
        59–60, 62
"Rosalita," 29
"Santa Ana," 80, 81
"Seaside Bar Song," 245
"She's the One," 20
"Sinaloa Cowboys," 24, 248, 266
Sisyphean interpretation of,
    209–210
and Socrates, similarities between,
    235, 239–244, 246, 250–53
as Socratic revolutionary, 63–67
Songs, 230
"Souls of the Departed," 232, 248,
    250
"soulwork" in, xiii–xiv
specific names in, 223, 265–67
"Spirit in the Night," 79
"State Trooper," 123, 170–71, 190
as storyteller, 134, 147
on storytelling, 230
"Straight Time," 23, 28, 197, 198,
    199, 200, 202–04, 206–07,
    210, 248
    as Sisyphean, 207–08
"Streets of Philadelphia," 79, 232
suffering in, 129
talking guitar of, xiv–xv
"Tenth Avenue Freeze-Out," 224,
    267
themes in, 163
and threshold of responsibility,
    103
"Thunder Road," xi, 93, 98, 99,
    141, 145, 162, 186, 191, 209,
    214
    a capella version, 146
    event in, 135–36, 138–39
    and redemption, 142
Tracks, 26, 80
transcendence in, 183–84, 191
Tunnel of Love, 22, 23
universality in, 186, 233
"Used Cars," 191
Wendy in, 104–06, 116–18

Printed in the USA
CPSIA information can be obtained
at www.ICGtesting.com
JSHW012020140824
68134JS00033B/2789